Fixing Prices

T0327389

Fixing Prices
A Century of Setting, Posting and Adjusting Retail Prices

Franck Cochoy

Professor of Sociology, University of Toulouse Jean Jaurès, Senior Fellow, Institut Universitaire de France, France

Johan Hagberg

Professor of Business Administration Specialising in Marketing, University of Gothenburg, Sweden

Hans Kjellberg

Professor of Marketing, Department of Marketing and Strategy, Stockholm School of Economics, Sweden

Edward Elgar
PUBLISHING

Cheltenham, UK • Northampton, MA, USA

Published by
Edward Elgar Publishing Limited
The Lypiatts
15 Lansdown Road
Cheltenham
Glos GL50 2JA
UK

Edward Elgar Publishing, Inc.
William Pratt House
9 Dewey Court
Northampton
Massachusetts 01060
USA

Paperback edition 2024

A catalogue record for this book
is available from the British Library

Library of Congress Control Number: 2023936885

This book is available electronically in the **Elgar**online
Business subject collection
http://dx.doi.org/10.4337/9781803929255

ISBN 978 1 80392 924 8 (cased)
ISBN 978 1 80392 925 5 (eBook)
ISBN 978 1 0353 4302 7 (paperback)

Printed and bound by CPI Group (UK) Ltd, Croydon, CR0 4YY

Contents

About the authors

Franck Cochoy is Professor of Sociology at Toulouse Jean Jaurès University, a researcher at the LISST-CNRS, and a Senior Fellow of the Institut Universitaire de France. He works in the field of economic sociology, with a focus on market devices. Recent publications include articles in the *Journal of the Association for Consumer Research, Marketing Theory, Science, Technology, & Human Values, Social Studies of Science, Journal of Macromarketing* and *Socio-Economic Review.*

Johan Hagberg is Professor of Business Administration Specialising in Marketing at the University of Gothenburg. His research revolves around the digitalization of retailing, consumption and markets. Recent publications include articles in *Consumption Markets & Culture, Socio-Economic Review, International Journal of Retail & Distribution Management* and *Journal of Macromarketing.*

Hans Kjellberg is Professor of Marketing at Stockholm School of Economics, where he heads the Department of Marketing and Strategy and the Centre for Market Studies. His research focuses on economic coordination in general and the organizing of markets in particular. Recent publications include articles in *Journal of Business Research, AMS Review, Journal of the Academy of Marketing Science* and *Environment and Planning A: Economy and Space.*

Acknowledgements

This book is the result of a series of fieldwork sessions, at the US Library of Congress in June 2015, at the Gothenburg University Library from November 2015 to March 2016, at the New York Public Library in January and March–April 2016, in our home offices in 2020 and the subsequent analysis, over several years, of the data collected. It combines original material with a series of previously published articles and chapters;[1] all of these previous works were developed, updated and reworked.

Financial support was provided by The Swedish Research Council, project Digcon: Digitalizing consumer culture [Grant number 2012-5736]. We warmly thank our colleagues in the Digcon project: Magdalena Peterson-McIntyre, Lena Hansson, Niklas Sörum at the University of Gothenburg and Jan Smolinski at the University of Toulouse Jean Jaurès. A special thanks to Bastien Soutjis, who contributed to Chapter 7 of this volume.

We would also like to thank some other people who have helped us along the way: Michel Callon, Barbara Czarniawska, Angela Pagan and her colleagues at New York Public Library, librarians at Library of Congress and Gothenburg University Library as well as Francine O'Sullivan and Sabrina Lynott-May at Edward Elgar Publishing.

We warmly thank *Progressive Grocer* for granting us permission to reproduce the images this publication rests upon.

Franck Cochoy   Johan Hagberg   Hans Kjellberg

LIST OF PREVIOUS PUBLICATIONS THIS BOOK IS PARTLY BASED ON

Cochoy, F., Hagberg, J. and Kjellberg, H. (2018). The technologies of price display: Mundane retail price governance in the early 20th century. *Economy and Society*, 47(4), 572–606. Reproduced with permission of Taylor & Francis.

Cochoy, F., Hagberg, J. and Kjellberg, H. (2019). The ethno-graphy of prices: On the fingers of the invisible hand (1922–1947). *Organization*, 26(4), 492–516. Reproduced with permission of SAGE.

---

[1]   See the list following.

Cochoy, F., Hagberg, J. and Kjellberg, H. (2020). The tower of labels: Labelling goods in the US grocery store (1922–2018). In B. Laurent and Mallard A. (eds), *Labelling the Economy* (pp. 233–70). Singapore: Palgrave Macmillan. Reproduced with permission of Palgrave Macmillan.

Cochoy, F., Hagberg, J. and Kjellberg, H. (2021). Price display technologies and price ceiling policies: Governing prices in the WWII and postwar US economy (1940–1953). *Socio-Economic Review*, 19(1), 133–56. Reproduced with permission of SAGE.

Cochoy, F., Hagberg, J. and Kjellberg, H. (2022). Reputation, trust and credit: Cultivating shopping practices in early twentieth-century US grocery stores. In V. Howard (ed.), *A Cultural History of Shopping, Volume 6: A Cultural History of Shopping in the Modern Age* (Chapter 7). London: Bloomsbury Academic. Reproduced with permission of Bloomsbury Academic, an imprint of Bloomsbury Publishing Plc.

Cochoy, F. and Soutjis, B. (2020). Back to the future of digital price display: Analyzing patents and other archives to understand contemporary market innovations. *Social Studies of Science*, 50(1), 3–29. Reproduced with permission of SAGE.

Hagberg, J., Kjellberg, H. and Cochoy, F. (2020). The role of market devices for price and loyalty strategies in 20th century U.S. grocery stores. *Journal of Macromarketing*, 40(2), 201–20. Reproduced with permission of SAGE.

Kjellberg, H., Hagberg, J. and Cochoy, F. (2019). Thinking market infrastructure: Barcode scanning in the US grocery retail sector, 1967–2010. In M. Kornberger, G. Bowker, J. Elyachar, A. Mennicken, P. Miller, J. Nucho and N. Pollock (eds), *Thinking Infrastructures* (pp. 207–32). Bingley: Emerald Publishing. Reproduced with permission of Emerald Publishing.

Soutjis, B., Cochoy, F. and Hagberg, J. (2017). An ethnography of Electronic Shelf Labels: The resisted digitalization of prices in contemporary supermarkets. *Journal of Retailing and Consumer Services*, 39C, 296–304. Reproduced with permission of SAGE.

Introduction: studying the display of prices

In today's consumer markets, in many countries, the display of prices is more or less mandatory and subject to detailed regulation: public authorities regulate where prices should appear, in what size the price information should be printed, the need to indicate the price per unit, and so on. In parallel to these regulations, which were gradually introduced over the past century, the posting of prices has been subject to repeated innovation, from the development and perfection of simple handwriting techniques, via increasingly sophisticated tools and mechanical aids such as price guns, to the introduction of barcode scanners and remotely controlled Electronic Shelf Labels (ESLs). Strangely enough, the social sciences have largely ignored these continuous and considerable investments made to organize and materialize prices. It is almost as if the mundane materiality of prices, which was meant to render them visible to market actors, paradoxically made them invisible to scholars. The purpose of the present volume is to correct this state of affairs by scrutinizing the development of price display.

For lawyers, policy makers and economists, prices are generally conceived as abstract values resulting from global power relationships and interactions between supply and demand. Even economic sociologists, ordinarily eager to criticize utilitarian and functionalist views of markets, have tended to share the view of their best enemies when looking at prices, although highlighting alternative causalities for their formation (for a comprehensive review, see Beckert, 2011). Whatever the discipline, numbers matter for what they express (Porter, 1995), rather than for how they appear.

For instance, in her book *Pricing the Priceless Child*, Viviana Zelizer (1985) shows that the way the valuation of children evolved cannot be restricted to market and demographic hydraulics; she explains how the basis for the value of children shifted from utility to sentiment, along a general process of "sacralization". This said and despite her insightful anthropological approach, Zelizer addresses the price of children in the same way economists do: prices are numbers expressed in dollars, with little concern for how these prices appear materially. It is unsurprising that Zelizer does not address the materiality of prices in this particular case, since this dimension is largely absent from the specific market she is studying. Hopefully, children are "priceless" not only in the sense of "sacred" but also in the sense of "lacking a price tag". Not so, it turns out: "The price tag of a black market baby rose from an estimated

$1,000 in the 1930s to $5,000 in the late 1940s. By 1951, some babies sold for as much as $10,000." (Zelizer, 1985, 199). However, the phrase "price tag" is used here in a figurative sense, which precisely illustrates the significance of the development we focus on. Zelizer's sentence would have been nonsensical prior to the developments that we chronicle in our study; due to the success of price tag technologies, the expression can now be used figuratively. In addition, Zelizer's remark explicitly refers to the black market, where physical price tags rarely exist. This is why, of course, she has to rely on "estimated" prices as a stand-in for physically manifest prices. Interestingly, however, in *The Social Meaning of Money*, when addressing how people handle their financial resources, Zelizer paid distinct attention to the way economic values leave their abstract dimension to take material form through "earmarking" practices, like putting money reserved for a specific use in a special marked envelope (Zelizer, 1994).

Similarly, in his book on the prices of contemporary art works, Olav Velthuis (2005) discusses the abstract character of prices. While he attends to the social and material world behind them, so to speak, he does not look at the materiality of the prices themselves. Accordingly, he unveils the relationship between prices and artwork size or artists' reputation. He insists on the meanings attached to prices: for instance, a high price may be seen as a sign of quality, of the previous owner's identity or of fraud. Velthuis thus presents prices as symbols and narratives rather than as palpable artifacts in themselves. Significantly, the book title is *Talking Prices*, not "*Writing Prices*" or "*Looking at Prices*" and the subtitle highlights the *Symbolic Meanings of Prices* rather than their objectified appearances.

Over the past two decades, the field of valuation studies has drawn extensively on the price/quality dichotomy. Notably, David Stark (2009) insisted on the multiplicity of orders that shape economic values; Lucien Karpik (2010) explained how quality goods like artworks, professional services, and wine are valued through a competition by qualities rather than prices; drawing on the notion of qualculation, Franck Cochoy (2002; 2008a), Michel Callon and John Law (2005) showed how contemporary market transactions articulate quantitative valuation and qualitative judgment. In *The Worth of Goods, Valuation and Pricing in the Economy*, Beckert and Aspers (2011) and the specialists of economic sociology they gathered explored these issues further. Based on various case studies, they show that the making of prices rests on a series of multidimensional valuation processes. However, these studies of the making of prices generally stop at the valuation stage and do not go as far as addressing the materialization one.

By contrast, we rather aim to complement the anthropology and sociology of prices and valuation practices by focusing precisely on the way those very prices are materialized. Our ambition is to look at the material character of prices, at the intersection of the market mechanism, marketing techniques, public regulations, and market devices. Or, to put it differently, our research objective is to go beyond the price/quality dichotomy by showing that prices themselves have qualities: they appear on special holders and in special places; they come with specific fonts, sizes, and colors. Our aim is to document and describe how such specificities contribute to orient economic cognition and decisions in several respects.

To this end, we investigate the relationship between seemingly insignificant, everyday price display innovations, like price tag devices, local managerial decisions about price formulations, and wider market changes like the introduction of regulations concerning price display, item pricing, and so on. Just as Paul Dourish (2022) shows that the material aspect of numerals matters – for example, the graphic difference between Roman numerals (X) and Arabic numerals (10) makes it impossible to conduct double-entry bookkeeping with the former, while the possibilities are infinite with the latter – we will show that each materialization of price display has a distinct impact on the economy. The setting for our inquiry is twentieth-century US grocery retailing and hence the crossroads between Main Street (individual stores) and Interstate (Federal regulations). The book is one tangible outcome of a project purporting to investigate price adjustment mechanisms and the roles of abstract procedures and economic rationality on the one hand, and the devices and arguments used to make prices public, acceptable and even seductive, on the other. As such, the book complements the few extant studies that go beyond the abstract mathematical dimension of prices to emphasize their multiplicity (Çalışkan, 2009) and materiality (Beunza et al., 2006; Grandclément, 2004; Muniesa, 2007) and show to what extent the materiality of prices contributes to the proliferation of various price-based valuation strategies (Stark, 2009). Primarily, it offers a historical, science and technology studies (STS) informed perspective that so far has been lacking in the study of prices.

To acquaint the reader with the issue of price display in markets and elaborate on how we have sought to shed further light on it, we first review previous work on prices in four disciplines, illustrating that price display has been curiously overlooked within the previous literature.

PRICE DISPLAYS – AN OMNIPRESENT, YET CURIOUSLY OVERLOOKED ASPECT OF MARKETS

Established Views on What Prices Are and Do

Four disciplines have paid considerable attention to prices, their function, and their role in society: economics, (economic) psychology, marketing, and (economic) sociology. In economics, prices have primarily been viewed as abstract indicators of value, produced by the price mechanism, and effective in directing resource allocation in society. In the words of Hayek (1945, 527), the price system is:

> a kind of machinery for registering change, or a system of telecommunications which enables individual producers to watch merely the movement of a few pointers, as an engineer might watch the hands of a few dials, in order to adjust their activities to changes of which they may never know more than is reflected in the price movement.

Under ideal conditions, this machinery works within a market thanks to what is known as the Law of One Price (see, for example, Goldberg and Knetter, 1997): identical products will sell for the same price (bar any constraints caused by information and transportation costs, trade restrictions, tariffs, etc.). Under ideal market conditions, neither sellers nor buyers have the power to influence the prices produced by this machinery; they are price takers. For this price mechanism to work, it is also assumed that market actors are rational and have information about available options, so that they can act on price signals.

Many contributions in economics have advanced a more realistic conception of both the production and consumption of prices in the economy. In his theory of monopolistic competition, Chamberlain (1933) suggested that sellers do have some degree of control over prices, either due to there being a limited number of sellers and/or due to the goods they offer being less than perfect substitutes. Rather than the pure competition case in which the price mechanism produces the price, all individual producers have some grip over price production in the economy. Conversely, following the lead of Simon (1955), the assumption of the rational and perfectly (price) informed actor was gradually chipped away at by several authors in the 1970s. To mention a few: Akerlof (1970) questioned the ability of prices to carry relevant information about underlying quality in goods. Williamson (1973) highlighted bounded rationality as one of the factors preventing markets from reaching competitive equilibrium. Grossman and Stiglitz (1976) argued that there was a cost associated with the acquisition of price information necessary for arbitrage in markets.

The more recent developments in how economics deals with prices builds on these insights but also on advances in (economic) psychology, most notably the growth of behavioral economics (see Camerer et al., 2004 for an overview).

Economics traditionally conceptualizes a world populated by calculating, unemotional maximizers that have been dubbed *Homo Economicus*. In a sense, neo-classical economics has defined itself as explicitly "anti-behavioral". Indeed, virtually all the behavior studied by cognitive and social psychologists is either ignored or ruled out in a standard economic framework (Mullainathan and Thaler, 2000). In contrast, behavioral economics has addressed two issues that have direct implications for how to understand the role of prices: how actual economic behavior differs from the idealized model and how such behavior matters in economic contexts (Mullainathan and Thaler, 2000). A key theme has been to understand how economic actors use various heuristics to simplify their everyday calculative behavior, for instance their processing of price information.

Most significantly, the developments in economic psychology have promoted a turn from actual to perceived prices, identifying and seeking to explain the disconnect between objective prices and the interpretations and responses of individuals to these prices. A milestone in this respect was the work of Kahneman and Tversky (1979) on prospect theory (for a review, see Barberis, 2013). Among other things, their work established the principle of loss aversion, that is, that individuals value losses more than gains. This can help explain observed gaps between the price at which individuals are willing to sell an item and the price at which they are willing to buy it (Kahneman et al., 1990). The principle can also be used to explain apparently uneconomic pricing behavior among sellers accepting a reduced (or even negative) margin for the prospect of gaining additional customers and sales (Urbany and Dickson, 1990).

The emerging psychological understanding of how prices are perceived has also had considerable influence on how prices are understood in marketing research. Most importantly, the insights from economic psychology concerning cognitive biases in how buyers perceive prices have been an important starting point for experiments and empirical studies of consumer responses to changes in pricing. At the most general level, the marketing discipline treats price as one of the parameters at a seller's disposal for positioning their offering in relation to competing offerings in the eyes of prospective customers (for a review, see Kienzler and Kowalkowski, 2017). Prices are thus not externally given (as in economics) but actively manipulated to increase sales and/or profitability and ensure a consistent offering. Prices are not simply aggregate outcomes, but are managed, influenced by social contexts, and imperfectly perceived.

Importantly, marketing scholars have stressed that pricing should not be regarded as a matter of costing but as a strategic marketing tool (Taylor and Wills, 1969). This view in turn has led researchers to: (a) study how customers perceive, process and react to price information (e.g., Grewal et al., 1996; Srivastava and Lurie, 2001; Biswas et al., 2006); and (b) investigate the effects of specific pricing tactics, such as price skimming, price bundling and price promotion (e.g., Chen et al., 1998; Basu and Vitharana, 2009; Spann et al., 2015). For instance, it is recognized that buyers may use price not only as an indicator of cost but also (lacking other information) as an indicator of product quality (Cialdini, 1984; Monroe and Lee, 1999). A special issue on behavioral pricing summarized the research front at the time as recognizing that (Maxwell and Estelami, 2005, 355): "consumers have difficulty processing prices accurately. They rely on cues to signal additional information and utilize heuristics to evaluate prices offered in the marketplace. They make comparative rather than absolute judgments and are influenced by subjective emotions as well as rational analysis."

In contrast to these first three disciplines, economic sociology conceives of prices as resulting "from the embeddedness of market transactions in institutions, social networks and culturally anchored frames of meaning" (Beckert, 2011, 757). Prices, then, are not the result of self-regulating markets, but of social processes and political power games. Compared to the other disciplines, however, the attention paid to prices has been relatively scant in sociology. Baker's (1984) classic study of price formation in two national securities markets is one important exception. Baker showed that prices in the studied markets were not simply aggregate outcomes but depended on the patterns of interactions between market actors. As a result, a growth in the number of buyers and sellers could result in seemingly counterintuitive outcomes (increased rather than decreased price volatility). Fligstein's (1996) work on markets as politics offers a second important contribution to the sociological understanding of prices. The central argument is that firms routinely act to stabilize their environment by reducing price competition, for instance by diversifying their products, by monopolizing markets, and/or by influencing State regulations.

The latter point brings up the key theme of how institutions may influence prices. While the role of institutions is attended to in some areas of heterodox economics (e.g., Commons, 1934; North, 1991), it is a mainstream argument in sociology. Obviously, the extreme version of institutional influence is direct price regulation, but this is only the tip of the iceberg. Numerous other regulations may affect prices, including, for instance, the extent to which effects of market transactions beyond those directly involved must be factored in by the transacting parties (e.g., environmental impact), the kind of information that must be made available by a seller (e.g., origin of produce, contents), varied levels of taxation on different types of goods and services, and so on. Such formalized regulations often differ across countries and industries, reflecting different cultural conventions, different conceptions of control, and indeed, different ideas about what may be legitimately sold on markets. Here, Zelizer's (1978, 1985) work on markets and morals offers key insights into the challenges of expanding the market economy, and hence prices, to areas "that are culturally defined as above financial relationships" (1978, 591). In such cases, Zelizer argues, a gradual process of legitimation is required in order for prices to gain acceptance and work in ways that resemble their role in less controversial market settings.

Different Responses to the Problem of Conveying Prices

All the disciplines discussed above agree that prices do not work unless relevant actors know of them. The disciplines have responded to this in different ways, however. For a long time, the standard response in economics to observations of breaches of the assumption of perfect information was to seek to correct reality to live up to this assumption by removing obstacles, improving the availability of information, and so on. During the past 25 years, this response has been developed further via the market design approach (Roth, 2007), for instance, by developing specific clearinghouse designs and auction algorithms (see, for example, Porat et al., 2008).

Economic psychology and, more recently, behavioral economics have instead sought to understand the various cognitive limitations and biases that affect price perception and hence develop a deeper understanding of the workings of less than ideal markets (see Thaler, 2016). But here as well, there has been a turn towards a more proactive stance largely linked to the growing popularity of *nudging* (Thaler and Sunstein, 2008) as a means of promoting socially desirable changes in consumer behavior that is characterized by "mindless choosing". Ironically, the abstract view of prices seems deeply rooted even in the minds of behavioral and technology-oriented economists. In Thaler and Sunstein's famous book on nudging, the authors recognize a wide variety of nudges, except prices in the material sense. They evoke several nudging schemes that play on monetary values – for example, clearer tariff information for complex services such as credit card services, cell phone subscriptions, insurance policies, mortgages (p. 93), charity debit cards instead of tax deduction for donations (p. 230), or a-dollar-a-day rewards for teenage mothers who avoid becoming pregnant again (p. 234) – but do not envision prices as technological nudges. It seems as if the authors forgot that price cards and price tags are among the oldest, most powerful, and certainly most widely spread, nudging devices used to entice consumers to make the "right" decision.

In many ways, nudging echoes what the marketing discipline has been preoccupied with for the better part of its existence (albeit not necessarily coupled with clear social desirables): identifying and testing ways in which to improve the market performance of individual products and services. As noted above, one key component of this has been to develop ways of utilizing price as an effective marketing tool, experimenting with different pricing structures, pricing tactics, and so on. Here, then, the objective has not necessarily been to improve the market as such, but rather how (primarily) sellers can improve their performance in the market. As a simple example: would a retailer increase profits by setting a high regular price on a good and then temporarily lowering it through "specials" compared to setting an "everyday low price"? However, as argued by Hagberg and Kjellberg (2015, 182), in most of this literature, "prices and price representations are conflated by focusing on 'perceived prices' (e.g., Gijsbrechts, 1993; Jacoby and Olson, 1977; Zeithaml, 1988). Further, perception-oriented pricing research prioritizes highly stylized experimental settings that drastically reduce the multiplicity of price representations facing consumers (e.g., Grewal et al., 1998; Srivastava and Lurie, 2001)."

Indeed, it is worth noting that in the rare instance when the format used to convey price information was the key research topic, a laboratory setting was used to secure "greater internal validity" (e.g., Zeithaml, 1982).

Within sociology, research on prices and price formation has focused on showing the social structuring of markets and its effect on the dissemination of price information, and on understanding the significance of price information across different social/cultural contexts. Since sociological inquiries have tended to be more "naturalistic", at least when compared to the idealized models in economics and the carefully designed experiments in economic psychology and marketing, the problem of price perceptions has not been as acute. In most studies, prices have been studied in their natural environments, so to speak. Nonetheless, like all the abovementioned disciplines, most sociological inquiries have tended to pay relatively little attention to the materiality of prices and have instead shared the common view of prices as just abstract values and focused attention on the rich tapestry of social factors that affect both the formation and use of prices in society.

Based on the above, it would be fair to say that how we come to know prices, in what form they are presented to us, and what role their materiality might have in markets are fairly neglected issues. That said, the topic has not been entirely neglected. Specifically, changes in regulations and requirements concerning the display of prices have triggered some research efforts, for instance, into the effects of unit price displays (Russo et al., 1975), or the above-cited work on consumer responses to in-store price information (Zeithaml, 1982). More recently, the technical possibilities of displaying prices linked to retail digitalization have also resulted in some studies of the effects of the provision of price information (e.g., Trifts and Häubl, 2003; Hanna et al., 2019).

We are certainly not the first ones to point out the lack of attention to the practical production and material display of prices. Indeed, during the past 15 years there has been a growing interest in precisely these issues. Among the pioneering works in this tradition are Kjellberg's (2004) and Barrey's (2006) studies of the practical work of setting prices in supermarkets, Beunza et al.'s (2006) development of a sociology of arbitrage in which the materiality of prices is crucial, Muniesa's (2007) study of the production of closing prices at the Paris Bourse, and Grandclément's (2008) work on the display of prices in supermarkets as a "jungle of paper". All of these contributions treat the formation and presentation of prices in markets as a practical problem that a wide variety of actors grapple with, including buyers and sellers, market providers, authorities, and politicians. They also explicitly recognize the material properties of prices. In the words of Muniesa (2007, 390) prices are: "material entities, always tied to concrete arrangements. Exploring their iconic, indexical and symbolic capacities [...] means considering, at least, three aspects: their material shape and display, the way in which they stand as a trace of something and, finally, their fit to a series of connections to other actions."

Studying Price Display in Markets as a Matter of Price Fixing

Against this backdrop, and following Muniesa's suggestion above, our approach in this book is to systematically inquire into the production and dissemination of prices in mundane markets. We do so by addressing three versions of the same question: *how are prices fixed?* The first version of this question concerns how prices are fixed in the sense of how they are decided upon. In other words, it concerns price *setting*. The second version concerns how prices are fixed in the sense of how they become attached to goods, or in other words how they are displayed at the point of purchase, that is, price *posting*. The third and final version of the question concerns how prices are fixed in the sense of repaired, or in other words, the *adjusting* of prices over time. A very practical challenge posed by these questions is of course what kind of study would help us answer them?

HOW TO STUDY THE DISPLAYING OF PRICES

In this book, we study the development of price display in the US grocery retail market for almost a century, from the 1920s until the 2010s. This ambitious time scope and choice of topic obviously presents methodological challenges. By stretching far back in time, it makes many modern digital methods untenable and prevents us from relying on classic observational methods and interviews. While accounting for historical events does not mean we must abandon all sociological and ethnographical methods, there are certainly advantages to be had by borrowing methods from disciplines that have made the past their primary concern. To this end, we have relied heavily on methodological cues from history and archaeology.

Empirical Setting

An important initial question for us was *where* and *when* to study price display. Five criteria were important here. *First*, we sought a market context within which price display had undergone considerable changes over an extended period of time that would still be possible for us to cover. *Second*, we sought a market context that would be evocative for readers in the sense that they could relate to it and perhaps even contrast our results with their own experiences. This led us to consider various mundane markets, most notably retail markets. *Third*, given the importance of regulatory developments hinted at in the beginning of this introduction, we sought a suitable regulatory context, in short, a context that had experienced the same regulatory changes. *Fourth*, to increase the relevance of our study, we sought a market context that could be considered a forerunner in that it influenced other market contexts, nationally and internationally. *Fifth*, we needed to ascertain the availability of data allowing us to explore these developments in some detail over the entire period. Taken together, these criteria significantly influenced our choice of the US grocery retail market in the twentieth century as a suitable market context for our purposes.

As any potential reader has a relation to the grocery retail market, our choice of the US grocery retail market allows our work to speak to readers in a way that a study of a more special market would not. The US grocery retail market has been a forerunner in the introduction of new retail technologies and formats throughout the twentieth century. During this century, this market has also undergone several significant changes during this period that have direct relevance for the display of prices, including the growth of self-service and chain stores, computerization, regulations, barcode scanning, and so on.

Methodological Approach

A second, and equally important, question was *how* to study price display in this context. We have sought inspiration both from sociology and ethnography and from disciplines that have made the past their primary concern. Thus, to explore the development and significance of price display technologies empirically we have employed a method we term the "archaeology of present times" (Cochoy, 2009). This is an innovative complement to classic historiographical research that mostly rests on the analysis of written materials, at the risk of overlooking the innumerable elements that people do not necessarily write about but that still constitute a major part of history. Like archaeologists, we base our analysis on the material forms that techniques of price display take (signs, shelf labels, price stickers, barcodes, labeling machines, digital shelf labels, etc.). This method offers one way of approaching our "material culture" (Cochoy, 2009; Prown, 1982; Schlereth, 1982; Witkowski, 1990). We combine this attention to material artifacts with the classic historical method of relying on written archival sources to gain knowledge about past events. More specifically, we analyze written documents in the form of magazine articles, a classic type of source in business history (see, for example, Bowlby, 2000; Spellman, 2016; Strasser, 1989), and occasionally complete them with varied secondary sources.

Here, the copresence of articles and advertisements, as well as the pervasive use of photographs and drawings in our source material, allowed us to supplement the historical method with an ethnographic gaze. Our approach thus combines the reading of written materials with the observation of pictorial ones; archival ethnography (Harper, 1998) paired with visual ethnography (Schwartz, 1989), so to speak. By paying attention both to human testimonies (mostly available in written form) and technical traces (accessible through pictures), we seek to achieve generalized symmetry about the contribution of human and nonhuman agencies (Callon, 1986). While, as mentioned, this method has been likened to a kind of "archeology of present time", we could also describe it as "ethnography of the past".

This method pays specific attention to the various material devices evidenced in historical sources but which often pass unnoticed in written accounts. Thus, our archival study attends both to the written texts and to the photos and images found in the magazine, allowing us to better account for the material aspect of the process.

Our Primary Source: the *Progressive Grocer*

To study how the display of prices developed in the US grocery retail market, we decided to rely on the systematic reading of one primary archival source, the *Progressive Grocer*, a trade magazine that was circulated for free among American independent retailers. This magazine was first published in the early 1920s and has remained alive and well since then. As such, it offers a unique window on the developments in the US grocery retail market for almost one century. Specifically, we follow the development of price display from the publication of the first issue of the *Progressive Grocer* in 1922 until 2020.

The *Progressive Grocer* is a US trade magazine that was launched to help the independent American grocery retailers modernize their businesses and resist the growing competition from chain stores, supermarkets and other large retailers (see Howard, 2015). One key message, repeated again and again in the magazine over the years, is that to remain competitive the independent grocers had to adopt modern techniques: new store fixtures like window cases and open shelves, new selling techniques like semi or full self-service, new tools such as slicing machines, delivery trucks or various forms of price display. In line with this remit, the magazine contains articles about the state of the retail sector and on how to improve business operations. In addition, since the magazine was funded by advertisers, each issue gathers a large number of advertisements from suppliers of technical devices and equipment designed to assist retail operations, as well as testimonies about devices and practices that could favor such modernization. Thus, the magazine offers numerous articles, surveys and pictures on the transformation of US grocery retail stores under the studied period. In particular, the pictures, cartoons and ads printed in the magazine provide a valuable window on the past in terms of the kinds of technologies US retailers could consider at a given point in time.

It is worth noting that our use of the *Progressive Grocer* as the main source of our account takes us beyond the narrow confines of a case study. The magazine works as a privileged point of entry to a repository of accounts that document both the mundane price display and price regulation practices for food at store level, overall policy discussions concerning the entire US market, as well as reflections on how the two are related. As such, it conveys important insights about the relation between behavior in the US grocery retail market and society more broadly. While the source focuses mainly on US grocery retailing and particularly the independent retailers that constituted its primary readership, it also includes material on developments from other countries, retail sectors and retail formats such as major retail chains and cooperatives.

Even if it is done systematically, basing our work on a single source is at first glance debatable, although it could offer a way of handling the overflows that often characterize business archives in more contemporary periods (Fellman and Propp, 2013). Careful historical inquiry usually requires the use of multiple sources and their subsequent triangulation (Tosh, 1991, 103–105). However, there are arguments in favor of our choice.

First, the *Progressive Grocer* is the leading trade magazine of its sector, with a readership which grew quickly: the publication was sent to 50 000 grocers when it was launched (1922, 05, 1; 1925, 07, 1 et seq.), that is, 20 percent of the professionals at the time, and this figure was extended to 75 000 professionals in the following decade (1936, 01, 9). Over time, its readership has changed into a more diverse group of retail professionals including CEOs, corporate executives, buyers and store managers particularly in the grocery sector, and in 2016 the total qualified circulation amounted to 37 381 (*Progressive Grocer*, 2019). It also gradually shifted from its initial focus on small stores to supermarkets, and thus reflected the evolution of a full industry. The magazine gathers inputs from various sources: contributions of journalists specialized in retail policies and techniques; insights into specific technical, commercial and legal issues by proclaimed experts; information about government regulations; facts and figures about competition (in particular chain stores and supermarkets); ads from suppliers promoting various retailing tools; articles reporting on experiences of individual retailers; and information about consumers, be it through professional testimonies or surveys.

Second, this wide and heterogeneous content allows triangulation of information within the source itself. Many of the articles and ads purport to promote particular techniques and pieces of equipment. As such, they do not necessarily provide an accurate depiction of actual use and business potential of these devices. In short, a lot of the information in our material is intended to promote rather than describe. Fortunately, our material from the *Progressive Grocer* also offers a wealth of "unwitting evidence" (Tosh, 1991, 106; see also Le Roy Ladurie, 1975) in the form of images, photographs and ads that are contemporary with the devices, but focus on other topics. For instance, we could observe a clear contrast between some of the promises and sales arguments linked to the use of price tags and the way such tags appeared in pictures illustrating other facets of the retail environment in our database. In short, this means that our empirical material is capable of offering a quite nuanced image of the developments we seek to account for.

The third argument is the advantage of following a single source continuously over a long period rather than intermittently covering multiple archives when trying to account for developments over time. We argue that following the *Progressive Grocer* provides a more systematic view of the array and timing of innovations, and a better chance of not missing small but nevertheless significant developments. That said, our approach is not strictly monomaniac: we have complemented our main source with other sources (see for instance our reliance on the full collection of US patents of price tags in Chapter 2, or ethnographic observations in contemporary retail outlets in Chapter 7) as well as with knowledge obtained from major works on similar topics (e.g., Bowlby, 2000; Chandler, 1990; Deutsch, 2010; Grandclément, 2008; Howard, 2015; Spellman, 2016; Strasser, 1989; Tedlow, 1990).

Data Collection

Our primary data was collected during a series of sessions at the US Library of Congress in June 2015, at the Gothenburg University Library from November 2015 to March 2016, at the New York Public Library in January and March–April 2016, and from our home offices in 2020. Through these sessions, we were able to browse every page of every issue of the *Progressive Grocer* from the very first issue of January 1922 to the December issue, 2020. All magazine pages containing information directly or indirectly linked to our project (e.g., on prices, price display and pricing technologies, store design and operations, merchandizing, retail format development, computerization, digitalization), were photographed and stored in a database. In total, this procedure generated a database containing about 15 000 magazine pages.

The pages in the resulting archive contain front covers, tables of contents, editorials, longer articles on topical issues, recurrent features such as "store of the month", interviews with prominent retailers, reports from experiments and studies conducted by magazine staff, short news flashes on new concepts, tools and technologies. The pages also contain a large number of advertisements from companies offering products and services to the readers of the magazine, including retail equipment manufacturers, retail service providers and producers of consumer goods. Most pages include both text and images related to the topics in question. Following a publication like the *Progressive Grocer* closely over almost a century, as we did, had a very clear and strong immersion effect. In leafing through several consecutive years of the magazine, we experienced that our reading of the journal de facto displaced us both temporally and spatially, from whichever library or office we happened to sit in on that day to early, mid- or late twentieth-century American grocery retailing.

Data Analysis

Once we had completed the data collection, we used Adobe Bridge to add codes in the metadata of each page file. These codes were inductively generated and concern both the *form* of the information found on the page, for example type of article, advertisement, supplement, table of contents, and the information *content*, for example pricing, store format, merchandizing, store operations. All three researchers contributed to this process by coding an initial set of magazine pages (spread out over the time period covered in our study). We then compared our proposed codes and developed a standardized coding structure based on our experiences. The entire database was then coded according to this scheme, along the lines of an indexing rather than tabular approach. During this work, we added new codes to the initial coding structure as new topics emerged. Since one magazine page can contain several items, for instance, an article, a news flash and an advertisement, the number of codes ascribed to each page varies considerably depending on page contents. The combination of our chronological file names and the initial coding provided us with a highly useful sorting device for exploring specific issues during specific periods. This allowed us to analyze subsets of the collected material along various thematic lines (such as writing price cards, price tag technologies, price policies, and so on).

Our analyses were then continued by following a three-step process. First, we sought out a subsection of the material by using the assigned codes and the chronological information found in the file names. Second, we examined the selected source material in detail, making running notes, copying central quotes, and extracting illustrative images. Third, we developed a thematically and/or temporally organized narrative on the topic in question based on the underlying source material. Specifically, our analytical approach always combined textual and visual ethnography (Pink, 2007). While we analyzed the actors' testimonies and viewpoints as expressed in writing in the articles and ads, the photographs, drawings and other illustrations found on the pages provided windows on the past. By sharing our database of magazine pages via a secure online service, we were able to work jointly on different subprojects despite being geographically separated.

Writing Up

In this book, we present our findings from our exploration of the development of price display in the US grocery retail market over a century. We specifically attend to the link between overall price movements in the US and the various tactics and techniques employed by US grocery retailers. As mentioned above, we show that *fixing* prices has a triple meaning: fixing prices is of course about *setting* economic values as economists understand it, but it is also about *posting* prices materially in retail settings, and *adjusting* them to changing material and economic conditions. And our historical account shows that the price economy can only be understood through the long but largely unknown interplay of these three dimensions.

The individual chapters are presented on the basis of thematic and chronological considerations. While several of the book chapters return to the 1920s as their starting point, the first three chapters more specifically focus on the first and second decades of the period (1920s–1930s). Chapter 4 focuses primarily on the 1940s and 1950s, while Chapter 5 focuses on the 1940s–1980s and the main focus of Chapter 6 is on the 1960s–2010. Chapter 7, which deals with the most recent developments from the 1980s to the present time, also comes full circle by relating later technological innovations with those of the 1920s.

Throughout the book, we analyze various forms of price display with associated practices and market developments, from showcards and price tickets (Chapter 1), swing tags and moldings (Chapter 2), batch sale and reference price moldings and tickets (Chapters 3 and 4), price pens, price stamps, price label printers and price guns (Chapter 5), barcodes (Chapter 6) and ESLs (Chapter 7). The chapters include specific attention to the emergence of price display from handwritten prices into printed ones (Chapter 1), successive developments of fixity and flexibility (Chapter 2), price display techniques and regulations (Chapters 3 and 4), item pricing (Chapter 5), as well as challenges to item pricing introduced by new price display technologies (Chapters 6 and 7).

Three main analytical themes are recurrent throughout the book. First, it explores the relationship between "micro-practices" of pricing and wider market changes in terms of general price levels, regulations, and power relationships between various market actors and reveals the mundane governance of price display. Second, it pays particular attention to the materiality of prices and shows how the material dimension of prices needs to be taken into account in order to understand prices and price transformation in practice. Third and finally, particular attention is paid to the long-term evolution of digitalization of price display in retail settings, by distinguishing three aspects of that process: indexing, numberizing, and computerizing, which over time has revolved around issues such as fixity and flexibility, standardization, universality and transparency.

STRUCTURE OF THE BOOK

Following this introduction, the book contains seven empirical chapters followed by a concluding chapter. Chapter 1 starts from the etymology of the term "digital" (from *digitus*, finger or toe) and shows that the display of prices in retail settings surprisingly rests on a *digitalization* process right from the beginning. The chapter focuses on a crucial and transitional period: the move from coded to open prices in retail stores in the early twentieth century. The chapter details how and why the grocery business went from concealed, coded prices to open, public and "indexed" prices (i.e., prices referring to a given set of numbers but also prices retailers point at, as if they showed them with their index). It explains how this shift was made by means of sophisticated (hand) writing devices and elaborate writing methods. All in all, the chapter traces how the fingers of the invisible hand progressively and ceaselessly moved to rewrite the big book of the contemporary market economy.

Chapter 2 reviews the spread and evolution of price display technologies, notably mobile and adjustable price tags for store shelves. It shows how the invention of price tags helped spread prices onto the shelves as well as introduce a subtle equilibrium between fixed, public prices for every consumer and removable prices for the grocers. It reviews how this new technology was refined, through the introduction of "swing tags", which built a better vertical association between the goods and the underlying prices, and "price tag moldings", which afforded improved lateral placement of prices. By disclosing prices, tags introduced a profound cultural and economic change: they empowered consumers, weakened service, and favored powerful actors like chains and supermarkets.

Chapter 3 focuses on the development of "price cutting" strategies that rapidly spread after World War I. These strategies mobilized price display as a weapon for aggressive price competition and rested on the use of new techniques like batch sales and the use of specials to attract consumers. However, the widespread use of price cutting techniques led to the development of price wars that worked as both a source and an effect of deflation and economic decline. This forced retail professionals to critically examine their former practices and subsequently led to counter-measures such as "resale price maintenance" policies as well as ad hoc public regulation. Eventually these transformations produced several new pricing methods and tools, but also altered the identities of market actors (manufacturers, grocers, consumers, regulators) and modified power relationships in the US grocery market.

Chapter 4 explores the postwar era of inflation and governmental "price ceiling" policies. Government and market actors joined forces to handle various problems associated with the price ceiling policy. The hybridization of regulations and retail management practices contributed to reshape price setting in the retail market. It led to the spread of "stereoscopic prices", that is, the simultaneous display of offered price and reference prices, which gave rise to new forms of price competition and reshaped product qualification and pricing processes.

Chapter 5 addresses two major interrelated developments in price display: the development of "item pricing" as a way of bridging the gap between shelf prices and checkout operations, and the development of various supportive technologies, such as price pens, price labelers, price stampers, and so on. Not only did these technologies help stabilize prices and allow them to travel with the goods, but they also enhanced prices with quality information, thanks to the graphic possibilities associated with the new technology of paper stickers. The technique was soon transferred to "price guns", allowing direct labeling (and relabeling) of prices on every product in the store. The expression "price gun" emphasizes the replacement of negotiable prices by prices that appear as "take it or leave it" ultimatums. These imposed fixed prices are distinctive features of the contemporary economy; they favor the brand logic and express the new managerial control over previous "free" price adjustments.

Chapter 6 explores how cash registers and scales first, and later barcodes and related devices, contributed to build, then transform, the market infrastructure in grocery retailing. The appearance of barcodes and scanners in the 1970s was intended to further stabilize the link between products and prices, but also introduced a partial and ironic return to the original coded prices. The UPC barcode was originally intended to provide a unique identifier for individual goods and, as such, its spread had a structuring influence on the upstream grocery markets. Barcode scanning, on the other hand, purported to improve the efficiency of retail operations by reducing the amount of work spent on price marking and by improving the precision and speed of checkouts. But the success and continued spread of barcodes to virtually every product sold in grocery stores meant that they could be appropriated for other uses, such as loyalty programs, tracking of purchasing behavior, consumer analytics, and targeted marketing.

Chapter 7 addresses one of the latest developments in price tag history – the invention of ESLs. While ESLs represent one of the latest and most sophisticated incarnations of price tag technology, their presence is surprisingly still marginal, particularly in the United States. The chapter analyses the promises of the technology and the problems encountered since their introduction in the mid-1980s and onward. Since their inception, ESLs have been associated with promises to improve shopper experiences, to simplify logistical in-store operations, as well as to enable increased interconnectivity. However, problems surrounding ESLs have particularly concerned the item-pricing regulations, gaps between the promises of the technology and its practical feasibility, but also that alternative solutions proved more compatible with existing store infrastructure. The account highlights how the success of an innovation is a matter of both timing and environmental fit, where technologies such as ESL rarely appear in isolation, but must fit with the wider contexts, systems and infrastructures. A century after, digital prices are still dependent on previous practices and infrastructures, such as hand operations and paper labels.

In the final and concluding chapter, we summarize and discuss the overall findings from the chapters in relation to the three main analytical themes. First, it discusses the relationships between the various micro-practices of pricing accounted for in the chapters in relation to wider market changes, power relationships and the mundane governance of price display. Second, it discusses the materiality of prices and its importance for understanding prices and price transformation in practice. Third, it discusses the long-term evolution of digitalization of price display.

Throughout this book, unless otherwise stated, we use a simplified format when referencing specific source pages from the *Progressive Grocer*: (year, issue, page). All illustrations, photographs and excerpts that we use are reproduced with the kind permission of the *Progressive Grocer*.

1. Indexing prices: prices and the fingers of the invisible hand

Source: Progressive Grocer (1924, 07, 46).

Figure 1.1   Gold Medal flour is never used alone

The history of price display is closely linked to the move from counter-service to self-service. In counter-service settings, "Flour is Never Used Alone", the ad says (Figure 1.1). Flour is a magical good that multiplies sales in calling for eggs, milk, sugar, vanilla, baking soda, and many other ingredients. But if flour is never used alone, it is never sold alone either. The Gold Medal flour doesn't go from the manufacturer to the consumer directly; the possibility of self-service still belongs to an illusory future. The ad acknowledges the present state of commerce and foreshadows the possible next one it dreams about.

As far as the present state is concerned, the manufacturer has no other choice than to meet the worldview of the counter-oriented grocer. If the big bag of flour is placed on the counter, it is placed there so that it can be taken not by the consumer, but by the grocer. The flour company delivers the bag to the professional so that the latter can open it, place its content in an opaque chest and then sell it in bulk like the generic "sugar" in the back, thus hide the brand and take full control of the sale, both in terms of price and quality. The sale of flour is necessarily mediated by the grocer, who can sell it as he wishes. This said, while acknowledging the rules of counter-service, the ad also pushes a new approach that discreetly promotes the new brand and package economy: the Gold Medal brand is clearly put forward; other packaged and branded products are displayed in the back, and more importantly on the counter, implicitly suggesting that, in the end, Gold Medal flour will be asked for by the consumers, and sold in the same way.[1]

Of course, this was just one ad; the chosen figure is a drawing, a rhetorical device, a fiction. But this fiction, featuring the archetypal store of its time, may tell us more about commerce in the early twentieth century than a thousand pictures of real retail outlets. Indeed, it is telling that a large brand, in order to seduce grocers, still had to replicate the service grocery store, with its thick counter and powerful grocer who would remove the brand and decide how to present and price the good. In the old grocery business, the grocer was king. He could turn his back to the customer; the goods were displayed behind the counter and their prices not even shown. Even if things were now changing (packaged goods began to invade the store, first on the shelves and then on the counter), the grocer still controlled what packages were displayed, how they were priced, and – as the grocer's hand on one specific box illustrates – which packages were selected in the end.

---

[1] At the time, the flour industry was indeed engaged in a new marketing effort based on the introduction of brands and advertising aimed at differentiating products that had been up to then considered as the same, because the grain came from the same fields in western Minnesota and North Dakota, and was milled with the same types of machines and with the same techniques (see https://www.mnhs.org/millcity/learn/history/flour-milling).

FROM CODED TO OPEN PRICES

As noted by historians of retailing, the access to price knowledge in traditional counter-service grocery stores was often restricted. Nineteenth-century retailers were used to hiding prices: they often marked them at the bottom of the merchandise, but in the form of enigmatic encrypted signs whose meaning was accessible to them only, thus enabling them to both know the cost of each item and adjust the selling price to each customer. As reported by Susan Spellman (2009), various techniques could be used in this respect. One of them consisted of using a game of tic-tac-toe, with numbers 1 to 9 placed on the grid (see Table 1.1).

Table 1.1   *Tic-tac-toe-like price code*

1	2	3
4	5	6
7	8	9

Each angle of the grid surrounding a given number would represent it; for instance, $1.35 would be noted by:

⌐⌐⌐

This coding system, with its bar-like simple straight strokes placed at the bottom of each package, foreshadowed the barcodes that invaded retail stores much later; see Chapter 6.

A similar and frequently used technique was to code each number as a letter of the alphabet. To this end, one used a word made up of ten different letters, such as "regulation", and assigned "R" to 1, "E" to 2, and so on (see Table 1.2).

Table 1.2   *Alphanumeric price code*

R	E	G	U	L	A	T	I	O	N
1	2	3	4	5	6	7	8	9	0

According to this scheme, \$1.35 would be coded as "RGL". This practice was fully indexical in Garfinkel's (1967) sense: the meaning of each price was determined by the particular market transaction context (retail store) and how the coded purchasing prices were converted into particular retail prices. The retailer used these hidden prices[2] as the basis for bargaining with each individual consumer, as noted by Christine Frederick, a pioneering progressive consumer activist in the early twentieth century:

> I thought that the best way to do my family marketing was to ask the dealer his price and then Jew him down.[3] That, I am told, was the attitude of all consumers in this country fifty years ago. This condition existed because at that time all dealers and merchants overpriced their articles, and the shrewd buyer was the only one who could get the best trade or bargain, after hours of talk and discussion. (Quoted in Strasser, 1989, 270)

As the retail space was transformed through the introduction of "open display", these coding techniques lost their relevance and power. Open display was a transitional method between counter-service and self-service. The approach developed throughout the 1920s, based on the idea that consumers would buy more if they had visual access to the goods. To this end, the opaque barrier of the counter was relegated to the periphery of the store, while "mass displays" of goods, packages and cans invaded store windows, and glass showcases and open shelves stocked from top to bottom appeared inside the stores (Cochoy, 2015a).

This new approach was the result of both unintentional effects and deliberate efforts. On the (more or less) unintentional side, packaged and canned goods played a major role. Given their standardized flat tops, these goods could be easily piled up to offer increased visual access. Being hermetic and solid, they reduced the risk of spoilage or damage and thus the reluctance of retailers to provide direct access to them. Last but not least, their opaque and regular surface favored written descriptions of their content, hence helping the products inform the consumers directly about their characteristics, and thus bypassing the mediation of the retailer.

---

[2]   It should be noted that the historical movement for price disclosure, far from being limited to the grocery sector, also concerns other markets like the market for alcohol beverages in the Nordic countries or real estate in other parts of the world. Conversely, some sectors still resist price display, like lawyer services in France for instance. Last but not least, in the United States, price display in contemporary grocery settings is by no means hegemonic depending on various State regulations.

[3]   We strongly disapprove of this expression, which reflects long-standing prejudices that unfortunately still can be found today, although they may not be expressed as bluntly as in the quoted text.

On the more deliberate side, the features of open display arrangements were energetically promoted by furniture providers. These were eager to show that a shelf was not just a shelf anymore so that old fixtures had to be replaced with new ones. They promoted shelves where vertical separations were removed in order to get rid of these opaque blinders that prevented you from seeing the goods from any angle. They also pushed brand new window showcases, which helped consumers inspect the merchandise while still preventing them from touching it. The open display concept, initially formulated by the Dayton company, a major store equipment provider, was later systematized and promoted by the *Progressive Grocer* itself through a national campaign to convert grocery stores in order to benefit from its potential and merits (Cochoy, 2020). The open display idea was a subtle compromise between service and self-service that served as a transition between the two. The consumer could now see the goods without touching them, and while the grocer preserved his service-oriented professional identity and operations, he avoided the risk of having the goods spoiled, damaged, or even stolen.

The notion of "open display" comes across as a purely qualitative approach, aimed at reshaping the sensorial and cognitive relationship between customers and goods. But even if open display initially was about qualitative and cognitive changes, it soon had a dramatic impact also on quantitative and calculative dimensions by requiring changes in pricing. The key feature of open display is the direct visual interaction between consumers and products, without retailer mediation. This reconfiguration of the buying relationship from a triadic to a dyadic one raised the issue of price display. If consumers were learning about the goods on their own, it made sense to make prices part of that setting. After all, price is one key dimension in qualifying products for exchange (Callon et al., 2002).

The *Progressive Grocer* quickly acted on this issue, pushing its readers to adopt price display practices. But achieving this goal was not easy. The first 25 years of the magazine provide ample illustrations of the fact that modern price marking techniques and price tag technologies were far from systematically and ubiquitously used. Indeed, there are several indications that the uptake was quite slow: first, counter-service had a remarkable endurance. Despite the magazine's crusade for open display and self-service, counter-service and semi-self-service remained the dominant modes of exchange until the late 1940s (1949, 04, 59). Second, and closely linked to the slow evolution towards self-service, there are innumerable pictures of store interiors lacking clear or systematic price marking. Third, the persistent pushing of the issue by the *Progressive Grocer* throughout this time period signals that it was far from resolved. So, why did the problem persist? Why was price display resisted? One of the major reasons can be deduced from cartoons published on the matter (see Figure 1.2).

Source: Progressive Grocer (left: 1938, 07, 149; right: 1948, 11, 168).

Figure 1.2   Price display competition

Both cartoons highlight one major risk of price display, namely that it would alter market competition by triggering an inescapable (vicious or virtuous, depending on who you ask) spiral of price cutting. Displayed prices work as indexes, in the "scale" meaning of the word: they facilitate price comparison and thus favor (possibly destructive) price competition. However, an evolution can be seen over time. The first cartoon reminds us of the old coded prices, even if the idea of hiding prices has been abandoned, so that the only remaining option is an absurd coding of product names. In the second cartoon, published 10 years later, the possibility of coding prices is gone, and instead, we see a foolish and destructive game of pure price competition between retailers who were previously good neighbors. Behind any humorous fiction lies a serious anxiety, and the *Progressive Grocer* knew it well, given the repeated efforts to reduce the worries of its readership by showing them that price display, even if inescapable, could present an opportunity rather than a threat. Behind this shift in price display regime is the opposition between prices as the results of for-mulation strategies (produced by market agencements with fixed calculation rules, like cost plus margin; Callon, 2013) and prices as spontaneous outcomes of fluctuations (resulting from the meeting of supply and demand).

The ones to convince about the new pricing regime were the retailers rather than the consumers. As far as the latter were concerned, the *Progressive Grocer* expressed the point of view of a fictional consumer who stressed the emancipatory qualities of self-service and posted prices.

> I like to go where the goods are all price-marked. Like every other woman, I have a bargaining instinct, but I don't like to argue about prices. I want to be able to look at the article and read the price myself. And that's why I buy at the chain store. To

tell you the truth, I don't care for the manager, but I don't have to talk to him much. [...] I just go abou' [sic.] comparing prices, and when I see something that the price tells me I can afford, I sell it to myself. [...] And if there is anything I hate, it's to have about half a dozen curious women around when I ask the price, and then have to decide that it's too much. It's terribly embarrassing, and when I try to escape by paying more for the article than I intended to spend, it gives me no pleasure. I am a little sensitive about these things, so I go where I won't be embarrassed. [...] Priceless groceries always make me think I'm going to have to pay more than somebody else. If they are marked, it means that I will at least get a fair deal. (1928, 12, 42; 94)

Apart from a contradiction (how can a subject have a bargaining instinct and like fixed prices?!) and some well-known prejudices that may indicate a male author (women have nature-like drives; being a woman is being curious), what is said makes sense: the idea that, during a transaction, the mediation of grocers or the presence of other customers was experienced as a painful social pressure has been documented and confirmed by subsequent scholarship. Business historians and market sociologists have pointed at the burden of social interactions in retail settings, particularly for women exposed to various sorts of harassment in this rather chauvinist environment (Deutsch, 2004). From this perspective, self-service had a welcome emancipatory power: it allowed consumers to privately choose the products they like at the price they wish, without fearing the moral or social judgment they previously had to suffer from both retailers and peers (Du Gay, 2004; Deutsch, 2001).

Another article published by the *Progressive Grocer* legitimates this view with additional arguments. A first one is that price tags help consumers save time, and more or less implicitly suggests that faster sales may increase store attendance, sales volumes and thus profits:

Customers are inevitably drawn to such a store [i.e. a shop where goods are "neatly priced" from "window" to "store interior"] because it saves them time. It gives them the satisfaction of feeling well informed without having to ask questions. Remember that many a shopper is a timid soul who hesitates to ask the price of an imported box of water wafers for fear it will be too expensive and embarrassing to admit it. Price tags, plainly displayed, eliminate this situation. (1931, 01, 28–9)

Another very subtle yet more theoretical argument is that customers, given their budget constraints, will not spend more than what they planned for during each shopping trip. The hope of getting more money from the customers by overpricing individual goods thus becomes illusory: the purchase of expensive goods will be compensated by the purchase of cheaper ones or by a reduction of the shopping list (maybe not during the first visit due to the lack of price information, but during subsequent trips, based on the costly experience of this opacity). By contrast, price tags will rather help people spend all the money they are ready to allocate to their provisioning operations: "Remember, too, that many a housewife runs her home on the budget system and must do the buying for her table accordingly. Price tags hanging from the shelves give her the opportunity of figuring ahead what she can afford to buy" (1931, 01, 29).

Last but not least, the article underlines that the preoccupation with prices is both central and inevitable in market settings. Using price tags is a way of anticipating and responding to this: "The most valuable store to the woman who is marketing [sic.] is the one that anticipates her questions and answers them before they are asked. The most important among these is 'How much?' The answer should be taken care of by the price tag" (1931, 01, 114).

By showing that consumers did not have to be convinced about the merits of price tags, and doing it through the figuration of the consumer's point of view, the reluctant grocer was invited to share this view and change his mind. In order to secure this change of viewpoint, the articles relied on a well-chosen metaphor: "Goods that are displayed without a price are as unsatisfactory as listening to a football game over the radio when the announcer neglects to tell the score ... and people will invariably infer that the price is much higher than it actually is" (1931, 01, 29).

The bet behind the football metaphor used by the (female[4]) journalist is clear: the chauvinist grocer will be more inclined to adopt his female customer's point of view if the reasoning behind her behavior is expressed in terms of his own male interests, tastes and preferences. This rhetoric is also traceable in the fictitious consumer testimony reported above that presses where it hurts: it implicitly promotes self-service ("I sell it to myself"). Moreover, it stresses that refusing price display for fear of competition ironically favors the independent grocer's most feared and hated enemy, the chain store ("I want to be able to look at the article and read the price myself. And that's why I buy at the chain store"). Price display is presented as the inescapable companion of open display: "If I price my goods, I will open the door to competition, but if I don't price them, I will lose against competition, because non-priced goods will be systematically interpreted as too expensive." The lesson is clear: trying to avoid competition is the best way to become its victim, much like the unfortunate driver who, after losing control of the car, stares at the tree he or she desperately tries to avoid rather than keeping his or her eyes on the road, as a trained pilot would:

> An objection has been raised that priced merchandise invites the nearby competitor to practice consistent underpricing. The average grocer tends to take this point

---

[4]   The signature of an article by a female contributor is exceptional in the *Progressive Grocer*. The article in question was written by Helen Augsburg (1931, 01, 28 et seq.).

seriously. Unless his store has a reputation for being high-priced and actually is, he should think less of the subject. As stated before, the inference of the customer is that the unpriced merchandise is always the most expensive. As a direct result, unpriced items are the slow sellers, regardless of what their price may be. (1931, 01, 116)

The irony of this mechanism is that it bears all the characteristics, wittingly or not, of a (doubly) "inverted adverse selection process". George Akerlof's lesson about the consequences of asymmetries of information in markets settings is well known: when a seller knows more about the quality of her product than her customers, the buyer, having no means of differentiating bad products from good ones, finds it rational to buy the cheapest. In the long run, the aggregation of such choices drives good quality products out of the market for the benefit of opportunistic sellers (Akerlof, 1970). The price tag case introduces a first inversion of the Akerlofian adverse selection, since when prices are missing, the asymmetry of information concerns the price dimension rather than the quality of the products (which can be discovered by tasting the goods if sold in bulk, or inferred from the brand name if packaged). The second inversion comes later: instead of driving bad products out of the market for the profit of opportunistic sellers, the price asymmetry drives unmarked expensive goods and bad sellers out of the market, due to the shoppers' preference for priced goods. With asymmetries of information restricted to quality, opportunism is rewarded and honest players punished. When information asymmetries pertain to prices, it's the exact opposite: opportunism is punished, and market transparency rewarded, for the benefit of both retailers and consumers.

In case this consumer-centered rhetoric was not enough, the *Progressive Grocer* introduced two additional grocer-centered arguments. The first one was financial. It implicitly praised the new strategy of profit through higher volumes and lower prices that was winning over the former approach of limited sales of high-priced goods (Strasser, 1989). Thus, the grocer should seek to attract more customers by displaying and lowering his prices rather than restricting himself to an inward and opaque game of differentiated product markups:

> The old theory is that if the customer shows a desire for a certain article, the salesman should be able to sell it to him regardless of what the price might be. But experience has taught us that such transactions do not generally lead to building continued good will and therefore should be avoided. [...] the grocer must think less of competition of brands within his four walls and consider more the competition presented by his fellow retailers. [...] The neatly well priced window and store interior is today the biggest boon to rapid selling. (1931, 01, 28)

The second argument was organizational. It balances the somewhat negative view of price display as a front-office risk (lower margins) by showing
that the method can also work as a back-office opportunity. Pursuing
a profit-through-volume strategy increased both the assortment and the
number of staff members, and thus multiplied the number and complexity of
operations. Here, price display offered a way to control labor, speed up service,
and prevent errors:

> Considering the advisability and advantages of using price tags from your own
> standpoint, they eliminate beyond question the possibility of clerks making mistakes
> in quoting prices to customers. Every day we hear clerks calling across the store,
> "Hey, Jack … what's the price of this?" while the customer stands by waiting, and
> if "Jack" has a customer, she must wait too. (1931, 01, 116)

If it had been the grocer's responsibility to know how many prices he could
memorize and how he could achieve this, the same grocer now had to know
whether his clerks were as dedicated and gifted in performing the same task.
In this respect, the daily management of prices as well as their visual ubiquity
and permanence became a good way to teach prices to the personnel and thus
reduce possible mistakes:

> [A] man who is busy placing various items on the shelves will find it difficult to
> remember their prices. Studying lists is likewise of little aid in acquiring a thorough
> knowledge of the price structure because the average human memory is too short
> to remember a long list of prices without confusion. […] Price changes should be
> made by the checker himself or should look at each item on the shelf as he reads it on
> the change list. This makes the new prices much easier to remember. (1939, 02, 44)

In other words, the *Progressive Grocer* suggested training clerks to use
price lists and price tags as a way to learn the correspondence between each
product and its economic value, just as one engages children to play the classic
memory game. In the latter, the players have to identify pairs of images among
a large and mixed set of cards turned face down. The one who identifies the
greatest number of pairs wins. This approach to price learning foreshadows
the results of contemporary situated and equipped cognition. In particular, it
anticipates the results of Jean Lave and her colleagues' famous study on consumer arithmetic in grocery shopping (Lave et al, 1984). The authors showed
that the calculative abilities of shoppers are greatly improved when they
rest on the direct manipulation of goods, rather than on just abstract mental
calculations. For instance, by handling pre-packaged cheese items, a shopper
was able to perform a kind of physical "everything else equal" calculation and
detect a pricing error. But in the case of price tags, what is at stake concerns
store owners managing their employees to reduce mistakes when dealing with

valuable items. In other words, the memory game of price tags is presented as a way to overcome a classic principal–agent problem by providing an astute solution to strengthen the link between specific products and their economic valuation.

It is important, at this stage, to observe that the various arguments reviewed above were of course identified and repeated by price tag suppliers well before the journalists of the *Progressive Grocer* picked them up and tried to convince their readers to follow along. See for instance the messages in the advertisements of the price tag manufacturer Frank G. Shuman Co. already during the very first year of the magazine (Figure 1.3). These arguments anticipate the *Progressive Grocer*'s rhetoric in favor of price display, although in a more cautious, conservative and respectful way. The Shuman Company focuses on classic window and counter-service rather than on open display, at a period when these arrangements still dominated the market it intended to seduce. Moreover, eager to motivate rather than worry its prospective clients, the company preferred to evoke the glowing promises of increased sales rather than the threat of price competition:

> Can you remember 1150 prices? Only a genius could carry in his head all prices on merchandise carried by your store and during your busy day you haven't the time or patience to answer your clerk's call of "How much is this?" and to be looking up prices—put your time to a profitable use (1922, 04, 94); First of all the window shopper and the counter shopper want to know "how much does it cost?" The price makes the sale and an attractive price sign gets immediate attention to your prices and your goods (1922, 10, 82); Price tags turn the "Lukewarm" interest of Window and Counter shoppers into sales. Shroud the price in mystery and the possible buyer will walk away rather than bother to ask questions. Don't lose a single sale. Mark your goods clearly (1922, 12, 87); etc.

But whether presented in articles or advertisements, the arguments in favor of price display were just words, ideas, rhetorical devices, and as such they faced the well-known limits of language performativity (Austin, 1962; Butler, 2010; Callon, 2010). Indeed, the journal appears to have realized that words work much better if combined with things (Cochoy, 2008b), if soft discourses are based on hard facts, if logical propositions are put to the test.[5] To this end, the magazine decided to conduct an experiment and report its results. The resulting article was published at the end of 1948, that is, more than 25 years after the launch of the magazine and its first attempt to promote price display (1948, 11,

---

[5]   Even if of course and thanks to the sociology of science we have long known that such a combination never really quits the realm of language or rather the chain of "inscriptions" (Latour and Woolgar, 1979), but helps in moving from a weak rhetoric to a stronger one (Latour, 1987).

Source: *Progressive Grocer* (left: 1922, 04, 94; middle: 1922, 10, 82; right: 1922, 12, 87).

Figure 1.3   The rhetoric of Shuman's price tags

84–5). This lag shows the resistance or sluggishness of stores to adopt the new techniques, as evidenced by the dominance of the semi-self-service arrangement until 1947, that is, the year before the article was published. It also hints at the lack of regulatory measures to mandate price display (an important issue that we will address in greater detail in Chapters 3 and 4). Nonetheless, the results of the study were clear:

> With a price plainly in view, a customer has all the facts before her and she can quickly decide whether to buy or not to buy. Without a price, she is forced to guess, to try to read the merchant's mind. Needless to say, guessing games do not promote sales, and 2/3 of possible sales are lost, according to actual store tests conducted by The Progressive Grocer. (1948, 11, 84)

The study was conducted in the following way: after a trip through a set of food stores selected at random, the authors noted that price marks were frequently absent, blurred or illegible. They subsequently conducted a test in four stores, three with self-service and one with counter-service. This test targeted a selection of everyday products, mostly with national brands, like ketchup, pineapple, pickles, peanut butter, mayonnaise, and so on. The test was organized over two weeks. During the first week, prices were rubbed off and price tags removed from the goods and shelves; during the second week, the goods were instead priced both individually and on the shelves. The comparison between the sales figures obtained for each week clearly showed that "sales volume, both in terms of value and volume, was three times as great when merchandise was price marked as it was when not price marked" (1948, 11, 85). More precisely, the summary chart showed that the effect of price absence was always negative, resulting in a financial loss that varied between 42 percent (instant chocolate) and 93 percent (mayonnaise; grape jelly). All in all, 182 vs. 561 items were sold; $167.02 vs. $54.05 was earned, resulting in a sales loss of $112.97. The explanation for this spectacular result was self-evident following the reasoning we already encountered:

> [The customer's] inner thoughts are probably that [the unpriced good] is so expensive that the merchant is ashamed to post a price, or that the store charges whatever she appears willing to pay, or that the owner of the store is simply a poor businessman. Besides, many women are embarrassed when they have to ask a price. Whatever their thoughts may be, the result is usually the same. They simply don't buy. (1948, 11, 86)

To summarize, price display worked as a distributed price index. Distributed throughout the store aisles, this index was first involuntary and partial in Strathern's (2004 [1991]) sense of being both limited and far from neutral. It was an emerging effect rather than the outcome of a deliberate strategy. Its messy and scattered character was far from a "real" index, well organized, printed on paper and sorted alphabetically. However, as we just saw, both the journalists of the *Progressive Grocer* and the price tag manufacturers encouraged grocers to seize this indexical character of price display. The need to display all prices in a self-service environment and to memorize them contributed to "fix" prices, that is, to stabilize their level and print corresponding lists, rather than have them shift on the basis of local bargaining or global price fluctuations. But being aware of a strong positive effect of price display on sales was not enough: knowing that prices had to be displayed still left open the question of how to display them.

PRICE WRITING DEVICES

Prices are symbolic information pertaining to language. As such, they can be made public by being spelled out or written. But writing prices can be done in different ways. First, prices can easily be written by hand. This approach can be seen as the first step in a long process of price "digitalization", provided that we remember the etymology of the term "digital" (from *digitus*, finger or toe) and see the fingers that lie behind the digital. The grocery business can indeed be seen as an inherently digital business, whether "electronized" or not. Hence, looking back at previous high-tech devices offers one way to understand the present (Johnson, 2016).[6] Retailing is about *handling* the stock, the display, the delivery, the money; it is about picking, cutting and slicing the goods; all these operations are done by hand, with strong, agile, expert fingers.

In this respect, it is no wonder that the International Business Machines Corporation (IBM) was digital in the sense of finger-oriented before becoming digital in the sense of number-oriented. Through its Dayton branch, IBM started selling slicers, grinders, mills and scales as early as in the first part of the twentieth century. In other words, IBM empowered the fingers of retailers with mechanical tools long before it assisted their brains with electronic computers (see Figure 1.4, left). This finger orientation of equipment manufacturers also extended to the preservation of grocers' fingers by adopting a design that "can't catch fingers" (Figure 1.4, right).

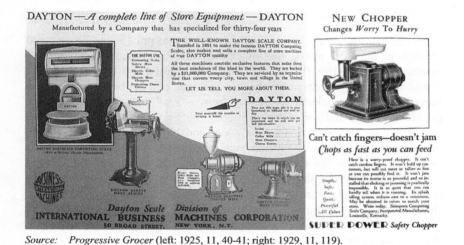

Source: Progressive Grocer (left: 1925, 11, 40-41; right: 1929, 11, 119).

Figure 1.4   *IBM and Stimpson's indexing machines: abandoning handwritten prices and preserving fingers*

The digitalization of prices followed a similar pattern, from handwritten prices to electronic ones, through their mechanization and subsequent computerization. Let us start when "digitalizing" prices meant indexing them, if we give to this word a dual sense: on the one *hand*, indexing means referring a price to a given set of numbers. Here, we refer to the price as a material entity, a given

---

6   We thank Nikhilesh Dholakia for suggesting this wonderful reference.

sign written on a prop, this entity being itself connected – indexed – to a range of values. On the other hand, we propose to take "indexing" as a synecdoche of handwriting, that is: using one's fingers – the index included – to materialize the value of prices. Price indexing, in both senses, was both practical and cheap; it did not require massive investments. It also allowed the grocers to retain a measure of service, serving self-service, so to speak.

But the introduction of (hand)written prices presented a dilemma. On the one hand, once prices were written, they were public and stable until replaced. On the other hand, what was written may have been presented badly, at the risk of misunderstanding, confusion, and error. As one of the articles on showcard writing nicely put it: "It is well to keep in mind that a showcard that cannot be read easily is as bad as no card at all" (1922, 02, 25). Writing is oriented towards general communication and universality. The alphabet and numerical characters have long anticipated the logic of the digital as the unambiguous, the stable, the universal, the logic of no noise, no loss, right versus wrong, 1 vs. 0. But writing also engages the body. The hand has always been the site of absolute singularity, from the unique destiny supposedly hidden behind our palm lines, via the use of fingerprints for identification, to handwriting as a differentiator between individuals, relied upon to guarantee the authenticity of personal documents and commitments (Pontille, 2003). Writing prices by hand thus faces a tension: how to create an accurate, unambiguous and universal meaning by relying on a form of communication full of idiosyncrasy? The solution was a dual digitalization process; it was about using the hand (and its fingers), but it was also about finding the means to get rid of the idiosyncratic character of such operations (abandoning handwriting), so that the resulting prices would be universally meaningful.

This was one of the major concerns of the *Progressive Grocer*. From its very first issue and throughout the 1920s, the magazine addressed this challenge in a series of articles devoted to the art of "showcard writing".[7] These articles, organized as monthly lessons given by lettering experts, were aimed

---

[7] "Easy to Make Show Cards with the Speed Pen" (1922, 01, 34 et seq.); "Speed Pen and Simple Directions Make Show Card Lettering Easy" (1922, 02, 25 et seq.); "Spacing of Letters and Words is Important in Show Card Making" (1922, 03, 25 et seq.); "How to make your showcards with very little practice" (1923, 06, 23 et seq.); "The simplest kind of letters for showcard beginners" (1923, 07, 25 et seq.); "An easy and useful alphabet for your showcards" (1923, 08, 23 et seq.); "How to use the speedball pen for making your showcards" (1923, 09, 32 et seq.); "Anyone can write good show-cards by these easy, simple rules" (1925, 12, 22 et seq.); "A few tricks in show-card writing told by an expert at the game" (1926, 02, 31 et seq.); "Show-cards lettered with a pen are easy and simple to make" (1926, 03, 41 et seq.); "How to make show-cards with any style of lettering" (1926, 04, 42–3 et seq.); "A lesson in Show Card writing" (1929, 03, 30 et seq.); "Make Artistic Show Cards" (1929, 04, 54 et seq.).

at teaching grocers the proper and professional way of writing "showcards" and "price tickets". What is new here is not the activity – the letter-painter was a well-established profession at the time – but the ambition to train all retailers in it. Subcontracting to professionals might be acceptable for painting a shopwindow or shop sign, a once in a lifetime activity (or even less, as in "Nnn & sons"), but not for daily writing practices. Here, the *Progressive Grocer* wagered that grocers attached to traditional service would accept a feature anticipating self-service if produced by their own hands. Handwritten prices would allow them to stick to manual operations and would work as an extension of themselves:

> The show card is a star salesman. It works 24 hours a day and receives no salary. How to write show cards is a handy thing to know and anyone can pick up the trick with a little practice by studying the articles which begin in THE PROGRESSIVE GROCER this month. (1925, 12, 22)

These articles present in detail the equipment, gestures and print standards that should be combined to achieve professional showcards and price tickets. As far as equipment is concerned, the appropriate paper, writing tools and ink play central roles: "All you need is: Smooth-finish Bristol board at a cost of about 25 cents a sheet, or any other non-absorbent cardboard or paper; one bottle good quality India ink, 25 cents; one set Esterbrook Speed Lettering Pens, Nos. 2, 3 and 5, $1.00 a dozen" (1922, 01, 35).

In another article, we learn that the required equipment could be acquired in the form of a tool kit, bringing together the appropriate tools (1925, 12, 23). But despite their generic character, these tools came with many options. Once a tool had been selected, a somewhat vertiginous set of choices appeared in terms of which version to use. For instance, the grocer opting for the Bristol board would have to decide on its thickness depending on the type of cards he wanted to produce:

> Showcard board, which is also known as Bristol Board, comes in several plys or thicknesses, coated on just one side or on both sides. The weight most commonly used by showcard writers is 8-ply boards coated on one side. Lighter boards will not stand up, and is only used where it is to be cut up into small price tickets. All Bristol Board comes in sheets 22 × 28 inches. (1923, 07, 68)

The type of card also affected the choice of writing utensils; brushes were recommended for large boards while pens were suggested for smaller price tickets and for performing quicker writing operations (1923, 09, 32). Once again, one choice led to another: *which* brush or *which* pen to use. One article focuses precisely on different kinds of brushes and their uses. It rejects "Camel's hair brushes" as inappropriate for showcard writing because of excessive limberness, and presents "Red Sable brushes in sizes 6, 8, 12 or thereabouts" as good tools to start with, given their stiffness and square ends (1925, 12, 23).

Another article focuses on pens, a kind of item also advertised in the magazine (Figure 1.5). It suggests using the "Speedball pen", made of a "shoe", or lettering surface, and an ink retainer. We learn that this pen, or rather "these pens", since they come in five sizes, multiplies the options, since "each of them offer[s] square or round points". The article tries to reassure the reader, by stating that the most popular one is the No. 3 round point (1923, 09, 32). Another article goes even further by being entirely devoted to pens whose variants are so rich that the journalist finds it useful to present and organize them along the kind of tree that naturalists developed for classifying the species of living organisms. Just as life can be divided between the animal and vegetable kingdom, "For sign lettering work there are two kinds of pens: the stub variety, similar to ordinary stub pens, and the flat shoe type, so called because each pen has a peculiar flat nib" (1926, 03, 41). This categorization is immediately refined with a subsequent division based on the nib being "either round or square, projecting from its point". As the classification tree is expanded further, the author explicitly assumes the taxonomist metaphor: "In the first class of lettering pens, the stub variety, there are five different styles. The style which most resembles the ordinary stub pen is called the Soenecken or 'round writing pen.' 'Textwriter' is another name for it" (1926, 03, 41).

The article continues to specify that the Textwriter comes in about a dozen sizes; it introduces "Music writers" as a "variation of the regular writing pens" having "three tongues instead of two". This feature gives the pen "greater spreading capacity and a more elastic 'feel'". It similarly presents the characteristics of the "Style C Speedballs", the "Marking pens", the "Shading pens", the "Peazant pens", and so on, their different capacities and uses, with a level of detail too extensive to reproduce here (Figure 1.5).

This entomologist-like description of forgotten technologies could make us smile. Being used to writing practices like keyboard typing and text tapping it is easy to reject the art of calligraphy and its old-fashioned tools. But this would be to overlook the sophistication and subtlety of the tools and techniques developed to master professional handwriting, and that are still in use today. Moreover, it would ignore that the tools and techniques created for digital (finger) writing have served as templates for contemporary digital (computer) painting, as evidenced by comparing the means for showcard writing in the beginning of the twentieth century with those offered by a famous photo editing software a century later (Figure 1.5).

As suggested in Figure 1.5, the software duplicates the logic of the past rather than creating a new one: the menu proposes a similar array of tools, similar choices between pens and brushes, similar possibilities to adjust

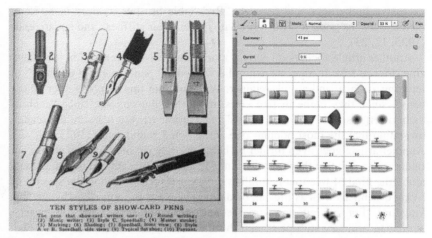

Source: *Progressive Grocer* (left: 1926, 03, 43; right: photo editing software, screenshot).

Figure 1.5   Finger and digital writing tools

thickness, softness, and so on. With digital technologies, handwriting and its techniques have been displaced rather than abandoned. Moreover and paradoxically, the digital still pertains to fingers even if mediated by electronic tools. Maybe even more so than in the past, given our frenetic moving and clicking, tapping and typing, touching and swiping. A recent example is the launch of iOS 10 for Apple mobile devices where one of the key new features was the ability to send handwritten iMessages.

The grocer could think that once equipped with his paper and brushes or pens he could start writing. But the *Progressive Grocer* shows that proper writing cannot be performed without carefully considering what to write, how to get prepared, and how to write it.

THE ETHNO-GRAPHY OF PRICES

What the grocer should write is not a showcard, but the words and numbers that go onto it. In this respect, the magazine sought to teach its readers that proper writing does not emanate from the hand but goes the other way. Expert writing is about ensuring that something from the outer world imbues the hand, so that the latter is capable of reproducing it. This external thing that must be communicated to the hand is an alphabet. Writing is about learning a model; it is about copying. Like language, writing precedes our existence; it is an external institution that exists before our birth and that we receive from others (Durkheim, 1950). As such, writing is about assimilating before performing.

As a consequence, proper writing requires education and thus a proper method. This is why the articles of the *Progressive Grocer* were delivered as monthly lessons, ordered in a step-by-step progression.

The first task is to learn *an* alphabet. The indefinite article "an" matters. As far as professional writing is concerned, it would be erroneous to take "an" alphabet to be "the" alphabet, that is, a generic, universal set of characters. Letters and numbers can be designed differently. Depending on their design, which may include straight or curved strokes and other twists, letters and numbers may be more or less difficult to reproduce, and the resulting effect could be different. In one of its lessons, the *Progressive Grocer* proposes to cope with this by starting with an alphabet made of straight strokes only (Figure 1.6) before moving to more complex character designs.

The alphabet model on the magazine page is to the grocer what the teacher's writing on the blackboard is to the pupil. Learning professional writing means going back to school, as the *Progressive Grocer* explicitly put it:

> You will remember practicing writing at school, how you were taught the free hand movement, and after a lot of practice were able to make beautifully rounded letters. It is not necessary to become a good showcard writer, but the same amount of practice that you did at school will make you a good letterer. (1923, 08, 25)

> Like at school, showcard writing skills are only acquired through proper study and practice. The task requires learning the design of the letters by heart, the order in which the strokes should be made, and the directions that should be followed [...]: Analyze each letter carefully and note the direction of each stroke. Follow the arrows with care, too. [...] As a last instruction, Practice, Practice, Practice. Work on the alphabet until you have the formation of the letters by heart. (1922, 01, 36)

> Study the forms carefully, following the numbered strokes until you can produce each letter from memory. (1922, 02, 26)

> Note the construction indicated by the arrows and practice each letter until you know without looking at the chart how the strokes are made to form the desired letter. [...] Keep this alphabet and set of numerals in front of you, copying them as closely as you can. The arrows on all the strokes indicate how each stroke should be made, and the figures on the arrows show the sequence of each stroke that makes up a letter or figure. The good rule, simple to remember is that all strokes are downwards or to the right, regardless of their position. (1923, 07, 25–6)

However, the *Progressive Grocer* stresses that even if the showcard writing lessons mean going back to school, this school is not for children. For instance, one of the lessons presented its school-like activity using the following metaphor: "Learning to write showcards is a good deal like learning to drive an automobile. You progress more rapidly by not attempting too much at the start" (1925, 12, 22).

Source: *Progressive Grocer* (left: 1923, 07, 28; right: 1923, 07, 29).

Figure 1.6   *The simplest kind of letters for showcard beginners*

Once reassured that he is not a child, equipped with proper tools and appropriate models, having learnt like a good pupil his "alphabet for beginners", could
the grocer finally start writing? No, not immediately. He first had to perform
some preliminary operations, like drawing the guidelines for the writing
operation:

> Rule the paper with guide lines about three-quarters of an inch apart for the capital,
> or upper case letters, and add extra guide lines for the tops and tails of the lower case
> letters (1923, 09, 33).

> First rule a sheet for 1-inch letters. Allow ¾-inch between the lines of letters to take
> care of the letters g, j, p, q, and y, whose descending strokes come below the line.
> Then draw the waistline, which is to mark the height of a, e, c, etc., and the bodies
> of the letters having ascending or descending strokes (1922, 02, 26).

The grocer also had to learn how to prepare the pen or brush, depending on
the chosen type of tool and objectives: "Dip the pen deeply enough to fill the
reservoir. Rest the under side on the neck of the bottle to drain off surplus ink"
(1922, 02, 25). "Your brush is loaded almost to the metal band, you distribute
the paint evenly with the back and forth motion on your 'palette.' When the
brush resembles a sharp chisel, it is ready" (1923, 08, 27 et seq.).

These preparatory operations are different from alphabet learning. Whereas the latter was mostly a cognitive task, preparing guidelines and loading pens or brushes are pragmatic activities; they are a matter of practice, a kind of operation that combines the mind (skills and meanings) with material objects and the body (Shove et al., 2012). Writing is a matter of mastering the spatial articulation between the writer's body, the writing tools and the writing setting (Lave et al., 1984). "Sit with the left of the body to the table. Place the paper squarely on the table, slightly to the right" (1922, 02, 25). "Draw all lines downward, or from left to right with a full arm movement" (1922, 01, 36).

Writing is also about mastering the temporal development of the same articulation, by finding the appropriate rhythm: "All […] letters are made with a free, rapid swing. […]. Good lettering is never made with a deliberate slow motion" (1923, 08, 25).

In order to perform this spatial and temporal accomplishment successfully, the contribution of the fingers is key. That is why this "digital-body" device receives particular attention, evidenced by several dedicated images (Figure 1.7). These are accompanied by precise instructions on how to hold the pen or brush and what kind of pressure to exert: "I merely wish to emphasize the importance of practicing with an easy, light swing, instead of cramping your fingers trying to make the brush stroke perfect and even from the very beginning" (1923, 08, 27). "The secret of making even strokes of equal width lies in holding the pen firmly, with the shoe flat on the surface to be lettered, and in practising diligently to obtain the desired grace in the letters" (1923, 09, 34). "Do not change the position of the pen, no matter what the direction of the line may be" (1922, 01, 36). "Hold the pen in the same position all the time" (1922, 02, 26).

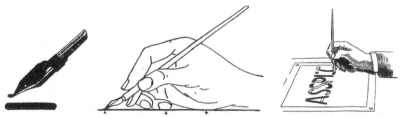

This drawing indicates exact position in which hand should be held. Follow it carefully. The cut at the left shows a No. 3 pen, full size and exact width of the line it makes.   *Hold the brush vertically, using the small and ring fingers to keep the hand steady*

Source: Progressive Grocer (left: 1922: 01, 35; right: 1925: 12, 72).

Figure 1.7   Handwriting techniques

Armed with knowledge about how to hold his pen or brush – obliquely for the pen, vertically for the brush, in both cases "using the small and ring fingers to keep the hand steady" (Figure 1.7, middle drawing and right caption) – the learning grocer can start exercising:

> Start near the top of the guide line with the first stroke of the letter A. The second stroke must overlap the first, beginning right on the line and forming the top. Now, play in the horizontal bar, away from you, not touching either of the outer edges of the letter. The next move is to finish the bottoms of the two uprights, with just a touch of the brush. (1923, 08, 27 et seq.)
>
> Remember that the round bill of the pen should be placed flat on the paper or card board and should be pressed down firmly to give equal thickness to all the lines. Rest at the beginning and end of each stroke, to give a rounded finish to each letter. (1922, 02, 25)

These instructions show that clear writing rests not only on following an external model, but also on finding the appropriate articulation between the general model and one's singular body ("Now, play in the horizontal bar, away from you"), success being closely related to the fingers' appropriate (im)pression ("pressed down firmly to give ..."; "Rest ... to give ...").

All in all, these instructions look as obsessional and detailed as ethnomethodological accounts of body torques, twists and other gestures (Schegloff, 1998). Indeed, they follow closely Garfinkel's advice of "paying the most commonplace activities of daily life the attention usually accorded to extraordinary events" (Garfinkel, 1967, 1). In this sense, we could indeed speak of the *Progressive Grocer* as being engaged in an ethnomethodological exercise. However, in the case of showcard writing, the precision of the description is not aimed solely at accounting for the innumerable and a priori meaningless bodily expressions that Garfinkel's disciples love so much, but rather at a quite opposite goal. Here, body and finger moves are described in detail not for the irreducible idiosyncrasy of mundane interactions, on the contrary to ensure that all practitioners, whatever their local settings, can perform the same action and produce the same effect, every time and everywhere, all over the US market. Here, finger writing is not a matter of indexical expression, but of index-assisted standardized communication! (With, of course, the help of other fingers.)[8]

---

[8]   Tim Ingold (2008) argued that the objective of anthropology is something distinct from ethnography, namely, to engage in correspondence (in the sense of intelligible interaction). From this perspective, the "ethno-graphy" of the *Progressive Grocer* is anthropological rather than ethno-methodological.

These lessons on showcard writing followed a progression. They started with a simplified alphabet whose characters were made from straight strokes only, postponing the learning of alphabets with curved letters and numbers to a later stage (1923, 08, 23 et seq.). The alphabet with "the simplest kind of letters for showcard beginners" raises a dilemma: it is easy to master, but its use is likely to reduce the effect of the finished sign. The result may well look professional in terms of execution, but still look amateur-like and simplistic compared to other available styles. Being a fully professional showcard writer would rather mean being capable of writing as a printer, and this is precisely the ambitious goal of the *Progressive Grocer*. As mentioned, the progression went from an alphabet with straight strokes to an alphabet with curved ones, "Single Stroke Gothic" (1923, 08, 27). But after this followed others, all clearly referred to as standard fonts borrowed from the printing industry, like "the Gothic" and the "Heavy Face Roman" (1923, 09, 33).

The lessons of showcard writing published by the *Progressive Grocer* thus have a common point: they show how the features of printed text could be introduced into the handwriting process. These features work like an oxymoron: they represent a return to the Middle Ages copyist monks and a move forward into modern printing at the same time! As outlined above, the alphabet is in itself digital in the modern sense of precise and unambiguous: no letter or number is subject "in principle" to being confused with another. The revolution of the printing industry (Eisenstein, 2005) pushed this characteristic further, thanks to the design, standardization and industrialization of fonts. Printing rather than writing solved the problem of often imperfect copy, stabilized the text, introduced a radical innovation in which the true change is that of no change: Gutenberg invented a means for permanence, reproducibility, universality. From this point of view, bringing the features of the printing revolution into handwriting, as the lessons in the *Progressive Grocer* do, introduces an amazing hybrid of handwriting and printing techniques that could be called "handwritten print". It is both a matter of handwriting (the fingers are put to work) and hiding it (the whole trick is to render the "handwritten" aspect of what is written invisible). This solution was thus both progressive (printing is the future) and regressive (handwriting is the past).

In this respect, "handwritten print" follows a dual pattern of modernization characteristic of the early years of the *Progressive Grocer* (Cochoy, 2015a). The first version equated modernizing with *improving*; it was about making use of past knowledge, skills and techniques but bettering their features. For instance, and as we saw with the IBM machines above, service can be kept and modernized by being mechanized. The same kind of modernization was also promoted upstream and downstream, by pushing the use of telephones and delivery trucks to improve ordering and delivery services. The second version equated modernizing with *replacing*; progressing by turning one's back on the past, substituting new ideas, methods and devices for established ones. This is what happened when service, credit and delivery arrangements were progressively abandoned for self-service and cash-and-carry. Handwritten print proposes a combination of the two: it retains retail service by improving writing patterns and replaces price bargaining and coded prices with open price display.

At the time when the *Progressive Grocer* introduced this twofold modernization, the typewriter and the associated print-like texts were spreading across the United States (Adler, 1973; Beeching, 1974; David, 1985). This was evident in the retail business, to which the companies that provided typewriters also provided cash registers: Burroughs, Remington, and so on. During this period, the printing industry was mediating print content, particularly in the field of advertising. From the mid-nineteenth century, this industry experienced dramatic changes that rendered it a prominent role in the development of the US economy. The Fourdrinier machine lowered costs by making paper from poor quality rags and the Hoe rotary press helped speed and scale up print production (Cochran, 1972). These innovations supported the rise of newspapers, particularly the metropolitan dailies. The press circulated the commercial news of companies eager to reach a national audience at a time when broadcast media was not yet available: "By the 1870s, rotary presses and pulp paper made magazine and newspaper space cheap enough for lavish display, and firms trying to capture a national market for their brands began extensive advertising" (Cochran, 1972, 150–51).

The growing prominence of printed advertising in newspapers placed text messages and professional fonts at the core of advertising: it is no wonder that the first and leading trade journal in the field of advertising was named *Printers' Ink*. It should also be recalled that in its very beginnings, advertising relied more on text than images. Early advertisers were labeled "copywriters"; the first professionals hired by advertising agencies were often English professors with the writing skills (content-wise) required to write catchy messages and formulate commercial arguments (Strasser, 1989). As illustrated in Figure 1.3 and Figure 1.4, the advertisements published in the *Progressive Grocer* largely reflect this strategy. While they included drawings and pictures, often in color, they mostly relied on text in accordance with the dominant definition at the time of advertising as a linguistic rhetorical device.

But copy writing is not just a matter of content; it is also a matter of professional and codified forms. Fonts played a prominent role in this respect, as illustrated by the use of the Agathe font and the innovations it led to. Conservative printers often imposed this font on copywriters. It thus worked as a vehicle but also as a brake for advertising communication: the Agathe font publicized commercial messages at large, but it also restricted their expression to a poor and sad single-sized and "text only" appearance, until the publisher

Robert Bonner had the idea to bypass these limitations by printing the same little ad repeatedly over several columns and full pages, creating a mass and attraction effect close to that of an image (Presbrey, 1929). Grocers and consumers of the period were thus immersed in this printing atmosphere, full of printed magazines, newspapers, ads, special characters, and popular fonts. The printing industry set a standard, a "one best way" for advertising communication, and it was in the grocers' best interest to get as close as possible to the printing culture of the time if they wanted to work as good professionals and modern communicators. Thus, they should complement the copywriters with their new identity as print copyists: "Follow the advertisements in any newspaper and familiarize yourself with the method of display, that is, where to use capitals, and how to emphasize the desired word or sentence" (1923, 07, 26). "Price tags that are poorly lettered by hand and carelessly cut from odd pieces of cardboard or paper have a decided tendency to make both windows and store displays look tawdry, junky and cheap" (1931, 01, 114).

But as mentioned above, designing showcards and price displays using "handwritten print" was a compromise between two worlds. As such, it was inherently unstable and could not last for long, at least not in isolation. It had one foot – or rather one finger – in the past, and the other in the future. In terms of the history of technology, handwritten prices could be described as a "reverse salient". When a system is changing, some element from the previous state of the system may not develop. This element could then work as a "reverse salient", slowing down or even hindering change. But this also creates opportunities for an innovator who may find a way to get rid of the salient by creating a new solution that is compatible with the new technology (Hughes, 1983). The move towards open display and later self-service, and the induced necessity of price display in a context of generalized printed information, put handwriting in a similar position. "Handwritten print" was the first solution to this, but it was far from the final one.

HANDWRITTEN PRINT; PRINTED HANDWRITING

The need for more and better price information opened the door to external assistance and further improvements. The first of these followed the IBM approach discussed above, introducing machines to assist writing, while later ones instead offered full substitutes. The first category gathers a set of astute devices exemplified in Figure 1.8. While these devices still require the contribution of the grocer's hand, this contribution varies greatly from device to device and points towards a more systematic evolution.

The solutions in the middle of the figure are still very close to handwriting. Both rely on the principle of the stencil, and as such they still require writing the letters by hand. In the picture of the "showcarder", we see the hand of the

Figure 1.8   Mechanical writing devices

writer tracing the signs through the stencil, and in the ad from the National Sign Stencil Co., there is mention of black and red ink, brushes and an alphabet. But by providing templates and technical assistance, these devices help the writer achieve a more standardized, print-like type of writing without having to learn tedious lessons of calligraphy. This is explicitly stated in the ad from the National Sign Stencil Co.: "Requires no knowledge of sign painting. Anyone can get perfect results." Indeed, it is proven by way of a sample: "The caption below is the exact reproduction of lettering stencil with No. 10 outfit."

The solutions presented to the left and right in Figure 1.8 are of a very different nature and represent full substitutes to handwriting. In these ads, the hand of the grocer is still required, but no longer for writing: the hand just has to rotate a wheel, just like the grocer who slices ham with an IBM slicer (see Figure 1.4). As its name implies, "Rotospeed" puts the accent on the rotary movement that replaces writing and on the speed and ease of the operation:

> Without the use of type or cuts, without an experienced operator, without muss or delay, the Rotospeed prints clean-cut letters, attractive circulars, bulletins and prices lists, from twenty to a thousand copies and on any size paper from a 3 × 5 inch card to an 8½ × 16 inch sheet. It prints illustrations, headlines, pictures, prices and facsimile signature all in one operation at a very small cost.

But if a lot is said about the output, with its amazing variety of documents, both in terms of content, volume and size, nothing is said about the input. We learn that the original is exactly and efficiently reproduced, but the way it is first generated remains undisclosed, probably because it needs either to be a printed original coming from the outside, or a written one made by the grocer himself, possibly in a very old-fashioned way.

The Price Writer displayed to the right in Figure 1.8 proposes a more advanced and incremental solution. It works like the Rotospeed by duplicating an original thanks to a rotary system. It requires no prior skills ("no special training required"), and the result may be obtained in a similar range of sizes. But it does more: this time, there are two rotary devices instead of one: the "price writer" supplements the rotary handle aimed at moving the cards with a "knob" aimed at selecting predefined elements for their duplication:

> Anyone can operate [the Price Writer]; all sizes of cards (3 ½ × 5 to 11 × 14) handled. Operation is simplicity itself; no special training required. Just insert the card, turn the knob to the desired printing character, pull down the handle. [...] Wide range of words available, in addition to the figures, dollars and cents, etc.

In other words, this machine proposes to combine preprinted words, numbers and signs as a typesetter does with individual characters. With the "price writer", the grocer was both the writer and the publisher. As the figure shows, and given the finite number of characters, the range of documents that could be printed with this device was certainly more limited than what could be done with the Rotospeed, but this time the input was at least clearly defined and referred to professional fonts for a professional, printer-like result. But the logic of typesetting could also be used in a simpler way, by assembling preprinted individual characters and placing them on an appropriate support, without the need to print the resulting assemblage. In fact, companies specialized in price tag systems had proposed this approach for years. In other words, and thanks to these companies, price tags became to retailers what fonts are to the typesetter.

* * *

The early history of price display that we have accounted for goes from handwritten prices to printed price tags; from lessons about how to handle a pen with one's fingers to advertisements for technical devices aimed at doing the same job. Shaw and Slavsky's "right hand" and its fingers replace previous ones (Figure 1.9). The argument of Shaw and Slavsky, a leader on the price tag market, is quite ambiguous. The ad refers to the hand, but only symbolically, as if professional fingers were not used in the self-service environment. Here, the "right hand" means "the appropriate hand" rather than "the writing hand". It is mobilized to illustrate a particular typology: four fingers cover the four major departments of a self-service store (groceries, meat, dairy, produce) and the thumb designates the price tag devices needed for their management: "the fifth and most important digit is your <u>how to price to sell system</u>." The "right hand of your business" suggests that another hand is working for you, like the previous invisible hand of the market.

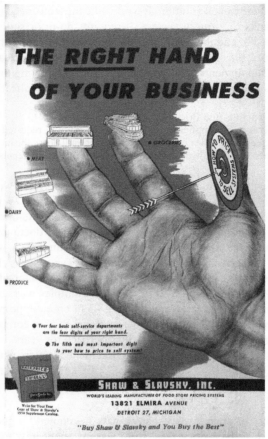

Source: *Progressive Grocer* (1950, 04, 237).

Figure 1.9   Shaw and Slavsky's right hand of business

More generally, price tags are and will always be a matter of *dexterity*. As we will see in the following chapters, fingers have not disappeared in the process of price "digitalization", but have been mobilized differently: handwritten precision has been replaced by handy manipulations. Prices must be both flexible and "fixed", but their manipulation should be reserved to professional hands. This process of price indexing (see above) never stopped, but was ceaselessly redefined, from handwritten prices to printed price tags to Electronic (*digital*, i.e., fingers-related according to the etymology) Shelf Labels. Prices rest on finger-related operations; mundane hands are continuously working hard behind the invisible hand.

With price tags, the retailing world moves from price handwriting to price typesetting. In terms of the overall digitization process, one may say that after having been "de-fingerized", so to say, prices were "numberized" (even if the two processes largely overlapped). The numberizing process was fourfold. First, numberizing prices meant expressing them with generic, standardized numerals. This kind of expression removed the confusion and imperfections associated with handwritten prices, whether traced with professional training or not. It also helped grocers stick to the printed standards adopted in the economy and society at large. Second, numberizing prices was about multiplying them in the retailing space, as stars blossom in the sky as the night grows darker. The easy combination of individual numerals helped spread them everywhere. Third, numberizing prices meant animating them. Thanks to appropriate technologies, prices were not only made present, but they were also changed and displaced appropriately. Fourth and more importantly, numberizing prices pertained to playing with numbers: by easing both the display (spatially) and change of prices (temporally), price tags favored the introduction of new price strategies based on price-based competition schemes that contributed to large economic changes as well as to new price regulations.

As we will see, this numberization process involved two steps. The first was the invention of price tags that spread and fixed the price of goods in the retail space. This technology associated printed price tickets (that one combines to set a price) and a clamping or molding system (to fix the prices on the shelves), which will be further explored in the next chapter. The second step was the use of price pens and "price guns" that diffused prices even further by displaying them not only on the shelves, but also on the goods themselves (a topic we will return to in Chapter 5).

2. Tagging prices: the proliferation of price tag technologies

Like many other pieces of self-service equipment, price tags quickly became a new "B(usiness) to B(usiness) to C(onsumer)" business; the devices were offered by firms to other firms (B2B), but the offer was made with the argument that the tags would help the buying firms to sell more to their customers (B2C). As part of the B2B orientation, price tag manufacturers insisted on the assistance provided by their equipment to retail operations: "no chance for mistake", said, for instance, the Edward J. Cook Co. But the same price tag manufacturers also stressed the selling power of their devices, that is, their supposed B2C advantage: "half the selling job is done for you", claimed Disc-O-Tag. Seducing the seducers with a promise of seductive power is extremely powerful; the seducers have no other choice than acquiring the seduction device if they want to test its alleged appeal ... at their own risk, without any guarantee of payback (Cochoy et al., 2016).

The price tag business was both "lateral" and opportunistic. It was "lateral", in the sense that price tag technologies emanated neither from the retailers nor from the consumers but from outsiders. The growing number of price tag companies saw them as a business opportunity taking advantage of the development of open display and self-service and the associated need for improved price information. Hence the numberizing process discussed at the end of Chapter 1. This numberizing movement evolved first from price cards to fixed tags, then from fixed tags to "swing tags", and from "swing tags" to price moldings.

PRICE CARDS

Price cards were an outcome of price writing skills. As illustrated by Figure 2.1, the introduction of price cards was closely linked to the transition from concealed to open prices and from service to self-service. They came along with branded canned goods, as a way to "heat up" the shopping environment. Like the printed labels on canned foods, they spoke directly to the customers, without the grocers' mediation. However, neither the branded labels nor the price cards were necessarily made directly accessible to the consumer; they were rather used as an appeal, well protected behind the store window, to bring the consumer inside, and then reintroduce the service, the discourse, and often the substitution strategy of the retailer.

Note how well the merchandise is arranged to display each item distinctly and to show the price of every article

Source: *Progressive Grocer* (1922, 08, 15).

Figure 2.1   Price cards in a shop window

In the same way that consumption patterns were changing from the production and subsequent consumption of homemade goods to mass consumption of branded products, price tags meant switching from "grocery made" price cards to the use of third-party devices. As such, they started the business of specialized price holding systems (Figure 2.2). Just like handwritten prices, homemade wooden price holders helped lower the costs of price display, involving grocers in their management, and thus moving prices inside the store, and easing the adoption of price display at the same time. Then, just as mussels anchor where stones abound, new species of price display solutions colonized the shelves.

Home-made wooden sign holders made of 1½ inch half round hard wood moulding. Simply saw a slit in the top big enough to hold the sign

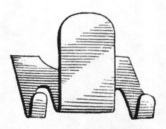

Every store should have holders to keep cards neatly in place. A holder like this doesn't cost much and does away with the evil practice of using pins which damage both goods and cards

These metal sign holders come in two sizes. The one shown here is for all signs measuring 5 by 7 inches or larger. There is a smaller one for 4 by 5 signs and price tickets

Source: *Progressive Grocer* (top and left bottom: 1922, 11, 31; bottom right: 1922, 07, 94).

Figure 2.2   Price card holders

PRICE TAGS

The first generation of price tags were *fixed* ones (in the sense of "nailed" or "clipped"). Figure 2.3 shows that no less than seven different varieties of such systems were offered within only 5 years. All these systems, despite their differences, offered distinct holders aimed at displaying individual fixed prices. More precisely, they were made of two elements: a series of removable and combinable paper cards, and a hard wooden or metallic slot aimed at receiving these cards, and fixing them on the shelf. With this sort of price tag, prices were fixed in two distinct ways. Not only were they fixed "externally", in terms of spatial position, but they were also fixed "internally", in terms of "price level", with the same price displayed to the eyes of everyone at least for a day. In a sense, the price tags also standardized consumers by leading them to adopt the view of a good and its price as inseparable.

Source: *Progressive Grocer* (from left to right and top to bottom: Edward J. Cook Co. (1922, 04, 94 a); The Disc-O-Tag Co. (1923, 03, 100 a); The Hopp Press Inc. (1923, 03, 100)); The Frank G. Shuman Co. (1922, 04, 94 b); John Ph. Kern (1923, 05, 102); Perfection Price Tag Co. (1924, 01, 100); The Price Tag Co. (1927, 05, 131)).

Figure 2.3   Price tags

As far as the physical fixation is concerned, the fixation of price tags was often twofold: first, many of these solutions were designed so that the price tag holder was firmly attached to its shelf; second, the same devices were often conceived so that price cards could not slide laterally. However, a closer look shows that the fixation of prices was subtler than one might think at first sight. This fixation, far from being intangible, was rather meant to be reversible. Let's consider an example: the "price cards" and cardholder of The Hopp Press Company and the corresponding patents – a pioneering device on the price tag market.

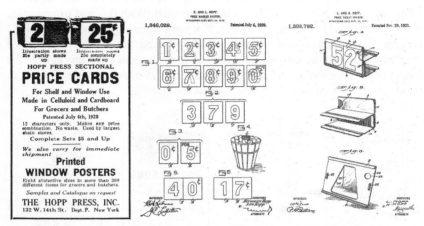

Source: *Progressive Grocer* (left: 1923, 03, 100; middle: Patent no. US 1.386.028; right: Patent no. 1.398.782).

Figure 2.4   Hopp Press: fixed price tag and patents

On the one hand, the cardholder is made so that the cards cannot slide out of their slot once they have been placed there, thanks to the two little lugs (labeled 22) that serve as stoppers. As the patent states:

> it is apparent that the present invention provides a new and novel form of ticket holder in which the body portion thereof is formed with lugs, said *lugs serving to prevent sliding movement* of the tickets relative to each other and to the holder, and *thus retain the tickets at all times in proper display position.* (Emphasis added)

On the other hand, the same cardholder is also designed so that the cards could be easily removed and replaced:

> Furthermore, by *providing the base of the holder with a cut-out portion in order that the edge of a ticket may be grasped and flexed*, the tickets may be readily removed without defacing the edges thereof, thus rendering the *tickets capable of indefinite use.* (Emphasis added)

The same is true for the holding part made of a "resilient U-shaped clamping member 10 in order to retain the base and the clamp in operative position" (see Figure 2.4, right). Such a clamping system was of course meant to be able to both hold and release its position.

The concluding paragraph comes back to this ambivalent combination of fixity and flexibility, and presents it as the distinct feature and contribution of the invention:

> We claim: A ticket holding device for flexible tickets comprising *a main body portion provided with oppositely disposed side flanges* in which a ticket is adapted to be slidably mounted, lugs formed integral with said main body portion, said *lugs being formed on the ends thereof to prevent longitudinal movement of the ticket* in the side flanges after the same has been positioned therein, and *a cut-out portion formed in the body portion to permit of engagement of the ticket to flex the same over the end lugs to permit of its removal from the body portion*, substantially as-described. (Emphasis added)

Far from being restricted to the solution offered by Hopp Press, this "flexible locking" feature soon became the main characteristic of the technology.

In order to be noticed and read, price tags had to be high and large enough, but this often clashed with the wooden shelves of the times, which in most cases were thinner than the height required for proper price display. As a consequence, many fixed price tags were designed in a way that "overflowed" the edge of the shelf, as can be seen from the solutions offered by Hopp Press, Edward J. Cook Co., and Disc-O-Tag (Figure 2.3 top left and Figure 2.4 top right). However, such designs faced the dual risk of either hampering the movement of goods, since these overflowing tags "blocked" the sliding movement of goods from shelf to consumer, or removing or damaging the tags. Indeed, picking a good from the shelf could damage the tag placed in front of it. This problem was manageable in the early period, when most stores operated as counter-service stores. Trained professionals could learn to handle the goods with the necessary care. But the spread of open display, then self-service arrangements, and thus the growing intervention of less skilled or cautious customers, led to the development of an alternative solution. This solution plays along the vertical axis of price display, by replacing fixed tag holders with "swinging" ones designed and offered by two companies: the Clamp-Swing Pricing Co. and the Swing-Tag Co. (Figure 2.5).

SWING TAGS

These tags were still overflowing the shelves, but instead of being placed on the same shelf as the product it referred to, and thus overflowing from bottom-up, the swing tag was mounted on the shelf above, and overflowed top-down. It is important to note the contradiction between the patent advertised by the Swing-Tag Co. and the features presented in the "March 21 1922" patent explicitly quoted in that ad (Figure 2.5, right): the patented price tag still had a fixed design, but in the ad it had been turned upside down, from standing

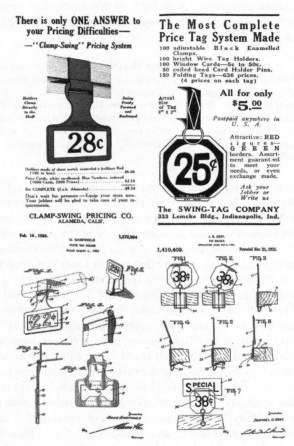

Source: *Progressive Grocer* (upper left: 1929, 08, 115; upper right: 1931, 06, 32; lower left:
Patent no. US 1,572,994; lower right: Patent no. US 1,410,402).

Figure 2.5   Two swing tags and their patents

to hanging, from rigid to swinging, by the discreet substitution of a simple
flexible loop for the fixed one. Irrespective of the reason behind this change,
the new solution mimicked the one proposed 2 years earlier by the competing
Clamp-Swing Pricing Co. and became the dominant solution in the price tag
market.

The hanging position had a triple advantage. First, it clearly indicated to the consumer that the priced product was the one placed below or behind it:

> the tag itself hangs directly in front of the goods and does not leave any doubt as to the goods to which it is to be applied as distinguished from a card placed on the front edge of the shelf, which creates doubt in the mind of the purchaser or the clerk handling the goods as to whether it applies to the goods on top of the shelf or to the goods placed on the shelf beneath. (Patent no. US 1,572,994)

Second, the hanging display reduced both the likelihood of hiding parts of the product and the chance that the two would collide. But even if such a collision occurred, there was no risk for the integrity of either the tag or the good. This was the third and main advantage. Thanks to the swinging feature, the tag stayed vertical and readable when untouched, moved aside if brushed by the grocer or the consumer, and then returned to its original position: "Clamp-Swing Prices swing freely forward and backward when goods are removed or replaced" (1928, 04, 71). "They swing clear when goods are removed" (1928, 02, 101).

The swinging feature was just an adaptation of the magic of the hinge to price tags, this incredible invention that with little effort turns a door into a wall when closed, and into a hole when open (Latour, 1988). A decade later, in the late 1930s, the hinge came to support the conversion of a shopping cart from a shopping basket, when placed on the top of a vertical rear gate, into a "shopping park" for other carts, which push the gate up when they collide into it (Grandclément, 2006). In the 1920s, the same hinge solved the possible conflict between fixed price display and product movement, and thus favored the transfer of service operations to the consumer.

Of course, there is often a difference between the utopian world described in advertisements and the actual implementation. This makes it relevant to check the information provided by looking at how advertised tags appeared (or not) in real retail settings (Figure 2.6). This "reasonable skepticism" about ad claims is not the exclusive privilege of researchers like us, but a concern shared and expressed by the actors themselves. The ad on the left in Figure 2.6 is well aware of the possible doubts on the part of retail grocers. As a consequence, it tries to anticipate and counter their possible objections by presenting the new device and its promises, as well as demonstrate its practical use. Since we know the device, let us concentrate on the promises and demonstration.

As far as promises are concerned, it is interesting to note that with a remarkable economy of words, the ad tried to address consumers' as well as retailers' concerns. First, it relied on the "B2B2C" rhetoric identified earlier: suggesting that Swing-Tags "attract[ed]" consumers was a way of attracting the professional retailers who wish to attract them so much. Second, it subtly

Source: *Progressive Grocer* (left: 1929, 08, 115; right: 1931, 06, 32).

Figure 2.6   Swing tags in use (top right oval lens added)

indicated that service and self-service were not opposed but one and the same. Self-service was indeed presented as a service offered to the consumer; the idea was to "help [the service grocer's] customer to help-themselves". Last but not least, the price tags were said to improve the performances of both grocers and consumers: they avoided "price confusion" for the first group, and "save[ed] time" for the second group. But these were not the only arguments. The ad also presented the tag as the "tightest gripping shelf clamp known". Whether this claim was accurate or not is difficult to determine – Swing-Tag was both judge and judged. What the claim implies, though, is that clamping systems had shortcomings; they were prone to be hit, displaced and removed, hence the importance of the "swinging" system to overcome such difficulties by removing the physical constraints imposed by the tag holder ("swings freely any direction").

The competitor Clamp-Swing went even further, by accompanying the repetitive representation of the same tags in dozens of advertisements during the 1930s. At first sight, all Clamp-Swing's ads look the same, but when examining them more closely we see that they developed an amazing array of arguments. The way these ads evolved is very interesting: first Clamp-Swing claimed that the device was "Invented by a Grocer to Meet the Present Day Requirements" (1927, 02, 118), knowing that the best argument for a device from the outside was to pretend it emanated from an insider. Then, the manufacturer tried to increase its market share by indirectly attacking the competition (Swing-Tag): "They don't turn or twist", it said about its own product, thus indirectly pointing at its competitor's flaws (1928, 04, 71).

But the performative effect of words increases if the things they are supposed to do can be shown to be already enacted. Along this logic, the ad was supplemented with a twin demonstrative figure. On the one hand, it offered a free sample of the tags. The implicit suggestion was clear: if the tags were open to free test, it is because there were no reasons to worry about them; they worked, and thus did not really need to be tested! This view was supported by the second demonstrative figure, which appeared in the form of a photograph showing the device in use. The photograph was not just any photograph: "This photograph shows how Swing-Tags are used in the Model Grocery Store, established by the Louisville Grocers Assn., in co-operation with the U. S. Dept. of Commerce." By exhibiting a device supported both by the grocery profession and the government as part of a "Model Grocery Store", as part of a campaign largely advertised by the magazine (Cochoy, 2020), the device was made out as something grocers had no choice but to implement.

But do idealized pictures displayed in advertisements really match what could be observed in real retail settings? Were the advertised devices really put to practical use, and if so, how? The photograph reproduced to the right in Figure 2.6 provides an answer to these questions. It is extracted from an article focused on new strategies and devices for the display of fruits and vegetables (1931, 06, 30 et seq.). It presents new types of shelves (inclined and metal) with several pictures, figures and arguments, but does not say a word about the swinging tags that appear on the same fixtures and pictures. This suggests that swinging tags were in use, but were very discreet, at the risk of being overlooked, both materially and cognitively. Indeed, just like the designer of the ad to the left, we had to zoom in on the tags and highlight them with an ellipse to make sure that our reader would not miss them.

In fact, the swinging tags had been swinging not only on the shelves, but also in the general history of product display and price display techniques. Swinging tags were one of the distinctive features of the transitional open display era that eased the move from counter to self-service. On the one hand, the multiplication of swing tags was a consequence of the increasing importance of visual interactions between consumers and goods introduced by open display. Indeed, the open display approach called for instant, direct and complete information, hence for clearly posted prices. On the other hand, it is interesting to note that the same swing tags fit better with the old-fashioned wooden shelves than with the new open furniture: on the photographs in Figure 2.6, swing tags appear on classic shelves only, with their horizontal wooden planks required for the clamping system, and with their lateral walls that limit the width of the angles from where the products can be seen (on the consumer side), and restrict the possibilities of product display (on the grocer's side). The removal of these two last obstacles was closely linked to the introduction of a new generation of price tags and store fixtures.

Price tags eased the identification of products, supported impulse buying, encouraged self-service, and thus contributed to the generalization of the new strategy of profit through volume (Tedlow, 1990). The growth and acceleration of retail operations went hand in hand with the appearance of a new sort of price tag that proved able, as time passed, to fit with such changes. This innovation appeared for the first time in 1931 in an advertisement by the F.M. Zimmerman Co. (Figure 2.7).

PRICE TAG MOLDINGS

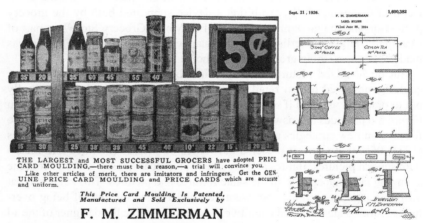

Source: *Progressive Grocer* (left: 1931, 02, 140; right: Patent no. US 1.600.382).

Figure 2.7   *F.M. Zimmerman's price card molding and patent*

At first sight, this ad constitutes a huge leap forward from the early twentieth century to our contemporary world: it introduces price tags as we know them today, with clear numerals, well placed below the products they qualify, put on a rail that travels the full length of the shelf and that allows them to slide left or right when needed. But a closer look shows that Zimmerman's system was not as modern as it seems. Of course, finding traces of pre-modern retailing is no surprise in an ad published in 1931. However, these traces were not only an involuntary sign of the times, but a deliberate reference to a previous period. Indeed, the Zimmerman Co. presented its innovation in a rather cautious and conservative way. Like many other equipment providers of the time, its main customers were still full service grocery stores. In order not to frighten their prospective customers, then, it made sense to present the new device in a way that did not represent too much of a break with their current situation. Thus, the innovative rail was prudently fixed on old-fashioned wooden shelves with vertical separations that you would find behind the counter, rather than on brand-new fixtures for open display that removed everything that could prevent the goods from being seen from any angle (Cochoy, 2015a). In addition, we can see that the cans on the bottom shelf were stacked vertically rather than horizontally, which would be typical for modern "facing" arrangements serving to catch the consumer's attention. The vertical logic fits better with the grocer's perspective: the professional knew what his products were and where he had to pick them up to serve his clients. The display logic was "one product, one column, one tag". This is confirmed by the patent, where the fifth figure shows that the "price tag molding" can also be used to name the goods with cards like "rice", "sugar", "beans", "flour" and "raisins".

All in all, Zimmerman's invention subtly balanced retail tradition and merchandizing modernity. The fact that the goods were generically named in the patent refers directly to the pre-modern state of grocery retailing where consumers, deprived of any precise and direct access to the products' characteristics and origins, had no other choice than to refer to goods by invoking the universal categories they belong to. In this setting, the retailers were necessary intermediaries for product information and supply who had the privilege to decide what to serve and could propose to their customers the products for which they got the higher markup (Strasser, 1989). However, the top part of the same patent staged the supply differently. It presented two products side by side: "'STAR' COFFEE" and "CEYLON TEA". Of course, this is not a modern kind type of choice, since just one unit kind of each product is proposed instead of many, as in contemporary supermarkets. The price given to the goods was not an item price, but a price per pound ("50 ¢" for the coffee, "95 ¢" for the tea). This kind of price implicitly indicates that the good was sold in a service store, so that the consumer had to rely on the grocer's intermediation to obtain what he or she wanted (or end up with a substitute more favorable to the grocer). But at least for the coffee, a specific brand was named, and this suggests that alternatives existed, and could be ordered. In this respect, the price tag feature strongly contributed to support the transition from counter service to self-service and packaged goods.[1] The shift from service to self-service was suggested also in the ad, even if prudently: in the photograph, only packaged branded goods were displayed with price tags, even if just one brand was made available for each particular good. Again, this suggest a compromise between the choice of the consumer and the preferences of the grocer, who has first to buy the device so that his customers may later buy the goods of his choice.

A last (but not least) characteristic of Zimmerman's system that made it a new, but perfectible solution, emerges through the comparison between the ad and the patent it rests on. The latter document acknowledges the reliance of the device on thin, old-fashioned wooden shelves. Indeed, it features the systematic overflowing position of the molding over the edge of shelves, at the risk of hampering the free movement of the goods from shelf to consumer (see the patents' figures no. 2, 3, 4, 6, 7 and 8). By contrast, the advertisement stages a situation where this problem had been opportunistically solved: if one looks carefully, one sees that the price tag moldings were attached to shelves that were thick enough to avoid the problem, so that the goods could be extracted by simply pulling them horizontally, without being stopped by the upper part of the device.

Easing the movement of prices from one side to the other, and consequently improving the movement of goods from the rear to the front, were the twin aims of price tag moldings. By facilitating better product information, the rails suggested fostering well-informed, thus faster and more numerous, choices. The joint channeling of price and product movements was the key feature of the device. In other words, moldings and price tags were to price display what rails and wagons were to the railroad industry. This analogy is more than just a pleasant metaphor. True railroads and price tag moldings were invisibly but truly articulated indeed: the development of the market for packaged goods was closely related to the unification of the US markets permitted by railroad networks and transportation (Chandler, 1977; Tedlow, 1990). What flowed with ease through railroad networks (i.e., goods and consumers) created bottlenecks in ill-adapted retail stores, and these bottlenecks were solved by introducing new "rail-like" features, like cars and delivery trucks outside the stores, or turnstiles, shopping carts, and price tag moldings inside them.

---

[1]   In so doing, the patent alternates product qualifying and product pricing, but also foreshadows the subsequent merging of the two operations. Indeed and as we will see with greater details in Chapter 5, price tags will later merge product qualification and product valuation, when it became possible to display both product qualities and product prices on the same label, and thus transform price tags into a "qualculation device", that is, a device that helps grounding economic judgment on price and non-price qualities (Cochoy, 2008a).

In order to understand this process, it is important to stress that the movement between global transformations and local innovations went both ways, just as railroads always travel back and forth. On the one hand, the flow of goods created opportunities for the introduction of devices to channel them better: when the offering of products grows and varies constantly, it becomes necessary to rely on devices that are capable of handling this growth and variation, and to adapt information accordingly. On the other hand, the development of such systems contributed to intensify and publicize the new flows and the new economy. The development of national brands, the adoption of profit-through-volume strategies, the rise of mass display and the development of self-service were seized by price tag manufacturers as powerful arguments to support the adoption of their devices, since they could present them as solutions for coping with such innovations. At the same time, once advertised in the *Progressive Grocer*, and implemented in retail outlets, price tag equipment talked and worked not only for their own spread, but also for the larger transformations they expressed and promoted.

Indeed, price tag moldings had (and still have) their own agency. Thanks to their rail-like design, they helped prices and goods move together, along with the daily changes in product supply: once placed in moldings, price tags could follow the goods as they moved. Conversely, once equipped with this easy way to move prices, conservative grocers were encouraged to move goods more often and differently than before. The continuous presence of price tags along the shelves responded to consumers' growing preference for self-service arrangements, and also taught them why such arrangements were preferable. Symmetrically, the ease of price setting and price moving through shelf moldings could partially weaken the resistance of many service grocers. Generally speaking, the new task of price display meant extra work for them and the self-service framework threatened to bypass their mediating and product-substituting power (Strasser, 1989). At the same time, the diversification of goods, the growth of product volumes, and the rising sales turnover put pressure on their memory skills (on the cognitive side) and their capacity to handle continual adjustments (on the material side) – two problems that price display devices helped them if not to overcome, at least to deal better with.

FROM WOOD TO METAL

If the design of price tags mattered, so did their physical construction. What made the efficiency, durability and reliability of train transportation is no doubt the steel construction of railroads, as compared with less reliable means of channeling transportation, like the often-unpredictable waters for boats or the imperfect macadam roads for cars. Similarly, some price tag manufacturers seem to have realized that the rail-like construction of price tag moldings required them to abandon the wooden construction adopted by companies like Zimmerman (see above), the Esdorn Lumber Corp. (1934, 02, 112) and Colonial (1940, 09, 215), and instead use a metal construction. This latter type was first advertised by the Dayton Co. in 1935 (1935, 01, 98) and soon became the new standard.

DAYTON *Metal*
MOLDING

★ Won't warp or split.
★ Creates the effect of steel shelving.
★ Hides sags and rough edges of shelving.
★ Displays cards at angle of greatest visibility.
★ Arrow on each card eliminates confusion.
★ Cards are locked in position but are easy to place or remove.
★ No clamps to hang crooked or fall off.
★ No dangling cards to destroy shelf displays.
★ Cards are on straight line between merchandise.

Amazingly easy to install. Molding finished in variety of colors. Price cards packed 1,150 to box, indexed, black, red or blue background all white characters. So economical that an ordinary price system seems high priced in comparison.

New literature, illustrating the new 1935 Deluxe Dayton Moisture Equipment for produce departments now ready. Mail coupon.

Patented

CORRECT DISPLAY

means retail success

Do you want to increase your sales?
Do you want to sell with less effort?
Do you want to keep all of your stock moving?
Do you want a more attractive store?

THEN you must look to display, must secure correct display, because this is the secret of modern retail success. Practically every outstanding success in retail merchandising is due to correct display. Whole stores are today being modelled to insure proper showing of goods.

But you can secure correct display in your store without discarding any of your present equipment—and without a large investment. Thousands of retail stores are proving this—as you will prove it. Let us send you information regarding the Dayton Display Fixtures—and the system of display which is revolutionizing selling.

Nothing else like this fixture; nothing else can fill its place; nothing else insures correct display so easily. Today—write us for literature.

The Dayton Display Fixture Co.
DAYTON   OHIO
1812 West Third Street

Source: *Progressive Grocer* (left: 1935, 01, 98; right: 1923, 08, 81).

Figure 2.8   Dayton Metal Molding and Correct Display fixtures

It comes as no surprise that metal moldings were introduced by the Dayton Company. As we learned in Chapter 1, Dayton was a branch of IBM specialized in the production of retail equipment that relied heavily on metal constructions. Dayton did not only manufacture slicers, grinders, choppers and the like; it was also one of the key developers and promoters of the open display concept. In the early 1920s, Dayton used open display as an argument for selling a new type of metal shelf that did not have vertical walls and hence allowed clear sight from every angle (see the right-hand side of Figure 2.8). Even if the price tag moldings did not fit directly with these shelves designed more than a decade earlier, they were the last contribution made by Dayton to a coherent and incremental range of metal-based equipment, going from service machines, to open display fixtures, to self-service devices.

Dayton's metal moldings were clearly more aligned with futurist self-service arrangements than with the open display shelves it had advertised a decade earlier. In its ad for the metal molding, the company tried to show that this new product, far from being just a variant of existing solutions, introduced a real breakthrough. No less than nine arguments were listed to back this up. The first arguments were logically negative ones, aimed at praising the qualities of the new device by implicitly stressing the weaknesses of wooden competitors. Just like the inventors of aluminum skis who insisted a few years later on the durability of their construction compared to classic wooden skis (Cochoy, 2015b), Dayton claimed that metal moldings "won't warp or split", like the available alternatives, whose wooden design was inherently subject to distortions inflicted by humidity or to breakage resulting from structural weaknesses, external shocks, or improper nailing. This is confirmed by the Zimmerman patent and its suggestion to affix the wooden moldings in the center, no doubt to reduce the risk of cracking, even if doing so ironically showed that this risk existed and was far from negligible. The ad for the metal molding thus sought to benefit from problems that grocers had experienced with wooden moldings and/or to make others believe such problems could occur.

Other attacks were directed at previous generations of price tag devices like individual shelf clamps and swinging tags. Here again, the targets were merely implied through the mention of negative effects that the new device avoided, but that implicitly afflicted competing solutions. The understated critique of swing tags suggests that these competitors were present and quite well known. The same critique was intended to teach the readers (us, and more importantly the grocers of the time) about the real and serious flaws in competing solutions. We learn between the lines that clamping tags "hang crooked or fall off" and that swinging tags "destroy shelf displays". This confirms our suspicions about these devices, and what their manufacturers often recognized by praising improvements supposed to alleviate such difficulties (see above: Clamp-Swing claimed that – understated: contrary to other solutions – its tags "can't turn sideways", 1927, 02, 118). A final type of critique consisted in criticizing competitors not for the features they had, but rather for the ones they did not have, like the "Arrow on each card", a feature aimed at showing the product that the price referred to. But saying that such arrows were needed showed at best that the device was still in its infancy, with no clear standard about how to "read the shelf", as if people were traveling a road without knowing on which side to drive. This confusion was in part fueled by the competition between shelf tags and swinging tags: the former were placed beneath the products; the latter were hung above or in front of them. At worst, the arrows indicated that price moldings were not inherently clear and that they needed additional maintenance to express clearly what they intended (Denis and Pontille, 2019).

Other arguments in favor of the metal moldings were positive. They aimed at praising their qualities rather than stressing the flaws of competitors. A subtle and clever argument of this type consisted in suggesting that the device would modernize your retail equipment without really changing it. The idea was that grocers with limited resources, or grocers reluctant to change, could test new arrangements gradually and at low cost, while keeping the rest of their store unchanged, both in terms of furniture and organization. The argument relied on a strategy that the company had used earlier to sell its metal shelves. Then, Dayton had suggested that one could adopt the new shelves without replacing existing wooden ones by simply covering them with the new device: "You can secure correct display in your store without discarding any of your present equipment" (Figure 2.8, right). Now, the company resorted to the same rhetoric and pushed it further. With metal moldings, Dayton suggested, one did not have to supplement classic shelves with new ones; one could even use the new molding as a way to keep antique furniture and prolong its life. Indeed, the molding was presented as having the double advantage of hiding worn and old-fashioned wooden fixtures (it "Hides sags and rough edges of shelving") and giving them the neat and modern look of metal ones: "Creates the effect of steel shelving."

Among other qualities, the ad mentioned the device's ability to "Display [...] cards at angle of greatest visibility", thus incorporating and pushing further the open display logic introduced by the metal shelves. It also signaled that "Cards [were] locked in position but are easy to place or remove". The "but" clause suggested that these operations could be more difficult using a competing solution. In other words, it linked a positive argument with a negative one against supposedly similar but in fact less "grocer friendly" devices. Finally, the ad stated that "Cards are on straight line between merchandise", once again implying this was not the case for other moldings, which seems doubtful. On the whole, the ad illustrated that positive advertising is also negative to some extent. Sometimes, ads go as far as introducing a rhetoric of "lying truth", giving the impression that a given feature of the advertised device is a distinct advantage when in fact it is shared also by competing devices.

Strangely enough, other possible advantages of the metal construction – even excellent ones – were not listed. The ad did not mention aluminum's better "slidability" (no risk that a splinter hampers movement), durability (no need of painting or varnish; tougher than wood) and "cleanability" (easier to wash and less sensitive to dirt).[2] The silence of the ad on such matters is certainly due less to poor judgment than to a lack of space and a need to prioritize among arguments. From this latter point of view, Dayton seems to have found it necessary to concentrate on arguments that positioned its pioneering devices in relation to its competitors.

Whatever the quality of Dayton's ad and product, further developments made metal moldings not only successful, but also standard, and eventually hegemonic. The generalization of metal price tag moldings followed a dual logic. On the one hand, these devices were simply added to existing solutions in the retailing landscape. The best illustration of this kind of "incremental" introduction of metal moldings is the catalog of the Clamp-Swing Co. Clamp-Swing had long been a major promoter of clamped swinging tags, as its name clearly indicates. However, on the other hand, the company also opportunistically included alternative systems into its product range, probably because the cost was low (these devices were very similar in terms of construction, thus easy to manufacture with the same materials and factory equipment) and because the possible rewards were high. It is well known that product diversification may bring stability to a business and allow companies to follow along as the market develops (Ansoff, 1957). Along this dual logic, Clamp-Swing ended up offering the full range of price tag systems we have reviewed, from fixed tags to swinging tags to price tag moldings, and also the first solution of individual showcards (1937, 02, 103) (Figure 2.9).

On the one hand, the proliferation of variants of a technology helps it colonize the world, a little like living organisms surviving and spreading in various environments through mutations of their genetic code. On the other hand, such a colonization process often leads to the selection of one species that ends up dominating the others. Metal price tag moldings worked as this kind of species.

In parallel with their spread, metal moldings were improved. Some of these improvements were more rhetorical than "real", and went along the trope of "lying truth" mentioned earlier. Three of the new providers – Modern Store

---

[2]   Here, we depart from the constructivist and asymmetrical approach adopted by Eric Schatzberg (1999) in his book *Wings of Wood, Wings of Metal*, where the author argues that the introduction of metal in the aircraft industry rested on social mechanisms, rather than on the qualities of the materials themselves. Since Durkheim we know that society no doubt has its force, that organization strategies are key and that individuals' social characteristics matter (social class, gender, education, race …). But we see no reason to think that material objects lack social characteristics and strength (for instance, aluminum is light, rustproof, durable, and so on), and that such characteristics also contribute to social action. Only a precise field study can decide whether the social or the material takes over the other (Latour, 2005).

Source: Progressive Grocer (1937, 02, 103).

Figure 2.9   Clamp-Swing pricing devices

Equipment (1947, 10, 138), Shaw and Slavsky (1947, 11, 27) and The Hopp
Press (1948, 02, 126) – presented their moldings as made from "extruded aluminum", as if something had been added beyond what was found in a normal
aluminum molding. However, given the shape of the device, the extrusion
process was certainly the only one available to make it! More subtle differen-
tiations also occurred, most of them introduced by The Hopp Press and Shaw
and Slavsky, who seem to have dominated the market as a quasi duopoly after
World War II.

Source: *Progressive Grocer* (upper left: 1947, 10, 138; upper right: 1952, 07, 166; lower left: 1947, 11, 27; lower right: 1948, 02, 126).

Figure 2.10   Metallic price tag moldings

The two companies advertised their products using both mimicry and differentiation. The basic idea seems to have been that in order to differentiate and stress one's major advantage, one should appear as similar as possible to the competitors in all other dimensions (Cochoy, 2002). See the two lower ads in Figure 2.10. On the left, Shaw and Slavsky praised the aesthetic and durable character of their extruded aluminum molding "polished to make your display look bright and snappy" and "built to last a lifetime". They also highlighted that their device prevented consumers from moving the tags thanks to the addition of a protective transparent plastic film – an issue and a feature we will address at length in Chapter 5. On the right, The Hopp Press similarly insisted on the robustness of its "Extrudo" aluminum molding – a construction that "will not rust or corrode" – and emphasized its nice look – a "handsome satin finish [that] remains clean and lustrous". Like its competitor, The Hopp Press emphasized "TAGS WILL NOT SLIDE OR SHIFT POSITION" and claimed that its moldings "propose a clear transparent plastic protector". In a nutshell, we understand that both moldings were similarly made of extruded aluminum, highly robust, aesthetical, with transparent films preventing the tags from being moved, so that the reader could end up hesitating like Buridan's ass between these two quasi-identical products (Cochoy, 2004). But as always with Buridan-based marketing rhetoric, The Hopp Press also astutely emphasized the only key difference between the two. The device showed a "solid but flexible" construction that "bend[t] around corners, creating an unbroken surface on island displays". This "decisive" quality was of course not just mentioned, but put forward in the picture, which clearly reproduced the same rail-like quality as the Shaw and Slavsky device but departed from it by bending it (materially and symbolically) into a distinct advantage.

Through the competing claims of the two manufacturers, we see how the two adopted and incorporated the very concept of open display and its transitional role towards self-service in their price tag moldings. Just as the windows of open display showcases provided visual access to the goods while preventing direct manipulation of them, Shaw and Slavsky's transparent film (a solution patented by the company in late 1948, see Figure 2.11) made prices visible while preventing consumers from touching them. "A transparent plastic strip slips into the outer slot and fits snugly over the price tag. Only you [the grocer] can change the price. Tags can be plainly seen, but not touched", the ad said. Like the curved angles of the open display "island-shaped" furniture they fit to (Cochoy, 2020), Hopp Press' moldings went beyond the segmented edges of old-fashioned shelves, brought safety as well as continuity in the display of products and prices, and promoted a shift from one kind of furniture to another.

However, and as evidenced by the pictures in Figure 2.12 – all of them extracted from articles focused on other topics than price tags – the spread of price tag moldings was gradual rather than sudden and took on various shapes rather than a unified standard form. In the upper left picture, it seems very hard to know the prices of the piles of items placed on top of the furniture. In the

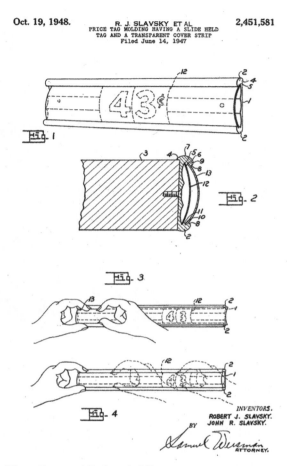

Oct. 19, 1948.   R. J. SLAVSKY ET AL   2,451,581
                      PRICE TAG MOLDING HAVING A SLIDE HELD
                       TAG AND A TRANSPARENT COVER STRIP
                              Filed June 14, 1947

INVENTORS.
ROBERT J. SLAVSKY.
JOHN R. SLAVSKY.
BY
Samuel Weisman
ATTORNEY.

Source: United States Patent and Trademark Office.

Figure 2.11   Slavsky et al. US Patent no. 2,451,581, 19 October 1948

upper right and lower left pictures, the situation is less messy. Helped by the disappearance of vertical walls and their replacement by less invasive brackets, goods have multiplied laterally and prices indicated with simple, large tags. In the lower left picture, however, we also see that the presence of a price tag for each specific item is far from systematic. Finally, in the lower right picture, we note the introduction of a more island-like type of furniture, equipped with continuous curved price tag moldings like the ones proposed by The Hopp Press. In all pictures, the moldings show prices only, without the names of

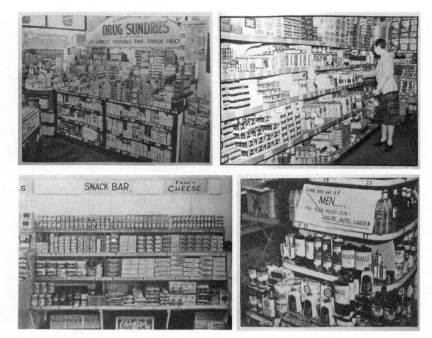

Source: Progressive Grocer (upper left: 1940, 01, 23; upper right: 1942, 10, 53; lower left:
1946, 11, 74; lower right: 1948, 09, 62).

Figure 2.12   Price tag moldings in various grocery stores

the goods. The lack of tags below some goods and the uncertainty about some
good–price relationships show how fragile, confusing and even useless the
device could be, irrespective of the modernity of the supporting device and the
claims of its manufacturer.

Moreover, even if they spread, price tag moldings were far from becoming
a standardized part of store furniture. On the one hand, the persistence of
a division between "naked" furniture and price tag devices preserved the
business of the companies that made and sold them as shelf extensions. On
the other hand, the same division between furniture builders and price tag
manufacturers hampered the full development of the latter, given the lack of
standardized and integrated solutions, and given the "optional" character of
their presence and the inadequate fit between certain fixtures and available
moldings. This situation was very similar to what we observed recently, for
several years, with QR code services. As long as QR code readers were not
provided as default apps for smartphones, many consumers did not use them,

either because they were ignorant about their existence, or because they estimated that the service rendered did not motivate the effort of installing the
software. In the late 1940s, however, there were signs of integration as price
tag moldings began to appear in the ads for refrigerators, at least visually. It is
very hard to know whether these "price tag molding equipped" refrigerators
incorporated solutions developed by the refrigerator companies themselves or
if they used solutions offered by specialized companies.

THE INTEGRATION OF PRICE TAGS INTO RETAIL EQUIPMENT

The relationships between refrigerators and price tags convey interesting
insights that become all the more meaningful if we return to their origins.
It would be wrong indeed to think that price tags appeared in a stable retail
environment. Contrary to what Jean Lave and her colleagues suggest with their
distinction between "arena" (the retail architecture) and "setting" (the part of
this architecture affected by consumers' actions) (Lave et al., 1984), the larger
frame is as flexible as the manipulated elements. The *Progressive Grocer* was
launched exactly when the refrigeration industry revolutionized the American
mass market and itself with it.

Home refrigerators had been introduced just a decade before (Anderson,
1953). In the advertisements for refrigeration devices that were found in the
early issues of the *Progressive Grocer*, the iceman and his expensive bill were
the main targets of new refrigerating solutions, implicitly indicating that this
antique profession was still dominating (1922, 05, 57; 1923, 07, 83; 1924,
01, 94; 1924, 05, 68, for example). The new devices, like price tags, came
from outside of existing equipment suppliers. A first category of refrigerators
adopted the astute rationale we saw above in which revolution goes hand in
hand with conservation: these machines, offered by the Lipman and the Baker
companies, were external cold generators conceived as add-ons for existing
fixtures (Figure 2.13, left). Another category went further by proposing new
fixtures with integrated cooling engines. The design of refrigeration devices
wavered between large and more or less opaque cupboards that fit with the
counter-service logic, and more open and transparent showcases that were
adapted to the open display logic.

The McCray refrigerator on the right in Figure 2.13 combined these two
logics. The old "wooden cupboard" style was there but it was also windowed;
as such, it hybridized counter service – this type of refrigerator still went
behind the counter but what was inside was accessible to consumers' sight.
The refrigerator depicted at the bottom of the ad moved a step forward/further
to the front of the service area, working as a counter and a showcase at the
same time. The food inside was still not fully accessible to the customers, but

Source: Progressive Grocer (upper left: 1926, 06, 125; lower left: 1926, 07, 116; right: 1923, 09, 109).

Figure 2.13   Early refrigerators

these customers nevertheless got a better visual access to it before making their orders. Refrigerators were thus both rigid and surprisingly flexible: they were solid and stable devices, but their design was unstable; it followed and enabled the evolution of the grocery business at the same time.

In the evolution and adaptation of refrigerators, price display occupied an important but paradoxical position. In some respect, the hesitation between opaque grocer-oriented safes and open consumer-oriented showcases in early refrigerators called for price display. But it took some time to see these devices fully integrating price fixing technologies. In some rare instances, the advertisements featured discreet price cards added to the shelves of refrigerated showcases (1926, 04, 94–5). But it was only in the late 1940s and early 1950s that they began to include "built-in" price moldings – see Butler (1948, 09,

171), Friedrich (1949, 05, 9; 1951, 08, 7), Federal (1951, 02, 235), Hussman (1951, 08, 98–9), and so on. These integrated price systems were sometimes presented as part of implicit partnerships between price tag and refrigerator manufacturers, as advertised by Shaw and Slavsky (Figure 2.14).

Source: *Progressive Grocer* (left: 1948, 09, 171; right: 1949, 04, 293).

Figure 2.14   Price tags on refrigerators

A 1957 ad from Hopp Press claimed that "The newer refrigerated dairy cases are equipped with both 1¼" and 3½" moldings" (1957, 11, 23), suggesting that the device had – or rather should – become pervasive and standard. Such evolutions were of utmost importance, since they evidenced the ability of price tag devices to shift from being independent market equipment to becoming part of a whole standardized and integrated display infrastructure, where product display and product pricing converged to form a single "qualculation" environment.

THE DILEMMA OF PRICE TAG REMOVAL

A distinctive feature of price tags was their ambivalence, being both stable and changeable. This helped to fix prices as non-negotiable values, but still allowed them to be revised when needed. This dual feature, however, was far from perfect. Just like a badly designed net may catch both the desired fish and unwanted species, removable cards could support both desired price shifts and undesirable card removals. The problem with removable price tags indeed was that they could be removed by … anyone. While this posed little problem in a service environment, where prices were displayed behind the counter and only within reach of the staff, it could become a serious problem in the new self-service setting. There, retailers were not the only people who had access to the price tags; if consumers could touch the goods, they could also handle their prices, and thus disrupt the match between the two. In particular, younger consumers were made out to be amused by playing with or collecting the removable tickets (Figure 2.15).

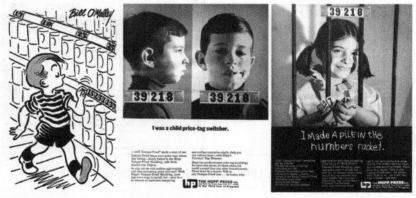

Source: Progressive Grocer (left: 1946, 10, 182; middle: 1966, 08, 5; right: 1965, 06, 5).

Figure 2.15   Tricky fingers

For many years, children were not an issue in retail settings since they were either absent or safely contained by appropriate means. Tracey Deutsch (2001) described grocery stores as a male, chauvinist environment, largely unfriendly towards women, even if women had to cope with it. It is easy to complement Deutsch's depiction: women unfriendly meant mother unfriendly, and what was mother unfriendly was child unfriendly in a period when social norms suggested child care was a mother's responsibility. In the traditional grocery store, children were considered a nuisance, because they presented a risk, notably in terms of spoilage or pilferage. The service store was particularly adapted to prevent such risks, thanks to its tall and hermetic counter that worked as a barrier to prevent undesired child activities.

The adoption of self-service changed the whole scene. With self-service, women experienced a greater freedom, relieved of the grocer's social control and harassment (Du Gay, 2004). The (slightly) emancipated women brought their children with them during their shopping trips. In the late 1930s, when the shopping cart was introduced, mothers diverted the device from its intended use as a rolling basket to an improvised form of baby stroller, at the risk of reducing its potential to support their shopping. Equipment providers seized these problems as well as the retailers' hostility towards children as a business opportunity. For instance, the Boston Metal Products Inc. proposed a turnstile equipped with a special apron placed below the turning arms that prevented "children from crawling through the gate" (1945, 11, 206), and shopping cart suppliers began to devise solutions that allowed the carts to carry children without affecting the shopping volume (Cochoy, 2015a). Price tag manufacturers worked similarly; they presented the problem that children could represent for price display as a real or hypothetical threat that should be prevented:

> The price tag molding has come into very wide use in grocery stores and markets both large and small. The molding is in the nature of a channel strip in which the price tags are inserted. The tags are easily slidable along the molding strip, and the displacement of tags by mischievous persons has become the cause of considerable confusion and annoyance and disputes with customers concerning prices. (Patent no. US 2,507,937)

For price tag manufacturers, fixing the problem of unwanted price moves was obviously an opportunity; it gave them an argument to extend and renew their product line by replacing the features they had been selling during the past three decades with new patented solutions. The new generation of price tag devices was aimed at firmly fixing prices so that "Children can't move 'em" (Freeman: 1949, 02, 184). At the same time, those prices had to be easily moved or removed, but only by the grocery professionals, as suggested by the Youngstown system that "Lock price tags permanently until you [the grocer] want to move or replace [them]" (1952, 07, 166). Hopp Press' humorous advertisements were aimed at promoting "Tamper-Proof", a patented system where removing a tag needed a special tool available exclusively to retailers (Figure 2.16) (1953, 10, 6–7; 1954, 04, 6–7). Interestingly, it should be noted that the argument of fighting pilferage, mentioned above, came after the introduction of this system.

Source: *Progressive Grocer* (1954, 04, 7).

Figure 2.16   Hopp Press Tamper-Proof

The working of these systems is best illustrated by Shaw and Slavsky's solution proposed 5 years previously (Figure 2.17). This device (the patented version in the upper part of the figure, and an improved version in the lower part with a "double lock" feature) helped the grocer clip price tags on to the molding simply by pushing with a finger. Once clipped, the tag was almost impossible to remove, except with an appropriate tool. In other words, fingers could be used to place the tags but not to remove them, thus preventing young customers from handling them. This system provided different users with different services: it offered changeable prices to professionals and fixed prices to customers. As such, it worked like Latour's (1988) door closers: it could be opened or closed when needed and by whom it was intended.

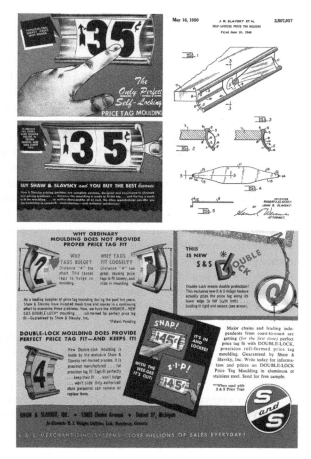

Source: *Progressive Grocer* (upper left: 1948, 10, 120–21; upper right: Patent no. US 2,507,937; bottom: 1956, 04, 40).

Figure 2.17 Shaw and Slavsky's "Permalock" and "Double Lock"

PRICE TAGS AS ULTIMATUMS: THE TENSION BETWEEN PRICE FORMULATION AND PRICE COMPETITION

By fixing prices materially on the shelves, price tags helped fix the price level in the store. At the same time, they allowed the grocer to adjust it as often as necessary. Far from being anecdotal, this ambivalent technical system, by being focused on the alternation between price fixation and price variation, contributed to reshape both the market economy and consumer society at large. Consumer society was reshaped, because price tags were one of the key elements of self-service. As such, they helped release consumers from their dependency on the grocer and introduced the new cognitive regime of product evaluation, based on the reading of symbolic information – prices on the shelves and brands and ingredients on the packages. Price tags also favored a dramatic shift in the functioning of the market economy. This shift was twofold. First, with price tags, transactions went from being based on opaque but negotiable prices to being based on transparent but fixed ones. Price tag technologies played an ambivalent role in the performation[3] of the self-equilibrating market based on price transparency and flexibility. On the one hand, by spreading and fixing open prices, price tags performed the transparency principle: for each generic good, a single price was provided for all customers. On the other hand, this was done at the expense of a relative abandonment of price flexibility: prices ceased to be immediately negotiable and instead became administered. Indeed, when they are displayed, prices become public and unambiguous, but also less easy to change (for the grocer) or to discuss (for the consumer). To put it in theoretical terms, price tags shifted prices from instantly adjustable values to what experimental economists label "ultimatums", that is, prices formulated by the grocer that the consumer only can "take or leave" (Güth et al., 1982; Camerer and Thaler, 1995).

Once redefined as ultimatums, prices became a matter of careful management. Because prices now had to be displayed before the exchange, they needed to be "pre-produced". Prices became less the result of a direct and instant negotiation between supply and demand than of complex a priori "formulations" based on markup calculations and other pricing techniques. This notion of formulation and its consequences has been clearly put (formulated) by Michel Callon:

> a concrete price is always established from at least one other price, i.e. it is only one element within a series (of prices) that precedes and extends it. We know this since primary school and the rule we were taught there: selling price = cost price + profit. [...] Let us agree to call price formulation the set of operations that move from a price series Pi to the price Pj: $Pj = f(Pi)$. [...] Identifying these formulas, their formation and the strategies to which they give rise, as well as their classification, their evolution and the moral, technical and political controversies they generate, certainly constitutes one of the essential tasks for the sociology of market agencements. [...] An agencement is a market one when it prepares, organizes and completes transactions that are settled by transfers of ownership giving rise to monetary

---

[3]   By performation, we mean the way economic theories end up shaping economic matters, according to the logic of "performative utterances" that enact the reality they describe (Callon, 1998; MacKenzie, 2004).

compensation, the amount of which (price) is obtained by applying a formula of the type $Pj = f(Pi)$. (Callon, 2013, our translation)

In other words, as ultimatums based on formulations, prices became the result of a production process rather than the outcome of a market equilibrating mechanism. They ended up being a characteristic of the goods close to[4] all their other qualitative dimensions, rather than a separate value dependent on market fluctuations only. And with price tags, we understand that this price management approach was not just a company business. Retailers continued the job of the factory; like their suppliers, retailers were fully productive. In this respect, the term "distribution" is too passive, too restrictive and mislead-ing, since when marketed, goods are not just distributed but re-qualified. Just like a built aircraft has to receive a final layer of paint in the airplane industry, goods distributed in retail outlets needed to receive a last layer of economic valuation. What is sold included its selling price; it is this new state of the good, and not the good that entered the shop, that is bought (Callon, 2013).

It is important, however, to remember that if price tags were designed to fix prices, they were also designed so that this fixation remained partial only. Callon is right to outline that prices are the result of complex price formu-lations, but it is necessary to add that such formulations are always highly fragile, challenged by competing offers, and thus subject to frequent and quick revisions. It is likely that consumers, who largely ignore the inner workings and cognitive legitimacy of price formulations, will favor a lower price over a higher one, whatever the sophistication and relevance of the formulations they rest upon, respectively. In other words, at the heart of the contemporary economy lies a tension between price formulation and price competition.

Price tags are precisely designed to support and manage this tension. By allowing the physical display and fixation of preset prices, price tags sustain the formulation regime, the management of prices, the "visible hand" of grocers over the invisible hand of market competition (Chandler, 1977). But by facilitating the quick, easy and cheap replacement of prices, price tags also acknowledge the importance of market pressure and price flexibility. With price tags, prices are fixed, but they are not cast in stone as a result of calcula-tions; they are provided in the form of "paper" or "celluloid" removable cards that are altogether resistant, cheap and mobile, ready to assist the low cost oscillation from managerial pricing policies to market price adjustments. All in all, with price tags, the invisible hand of the market and the visible hand of

---

[4]   "Close to", but not "like": while put near to the goods, the price remains detached from them. This "close but not equal" to quality dimension of retail prices has important implications, as we will see in Chapter 5.

the manager are neither opposed nor substituted like business history presented them; they rather go "hand in hand". Just as the binding of a ski provides a skier with a device that is fully rigid when she skies and fully flexible when she falls (Cochoy, 2015b), price tags provide grocers with a tool that helps them shift from price management to price adjustment, according to the circumstances, without compromising or blurring these two regimes. The idea is to allow the alternation between two very clearly defined states – a price well fixed for the day and to everyone's eyes; but a price still flexible for the days to come – like the "locked" or "unlocked" position of the ski binder, the "on" and "off" switches of electric devices, or the "0" and "1" of the digital world to come. In a way, such fixed prices favored the movement of goods: with clear and unambiguous fixed prices, consumers could make their decisions faster, without being slowed down by uncertain bargaining rituals or the necessity to rely on additional information given by professional intermediaries.

* * *

Until now, we have focused almost exclusively on price fixing (i.e., setting, displaying and adjusting prices) as material operations. These practices of displaying prices, changing prices, and moving price tags were motivated by fluctuations in the supply and prices of goods. At the same time, the new technologies also eased price variations. Of course, changeable prices were less flexible than retailers' discretionary prices. But they were more flexible than prices printed on the package: with price tags, prices could be changed collectively and on a regular basis. Price fluctuations, pricing formulas and price tag technologies thus combined to ease price changes. By offering the possibility to change prices at little cost, through the mere recombination of numerals, price tag technologies allowed for a new type of pricing strategy. With them, grocers could move from individualized price flexibility in the old system of bargaining, to systematic and transparent price changes. This strategy could be labeled "bargaining through volume": the little advantages granted individually and privately to consumers, thus with limited contagion effects, could become systematic and global, with a potentially huge impact on the whole economy, as we will see in the next two chapters.

3. Managing prices: price cutting strategies

The introduction of self-service led to a proliferation of price display technologies and associated price display practices. This impacted the economy and society at large by heating the tension between price formulation and price competition. In this chapter and the next, we examine this tension, its workings and consequences in greater detail by focusing on the development of "price cutting" strategies and "price ceiling" policies after World War I. Price cutting strategies were about mobilizing price display as a weapon for aggressive price competition; price ceiling regulation was about using the same devices as a way to fight inflation. The present chapter focuses on the price cutting strategies, while the price ceiling policies are the topic of Chapter 4.

As we will see, price cutting strategies depended more specifically on the use of new techniques aligned with a general profit-through-volume approach, like batch sales, and the use of specials to attract consumers in the hope of selling more profitable goods to them once in the shop. As is often the case with economic rationality, what seemed good from an individual perspective proved disastrous at the aggregate level. The widespread use of price cutting techniques led to the development of price wars that worked as both a source and an effect of economic deflation and bankruptcies. They exacerbated the effect of the Great Depression and forced retail professionals to critically examine their former practices. In order to overcome these problems, independent retailers and large manufacturers employed counter-measures such as "resale price maintenance" policies and eventually asked for ad hoc public regulation. Eventually these transformations produced several new pricing methods and tools, but also turned prices into corporate assets. Additionally, along the way, pricing devices altered the identities of market actors (manufacturers, grocers, consumers, regulators) and modified power relationships in the US grocery market.

PRICE CUTTING STRATEGIES AND TECHNOLOGIES

Let's start with a chart (Figure 3.1), which shows food inflation in the United States between the two World Wars (1915–1939) in terms of the monthly variation of the US food price index. The fluctuations evidenced in the chart

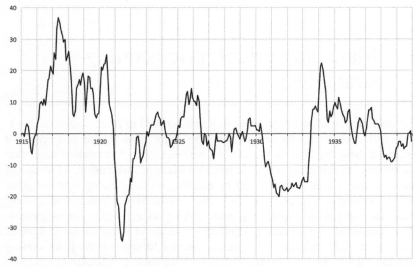

Source: US Bureau of Labor Statistics.

Figure 3.1   *US food inflation 1915–1939 (12-month rolling change in the food price index)*

are not the tiny ones we saw during the recent decades, following the impressive performance of monetarism (Friedman, 1960), but dramatic moves, with roller-coaster-like variations. But why and how do prices go up and down? The classic explanations are that national price movements are caused by external shocks, like wars, poor harvests, international macroeconomic fluctuations and so on, or by internal economic mechanisms like excessive growth in money supply, fluctuations in real supply or demand, or the expansion and subsequent burst of financial bubbles (see, for example, Gordon, 1977; Bernanke and Mishkin, 1997; Maćkowiak, 2007). These links exist, matter, and may even be prominent: to a large extent, the weight of aggregates, the impact of global shocks and the interplay of manufacturers, retailers and consumers are to the economy what hurricanes, tornadoes, atmospheric pressures and winds are to the weather: they work as strong and somewhat irresistible forces that market actors cannot but cope with.

   Such forces are also acknowledged by market professionals. In an article significantly entitled "Advance prices with the market, then you can come down with it", *Progressive Grocer* journalist Carl Dipman attributed the price escalation during 1918 and 1919 to the war, and the following peaks to the "feverish prosperity" that followed the Armistice. He explained that the dire price drop in 1920–21 – a decline of 59.3 percent within a year – was the consequence of overstocking: excited by the rise of prices and the hope of easy profits that came with the postwar prosperity, wholesalers bought too much and soon found themselves stuck with excessive stocks. To liquidate the stocks, they had no option but to cut prices, making thousands of them go bankrupt (1922, 12, 7).

But for Dipman, watching the economic records was not enough. The stronger the forces, the more one felt the need if not to control, then at least to mitigate or anticipate them. Dipman's stance was motivated and followed by immediate advice, urging retailers to continually adjust their prices to changes in wholesale prices and save the extra profit as a safety net in case of deflation. Instead of replacing the invisible hand of the market with the visible hand of managers (Chandler, 1977), Dipman thus proposed a compromise consisting in having both hands work together, by actively taking advantage of market movements. But he did not detail how this could be done; readers learned that prices had to be properly adjusted, but still had to discover through what means.

In the following, we show that price adjustments are neither just a matter of abstract and climate-like mechanisms nor one of managerial voluntarism and business strategies. They are also a matter of proper infrastructures, tools and mundane, manual operations. In other words, if price pressure matters, it is because actors make it matter. As Latour stresses, contexts are the results of contextualization efforts:

> Transforming the context into a certain number of people who represent interests and who all want to achieve the goals of those who they represent does not suffice to enable one to decide whether or not they will have any impact […], still less to calculate in advance what the impact will be. [...] Hence the idiocy of the notion of "pre-established context." The people are missing; the work of contextualisation is missing. The context is not the spirit of the times which penetrates all things equally. Every context is comprised of individuals who do or do not decide to connect the fate of a project with the fate of the small or large ambitions they represent. (Latour, 1996, 137)

In accordance with this view, we explore how retail actors contextualized prices. We do so by examining the price cutting practices that became a major concern during the interwar period, from the sharp deflation of 1920–21 to the Great Depression in the 1930s.

As the name suggests, "price cutting" concerns both a price decline and a voluntary strategy: if prices drop, it is often because someone "dropped" them; if prices are cut, it is because someone cut them. In the very same way that any domination supposes a minimum consent of those who are dominated (Weber, 1978[1922]), any deflation requires the participation of economic actors ... and sometimes even stems from them. As we will indeed see, price cutting was the outcome of the replacement of former bargaining habits by several new practices and technologies, including price displays, batch sales, the use of leaders and specials, and so on.

Bargaining

In order to be cut, a price has to be known. But known by whom, how, and when? The history of price cutting is the history of a shift from one regime of price fixing to another. As we know (see Chapter 1), the first regime was that of hidden yet negotiable prices (Howard, 2015). At the turn of the twentieth century, prices were often undisclosed (Hollander, 1965). Or rather, they were displayed in an asymmetric way: the retailer would mark his (purchasing) price at the bottom of a product by using a code that only he could understand (for instance, by using a specific letter for each numeral) (Spellman, 2009). By means of such a device, the retailer could know his cost and use it as a base for bargaining with each individual customer. The widespread use of such bargaining was even reflected at a Congressional hearing on pricing issues in the first decade of the twentieth century (Strasser, 1989, 270–71). Under this regime, price cutting was both systematic and limited: every transaction would include a price negotiation, often ending in a price reduction, but given the lack of publicity about the underlying prices, price comparisons and the related economic pressures on prices were effectively restricted. The price adjustment process was confined within the walls of each store and even within the frame of each individual interaction. The link between such local processes and wider economic developments was thus not readily observable. However, things were changing, due to the emergence of the new regime of price display, which altered both the local conditions for price fixing and the workings of the economy at large. This new regime started with the display of prices in shopwindows.

Cut Cards

The dramatic growth of the market for canned foods after World War I (Twede, 2012) helped promote price display: the longer shelf life of canned products afforded branded goods with stable prices as parts of the products' image (Strasser, 1989). The cans also replaced the sensorial examination of goods with a "literary" description of their contents that partially replaced the grocer's advice. This encouraged retailers to complement the description of quality with a corresponding description of price. Last but not least, the durability of canned goods made them highly suited for display in shopwindows, thus further encouraging the display of prices. Openly displaying prices changed the regime of price fixing. With open prices, there were no more "hidden cuts"; prices were displayed at the store front, offering both commercial appeal and a basis for price comparison and competition.

Source: Progressive Grocer (1924, 03, 14).

Figure 3.2   Cut price grocery

Far from abolishing bargaining, the open display of prices introduced a new way of price cutting that reinvented bargaining. It did so by bargaining before bargaining, so to speak. The price was duplicated; the retailer simultaneously showed one (supposedly regular) price that was cut and replaced by a lower one. Both prices worked together and strengthened the impression of a rebate. This transparency was of course only partial: the consumer did not know the underlying cost of the discounted goods, not necessarily their regular prices, nor the prices of the goods that were not advertised and that often helped cover the reduced markups, as Figure 3.2 suggests.

This shift from the regime of piecemeal price bargaining to the regime of open price display illustrates that prices depend on the specific price mechanism employed (Aspers and Beckert, 2011, 26–7). It also shows that such shifts may present interesting dilemmas. During the bargaining era, prices were fully flexible, but at the expense of a lack of knowledge; prices were adjustable, but at the individual level only, based on local businesses favoring service and customer loyalty (Tedlow, 1990). With the new price display regime, prices were largely available (although not systematically), but at the expense of becoming more fixed. Price display shifted prices from being immaterial and variable outcomes of commercial interactions into material and somewhat stable ultimatums: being openly displayed, prices were now the same for every customer and worked according to a new "take it or leave it" logic (see Chapter 2). The prices could still be changed, of course, but these changes did not occur instantly and for individual customers, but asynchronously and for the entire clientele. In other words, price changes now resulted from *ex ante* or *ex post* "global" decisions rather than from instant and singular adjustments. Along these lines, price display became a matter of private policies of "resale price maintenance" and later of Federal or State regulations (see below). The remaining flexibility concerned which prices to adjust and to what levels, rather than which customer to favor and by how much; conversely, on the consumer side, it concerned where to shop for what goods and at what price. While the displayed prices might be fixed within the store during any given day, their fixity was challenged both from the outside, via price competition, and from the inside, via new selling techniques that turned price display into a major marketing variable.

Batch Sales

After first being displayed on simple handwritten carton cards in the shopwindows, prices gradually colonized the store through more sophisticated devices. Strangely enough for a country that praises free market competition based on price adjustments, displaying price was fully optional rather than mandatory in the United States. Goods were simply assumed to have a "correct price", that is, a price set by the manufacturer or the retailer. For this reason, price competition in the grocery business was implemented less by market players or regulators than by price tag manufacturers. From the early 1920s, prices spread on the shelves, thanks to the rapid development of new price tag devices promoted by several companies including: The Hopp Press (1922, 01, 90), Frank G. Shuman (1922, 02, 86), Edward J. Cook (1922, 04, 94), Disc-O-Tag (1923, 03, 100), John Ph. Kern (1923, 05, 102), F.M. Zimmerman (1926, 06, 21), Clamp-Swing Pricing (1927, 02, 118), and Swing Tag (1927, 04, 154). The resulting proliferation of price display devices is one early example of the growing importance of professional market mediators and their expertise in the enactment of contemporary markets (Barrey et al., 2000; Araujo, 2007; Cochoy and Dubuisson-Quellier, 2013).

Of course, displaying prices for every product in the store added a new task to the retailing business. The price tag manufacturers wagered that this task would be more easily accepted if retailers got the means to do it faster, more easily and more efficiently. But these technologies not only assisted in displaying prices for given items; they also promoted new ways of pricing. One of these consisted in offering a special price for batches.

Source: *Progressive Grocer* (1930, 06, 61).

Figure 3.3   *Clamp-Swing, batch price holders*

As shown in Figure 3.3, Clamp-Swing offered a batch price card holder consisting of two parts: one for the description of a particular batch promotion ("3 lbs for", "2 Doz for", "3 for") and the other for displaying the corresponding price (respectively: "25¢", "63¢" and "50¢"). The advertisement that the illustration is taken from stressed that these descriptions and prices were not written by hand, but obtained by simply inserting preprinted cards: "A Style 'W' set includes 25 holders and 500 cards for any prices and every ordinary quantity including boxes, pounds, dozens, etc." This suggests that the use of the device was not just a matter of simplifying the retailer's job; it was also about transforming it by affording the use of the batch sale strategy in all its possible variations.

F.M. Zimmerman took this logic further by offering price card moldings that allowed retailers to advertise batch sales directly on their shelves, thanks

Source: *Progressive Grocer* (1932, 04, 115).

Figure 3.4   F.M. Zimmerman, batch price ticket

to batch tickets ("for") that combined with the usual price tickets to display promotions (see the fourth price from the left in Figure 3.4, "2 for 25¢").

Batch sales, organized along a "the more you buy, the less you pay" logic, go beyond cost accounting based on double-entry bookkeeping, where the selling price of a given good is systematically calculated in reference to the underlying costs in order to ensure a profit. (See Polanyi's [1966] famous example of the European side of the Dahomey slave trade where the price of slaves was based on their monetary cost.) Instead, batch sales predate ideas about activity-based costing (Cooper and Kaplan, 1988): by selling the same volume of goods through one transaction rather than two or three, significant operational cost reductions could be achieved. Batch sales further replace the fixed relationship between costs and prices with a dynamic and probabilistic bet about the power of price elasticity. In other words, batch sales introduce a sort of price cannibalism, where the price for the quantity sale destroys the unit price. As such, it supports the strategy of "profit through volume", that is, "selling many units at low margins rather than few units at high margins", which was at the heart of the transformation of retailing and the development of mass distribution from the late nineteenth century onward (Tedlow, 1990, 16). But with batch price holders, profit through volume appeared not only as an abstract strategy of buying in large quantities and selling at a lower price. The strategy was also implemented at the level of individual and selected goods: it was transferred to the customer, who was explicitly told to buy more in order to get a better price. In this respect, the batch price holders worked like the virtual batches of our contemporary supermarkets (Grandclément, 2004): the batch was made real by the price holder, but it did not exist at the product level: the consumer had the choice to "enact" it and get the rebate, or buy fewer goods and pay the regular price. "[T]here are so many bundles she can hardly carry them. As the clerk puts the three packages of breakfast food before her, she finds that they are too bulky. Finally she takes only one package and pays the regular price; the special is only on three packages" (1927, 02, 24).

As such, batch sales invented a kind of optional price cutting, possibly for the benefit of the customer (who could adjust her calculation depending on her resources, but also get lured by the selling technique), but definitely for the profit of the retailer. The latter could compensate the lower margins obtained on batches by the increased volume of products sold, by the virtual character of batches allowing lesser quantities to be sold at regular price, and by the promotional atmosphere created by colorful batch price holders, attracting store traffic and hopefully generating increased sales of other items.

Leaders and Specials

The idea of selective profit through volume introduced by batch sales was carried further through leaders and specials, two techniques aimed at proposing rebates for a few well-chosen goods that served to attract customers to the store. Again, the price tag manufacturers supported the implementation of the technique by offering "special" holders (Figure 3.5).

As before, the equipment provider sold both the device and the technique it supported; it did so along a performative logic that at once spread a merchandizing tool and the corresponding theories. Here, the idea of making profits through increased sales of low-priced items was supplemented with the idea of profiting from the attraction power of low prices to bring customers into the shop and then making them buy higher priced and more profitable items. The price tag manufacturer took an active part in this. First, it alleged the selling power of the device, by presenting it as a way to both benefit from existing customers and gain new ones: "Old customers buy more, new friends are made daily", the ad said (Figure 3.5). It also refined the spatial logic of specials that

"Special"—"Special Today"

Now the new Style H CLAMP-SWING puts added punch into these words.

Price every item in your store —feature your specials—merchandise like your competitor. Old customers buy more, new friends are made daily—say thousands of present users.

The New Style H

CLAMP-SWING

— is better looking
— has no wires to rust or scratch
— is built for years of service
— is finished in brilliant red lacquer; other colors: orange, blue, green or ivory, may be had to harmonize with store interior.

Put this powerful sales builder to work for you.

Clamp-Swing Pricing Co.
Alameda, California

Style H For use with Style S or J

Source: *Progressive Grocer* (1930, 02, 55).

Figure 3.5   Clamp-Swing "Special Today"

focused the customer's attention on a given product by supplementing it with a temporal trick: the special was valid "to-day" only. By suggesting that the promotion could be over the day after, the device urged the customer to seize the opportunity, thus promoting impulse purchases rather than thorough examinations. Clamp-Swing also promoted its special holder by contextualizing it (Latour, 1996) as part of the competitive race. The recommendation to "merchandise like your competitor" implies that competitors had already adopted the technique, leaving retailers who wished to remain competitive little choice but to implement it as well. The use of specials turned price from being a variable value determined via market interplay, to an internal quality set by the retailer for its distinctive marketing appeal. In other words, with such devices, price cutting did not appear as the result of a mechanical and remote price adjustment, but rather as a voluntary and strategic business initiative. This strategy was based on the idea that the special was a bait to attract customers to the store where they would hopefully buy other goods: "The cut-price article is generally used as a bait, and the loss must be made up on other articles [...] The price on a well known article is usually cut with the intention of causing the consumer to believe that all other articles in the store are proportionally low in price" (1924, 03, 15–16). "[The leader's] low price is not to make sales but to give customers the impression that all the store's prices are low" (1936, 06, 78).

This strategy was not exclusively linked to the emerging "open display" and "self-service" logic. Indeed, it was actually more efficient in the context of a full service store, where the retailer, by interacting orally with the customer, could actively reorient her towards more profitable items, once they had been attracted by the special: "Frequently when consumers come to the store to buy the leader attempts are made to 'switch' them, by window and counter displays, sales talk, other means, to a more profitable brand" (1936, 06, 78).

Specials were about having your cake and eating it: they offered all the appearances of lower prices, but were meant to increase overall traffic and sales of profitable items. All in all, these new pricing techniques amazingly succeeded to create opacity in the new regime of price transparency (i.e., price display). While prices were now being displayed, some were displayed more than others; just as a big tree hides the forest, a special could obscure regular prices. With specials, grocers had the means to tune competition: instead of bargaining with each individual customer, they just had to bargain with price display. They could increase front-stage competition (price comparisons through public price display), while reducing it back-stage (through the selection and staging of prices that matter). Whatever the prices, the new regime of price display was never fully transparent since the markups were not accessible to customers.

However, one should not be misled regarding the effectiveness of these practices. On the one hand, the quotes above give the impression that retailers viewed specials as a cynical and manipulative tool aimed at luring customers, without any sense of ethics and social responsibility (Figure 3.6). The price tag manufacturers obviously resorted to such rhetoric when contextualizing their solutions, and innumerable retailers were doubtlessly seduced by their promises. On the other hand, the success of specials triggered a price cutting craze that ironically ended up endangering the retail sector, to the point where its members developed strong concerns about it. Indeed, it is very important to stress that the quotes above are taken from articles aimed at critically examining

Source: *Progressive Grocer* (1927, 02, 24–5).

Figure 3.6   "Try a little chain store bait"

both the workings and effects of specials, with a remarkable reflexivity and
even a sense of guilt.

In fact, the grocery profession gradually recontextualized the specials from
powerful competitive tools to destructive weapons. An article entitled "'Try
a Little Chain-Store Bait, Says Pop" (1927, 02, 23 et seq.) nicely illustrates
the first contextualization. Pop Keener was featured in the *Progressive Grocer*
as an old, retired and experienced grocer who regularly offered advice to his
son about developments in the grocery business. In this article, Pop suggested
using the technique of specials from the chain store, both for its supposed
efficiency and to face the competition:

> The chain stores don't sell [the specials], Son. [...] They just advertise them. They
> merely create an impression. [...] there is method in their madness of almost giving
> merchandise away. They don't want to make sales on these specials; they want
> to make an impression [...]. They use them as the bait to bring customers to their
> stores. Once people are there, the clerks are trained to sell profitable things. [...]
> they [...] apply psychology. They pick out 10 or 12 items which are well known and
> used in every household. These they use as bait, if you please. They are the things
> which create the impression in a woman's mind that the chain store is an economical
> place to buy groceries [...] Now, I will make a suggestion to you, Son: Take the four

leading specials which the chain store down the street advertises and sell them at the same price.[1] (1927, 02, 24 et seq.)

According to Pop's advice, specials and the related price cutting strategy appeared as both the disease and the remedy, or the other way around. Pop clearly attributed the technique of specials to the chains, and presented independent retailers as its victims: "We can't even buy goods at the price the chain sells them", Pop said (1927, 02, 23). As a consequence, adopting specials was less about following the route to modernity – which was the overall *raison d'être* for the *Progressive Grocer* – than a means to survive. Largely, then, Pop's advice relied on the same contextualization as the advertisement by the Clamp-Swing Pricing Co. in Figure 3.5.

Another article published a few years earlier expressed the same idea in an even clearer way, by presenting the use of specials as "unfair price cutting" (1924, 03, 15). The article added "honest dealers often [felt] obliged to resort to 'leaders'". Saying that one does something because others are doing it, and because one is trapped in their game, was a way to mitigate and even eschew responsibility. Moreover, presenting independents as "honest dealers" who "[felt] obliged" to use specials clearly expressed regret and awareness that something was amiss in such behavior.

The problem was twofold. First, because prices not only signal economic value but also product quality, price cutting damaged the reputation of both the manufacturers ...

The price cutter [...] cuts into the sale of the legitimate manufacturer, who has established good will for his house or his product. (1924, 03, 16)

... and the retailers:

Price is generally cut on a "leader." The dealer who is in competition with the price cutter and sells the "leader" at a legitimate profit, is often held up by the consumer as a profiteer, and loses his good will and standing in the community, because the price cutter places him in a false light. (1924, 03, 16)

---

[1]   Here we have the classic economist version with a twist. Lower prices are supposed to reduce supply, which the specials seem to do: the retailer advertises a price at which it is less interesting for him to sell the good. The reduced price also seems to trigger increased demand, as economic theory predicts. The imbalance between supply and demand that this creates is then compensated by the sale of *other* goods than those with lowered prices. Meanwhile, the special has redirected demand towards the advertising retailer.

Second, and all things considered, in the article's own terms, price cutting meant to "fight fire with fire" (1924, 03, 15). Even in 1924, at a time when prices were if not stable then at least reasonably so compared to the deflation of 1920–21, grocery experts lucidly saw the use of specials as both bait and threat. The manipulators knew they could be punished by their very manipulation. Indeed, what was acceptable in the 1920s proved disastrous a few years later. At the store level, price cutting was about lowering prices as little as possible: the price was cut only on a few items and profits preserved through the sale of other items. But at the aggregate level of the economy, things were dramatically different. Price cuts started a vicious circle of price competition that contributed if not to create, then at least to accelerate deflation. Thus, however reluctant the retailers might have been, their large-scale adoption of price cutting techniques as competitive tools set the stage for a dramatic recontextualization of the new pricing regime just a few years later.

THE EVILS OF PRICE CUTTING

Source: *Progressive Grocer* (left: 1932, 08, 13; right: 1932, 09, 15).

Figure 3.7   *Let's face the facts on this crazy price cutting*

In the early 1930s, the *Progressive Grocer* published a series of articles where the magazine's journalists expressed serious concerns about price cutting: "Economist's Study Shows Price Cutting a Menace" (1932, 02, 74); "What about Price Cutting?" (1932, 06, 36); "It's Time to Stop Crazy Price Cutting" (1932, 08, 12); "Pop Keener Discusses This Price-Cutting Mess" (1932, 08,

12); "Let's Face the Facts on This Crazy Price Cutting" (1932, 11, 16); "The Grocery Trade Has Had Enough Price Cutting" (1933, 04, 28). The reiteration of such concerns (see also Figure 3.7 and Figure 3.8) shows the gravity of the problem: presenting again and again similar arguments against price cutting was like trying again and again to hit the brakes on a car racing downhill on a steep road.

He started something . . .   . . . that he couldn't finish

Source: Progressive Grocer (1933, 02, 17).

Figure 3.8   He "started something ... that he couldn't finish"

It is no wonder that this series of articles – published in 1932 and 1933 – linked price cutting to the Great Depression. But they did more than this: they expressed philosophical concerns about the conduct of the grocery business and the responsibility of retailers, beyond the general economic crisis; they presented an interesting analysis of the social dynamics behind price cutting practices; and, based on all these developments, they called for action by proposing innovative ways to stop and hopefully reverse the movement.

Diagnosis

As just mentioned, the articles voicing concerns over price cutting appeared at a very specific moment during the Great Depression: 1930 and 1931 were the worst years of the crisis, with a 30 percent aggregate drop in food prices (see above, Figure 3.1). As a consequence, Carl Dipman encouraged retailers to get out of the vicious circle: "It's time to stop uneconomic price cutting. It's time because this country wants to get back to normal business" (1932, 08, 12). Interestingly enough, this implicitly suggested that deflation was not just the result of an exogenous financial shock and the effect of uncontrollable market forces, but that store managers had their share of responsibility for it (as well as means to counteract it). In Dipman's view, price cutting was the combined

result of two developments: the economic Depression, which sharpened competition, and managerial techniques that had been invented a few years before,
which dramatically speeded up the vicious circle of deflation. "Price cutting
is nothing new. We have always had it. But the extent to which it is practiced
today is unprecedented in the food business. [...] The thing has been slowly
creeping up on us for ten years. Along came the depression and accentuated
it" (1932, 09, 14).

The irony of price cutting was that when the Depression accentuated the
price movement, techniques aimed at trapping the customers ended up trapping the trappers: "We certainly succeeded in converting [the housewife] into
a bargain hunter" (1932, 09, 77).

According to the *Progressive Grocer* (1932, 02, 74) the link between
price-cutting-as-deflation and price-cutting-as- merchandizing was acknowledged in a study commissioned by the New York Board of Trade in the
spring of 1931 and conducted by Professor Seligman of Columbia University
(Seligman and Love, 1932). In his report, the renowned economist acknowledged that price cutting was not just the expression of price decline, but the
result of pricing strategies. Stressing the "persistent use of leaders and specials", he concluded: "Predatory price cutting that creates cut-throat competition is dangerous to the welfare of retail trade, particularly in depressed times,
and no real benefit to the public in the long run" (1932, 02, 74).

Economic Ethics and Philosophy

The retail experts at the *Progressive Grocer* further developed the reflexive
self-criticism of price cutting as an expression of both the Depression and the
retailers' own practices. In "Pop Keener Discusses This Price-Cutting Mess"
(1933, 04, 28), the columnist revisited his previous advice to use a little "chain
store bait". This time Pop tried if not to apologize then at least to justify his
previous suggestion by introducing a subtle distinction between acceptable
and unfair price cutting, implying that his previous advice had concerned the
former type:

> Dear Son: [...] Incidentally, you remind me that I once advised you to jump in and
> offer specials because everybody was doing it. [...] I've advised offering specials,
> let me try to clarify this pressing problem [...]. [According to John Wanemaker, the
> founder of the department store], every proper retail transaction is a square deal.
> And a square deal means a *profit for both buyer and seller* [...] the unexplained
> special price contradicts the square deal principle. [...] Anybody could understand,
> for instance, the logic of the Clearance Sale, the Remnant Sale, the Demonstration
> Sale, and so on [...] certain unscrupulous dealers faked sale names. Witness the old
> fake Fire Sale, and the fake Closing Out Sale. [...] Gradually sale names came into
> use that explained nothing. Witness such names as Startling Price Sale, Howling

Bargain Sale, Greatest Sale on Earth—names merely sensational or wild exaggerations. [...] At any rate, unexplained specials became a trade habit. [...] why should we complain of customers being unreasonable when we have ceased to use reason ourselves? (1933, 04, 28–30)

Later, when reflecting on the transition from bargaining about hidden prices to open price display, Pop Keener equated the reliance on price specials to a generalized form of bargaining, as if modernity was indeed pulling the grocery business backwards: "Regular and fair prices were adopted as the modern ideal because bargaining was wasteful, consuming too much time. But we see price cutting madness restoring wasteful bargaining in a new form—shopping around and comparing the cost of specials" (1933, 04, 76).

According to this view, grocery retailers could not but consider their own price cutting practices as economic and societal nonsense: "All business in this industrial civilization is entitled to operating expenses plus a reasonable profit. When such tactics are assumed as to make impossible even operating expenses, industrial civilization is a failure" (1933, 02, 80).

Analysis

Beyond the diagnosis of its general meaning, a major concern was to assess what the vicious circle of price cutting did and who suffered from it. The negative impact of the practice included both its past observable effects ...

Ruthless price cutting depresses commodity and farm prices, dissipates profits of distributors and producers, and prevents the return of business to a sane and normal level. (1932, 08, 12)

... and its future predictable outcomes:

A continuation of ruthless price cutting will depress commodity prices, in turn restrict still further buying power, and finally delay the return of prosperity. (1932, 08, 12)

The author of the article also provided a clear example illustrating how such effects could come into existence: in response to a retail chain cutting the price of butter, competing grocers refused to buy the butter until they got a price enabling them to compete with the chain. As a consequence, the producer's stocks of butter increased to the point where the producer had to slash its price, so that in the end, everyone lost. This idea that everybody was suffering from price cutting was further argued by Carl Dipman. After having stressed that "As a trade, we have been carried away by this uneconomic price cutting", Dipman added that "By 'we', we mean chain stores, manufacturers, wholesalers, retailers and consumers. We are all guilty—not individually but as a group" (1932, 09, 14).

This point was developed in Dipman's account as well as in other articles and testimonies. The responsibility of every actor was stressed. Dipman explained that the chains were trapped in the vicious circle of price cutting they had introduced (1932, 09, 15), following a pattern where competitive weapons work the first time but then threaten the ones who devised them (see for instance how Frequent Flyers Programs soon trapped the airline companies [Araujo and Kjellberg, 2016]). Another article stressed that independent retailers did not escape the same vicious circle: "The independent stores, which the authors find are followers rather than leaders in price cutting, are forced by competition to meet cut prices and resort to the same tactics as the cutter. They must defend their profit margins by switching customers to other brands with a longer margin" (1932, 06, 36).

But retailing experts, whatever their own interests, did not forget to acknowledge that "The party most injured by price cutting [was] the manufacturer" (1932, 06, 36). The argument was that manufacturers did not only loose goodwill, because low prices were raising doubts as to the real value and quality of their products, but because price cutting was disrupting the trust relationships that were the foundation of efficient and profitable distribution channels: "What the manufacturer loses is much more important—namely dealer cooperation. [...] The retailer finds that to make a normal profit he must sell the consumer another brand. Thus manufacturer and distributor pull against each other instead of pulling together. The result is a huge economic waste" (1932, 06, 78).

Finally, some experts went as far as claiming that price cutting was also damaging to the consumers by stressing that depressed prices contributed to the population's impoverishment:

> Low prices, which are supposed to benefit the consumer most, in reality make him the greatest loser of all, a business specialist in Los Angeles said. With high prices, all could share abundance. With low prices, millions are idle, thousands are on the verge of starvation, and scores have jumped from high windows in self destruction. (1932, 11, 18)

To summarize, these articles point towards a reflexive re-examination of the contextualization of the price cutting practices that had spread among the retailers along with the new price display devices. Interestingly, while the Great Depression provided power to the argument, it was not used to exonerate the retailers. Quite the contrary, even in the face of such large-scale forces, the articles explicitly stressed the agency of the grocery retailers, that is, their capacity to make a difference (Giddens, 1993).

PRICE CUTTING POLICIES

Once the *Progressive Grocer* had shown that price cutting had become "crazy" to the point of being destructive for the entire grocery profession – "Further price cutting only demoralizes and destroys" (1932, 08, 13) – it could call for action. It did so pragmatically, arguing "all means were good", whatever their ideological foundations, provided they could contribute to the return of prosperity. According to this logic, the magazine's arguments relied equally on the liberal drive of individual rationality and on the new interventionist approach of the Roosevelt Administration.

Inverting Economic Anticipations

As far as individual rationality was concerned, the *Progressive Grocer* fought hard to invert economic anticipations by convincing its readers, according to a logic of wishful thinking that prices had reached a point where they could not but go up again. After the negative self-fulfilling prophecies that drove the country bankrupt, time had come for their positive counterpart to enact the return of prosperity. To this end, it was important to stress the appropriate moment ("now") when the prices had reached a "bottom" from which they could only increase, by repeating it again and again: "It's time to stop uneconomic price cutting. [...] Leading business men and economists are of one mind—that deflation and liquidation in food products has gone far enough" (1932, 08, 12). "We have *now* reached a point in this depression where wide scale price cutting simply aggravates conditions and continues the present unsatisfactory situation" (1932, 08, 14, emphasis added). "*Now* is time to stop this uneconomic price cutting" (1932, 09, 74, emphasis added).

Interestingly, the magazine seems to have been convinced that the counter-cyclic view would be all the more acceptable if it did not deny economic realities, but rather built on a factual assessment of the situation. Along these lines, it acknowledged that the Depression was inevitable, while at the same time stressing that it had reached its climax: "We have had very little to say about price cutting in these pages during the past two hectic years. This country was in for a period of deflation. Stocks and inventories had to be reduced. Prices had to reach a bottom" (1932, 08, 13).

The idea of a bottom was not just claimed, but supported by thorough economic reasoning, for instance stressing that as surpluses were now disappearing, prices would stabilize (1932, 08, 13). Implicitly, then, journalists at the *Progressive Grocer* knew that performative statements would be all the more performative if they were based on constative ones (Cochoy, 2015a). Accordingly, using numbers was helpful to convince retailers that price cutting had reached an extreme and thus had to be abandoned if you wanted to survive: "45% of the items of a grocery line do not carry a legitimate margin. That situation is grossly unfair. It places an unfair burden upon the other 55% of a grocer's line that must, as a consequence, bear more than a fair proportion of the overhead and operating expense" (1932, 08, 14). "Today approximately 75% of the food is distributed through dealers who resort more or less to the price appeal" (1932, 09, 77).

If statistics offered one argument, sociology offered another. To break the vicious circle of price cutting it would help to unveil the socially deceptive logic underlying it. If price cutting developed because independent grocers blindly copied the practice of chain stores ...

> Some independents are more interested in underselling the chains than they are in making profit for themselves. (1932, 08, 50)

... one way to convince the same grocers to change their behavior was to let them know (or believe?) that the chains were now beginning to abandon their own strategy:

> Even chain stores have come to the realization that price cutting has been carried too far. (1932, 08, 50)

> Chain stores are one after the other "upping" their prices. (1932, 09, 78)

Another original way to make grocers shift views consisted in developing a Smithian-like argument. In this particular case, the adjective "Smithian" does not refer to the Adam Smith of *The Wealth of Nations* and the drive of self-interest, but to the Adam Smith of *The Theory of Moral Sentiments*, and the idea of the impartial spectator, that is, the aptitude to adopt another perspective than your own (Smith, 1759). The magazine invited its reader to adopt the customer's point of view. The underlying and wishful reasoning was that grocers would be more inclined to abandon price cutting practices if they realized that the bait did not work anymore, because it had become both well known and meaningless to its main targets:

> From the standpoint of good merchandizing alone, ruthless price cutting has a doubtful value. The American housewife has been "specialed" to the point of boredom. The country has been so flooded with inferior merchandise [...] under the guise of "economy" and "specials" that the appeals and price cuts are more and more falling on deaf ears. The thing has been carried too far. Everybody has been doing it. [...]. The word "special" means next to nothing. The housewife is beginning to realize that so-called specials are for the most part not specials, and are in fact often shoddy merchandise for which she pays handsomely. When popular

brands are cut to ridiculous levels, she knows they are mere bait and that she will be hooked on something else. (1932, 08, 14)

Last but not least, a complementary strategy geared towards altering the grocers' views was to call for reflexivity and moral reappraisal by shaming actors and asking them to take responsibility for the societal consequences of their actions. The magazine counted on this shaming strategy being all the more efficient if it addressed both independent retailers …

> You independents who cut prices are contributing to the demoralization of the entire grocery industry. You are not only dissipating your own profits but are making impossible for others to make a decent living. [...] Don't be too anxious to "lick" the chains, for what does it profit you to run a chain unit out of your neighborhood and go broke yourself doing it? (1932, 08, 50)

… and chain stores:

> And to the chain stores: You have a grave responsibility in helping improve the present situation. [...] Don't be too much agitated by a few price-cutting independents. (1932, 08, 50)

All in all, moving out of the vicious circle of price cutting was presented both as being in the best interest of individual players and as a patriotic duty of every actor:

> Let's try gradually to raise the housewife's standards of quality and value to where they were before we turn them down. And let's remember as we return to sane merchandizing, we not only improve our own profit but we do a patriotic duty to our country in helping bring back normal business, a decent profit and a living wage for the other fellow as well as ourselves. Let's run our business intelligently with a sane, progressive policy and not blindly follow the lead of every blunderhead who parades his cut prices in screeching headlines in the public prints. (1932, 09, 80)

With these arguments, the *Progressive Grocer* offered a new contextualization of price cutting instead of the defunct idea that grocers had no option but to adopt these practices.

A Call for Resale Price Maintenance (RPM)

The hybridization between "liberal" and "national" dynamics logically led the magazine to complement its efforts to reverse individual anticipations with a strong call for legal action. Such a call was the explicit conclusion of the Seligman report endorsed by the magazine: "some form of price maintenance would be beneficial" (1932, 06, 36).

What does "price maintenance" mean? This expression alludes to a kind of regulation that would enable manufacturers to refuse to sell to price cutters and to fix the prices of their goods through special contracts with the distributors, rather than rely on the free market. Many actors were considering this option, both on the manufacturer and the government sides. As early as 1928, just before the crisis, a report from a Congressional subcommittee stated: "there [were] undoubted evils connected with the unrestricted right to sell trade-marked goods at any price which the seller thinks to his advantage" (1930, 01, 38).

Two points are particularly interesting with the RPM idea. First, it was a managerial method that some actors tried to convert into a legal scheme. But even when it was put into legislative efforts, RPM was both against the Federal regulation of prices (prices should remain the business of private actors) and against free market competition (prices should be fixed by companies rather than by the interplay of supply and demand). Second, RPM was both a macro and a micro issue. As a macro issue, the policy was part of the anti-chain movement in which small retailers and large manufacturers opposed mass retailers and consumer organizations (Deutsch, 2004; Howard, 2015). As a micro issue, RPM introduced a distinctive concern for prices as a material dimension of products; it focused on where and how to display them, for instance by printing them on the package (see below). As such, it strongly participated in the mundane governance of prices, at the crossroads of local price display and "global" price regulations.

In fact, the maintenance of retail prices started well before the price cutting craze of the 1930s, and even before the introduction of the price-focused merchandizing strategies reviewed above (Howard, 2015). The history of RPM is well summarized by the US historian Susan Strasser, who shows that this practice was introduced as a corollary to the development of branded goods and national brands.

> With the ascendancy of branded goods [...] the manufacturer — who invested not only in the equipment to produce Uneeda Biscuits or Kodak cameras but also in the apparatus for marketing them — had an intense interest in what happened to their goods after they sold them. Calling it "fair trade," manufacturers adopted price maintenance, a policy of setting prices not only to their own customers, the wholesalers, but also to retailers and consumers, sometimes by printing a price on the package. (Strasser, 1989, 269)

Before becoming part of legislative efforts, then, RPM was a business policy developed by manufacturers to extend their control over product quality to prices. As such, it falls within the scope of the corporate control mechanisms identified and reviewed by Neil Fligstein (1990). Strasser notes that pricing as a managerial decision became a matter of marketing strategy. It allowed selling different brands to different market segments; it was also a weapon to position one's brand in relation to competing ones. In this respect, price cutting could threaten the value of the product by suggesting that it was not worth its previous price. Lowering the price was not just about getting customers of a given product to switch from one retailer to another, it also modified the image of the product itself. With RPM, price shifted from being an externally attributed quality to an internal one. In this respect, RPM was a weapon in the war between large manufacturers and mass retailers. While the former sought to protect their goodwill, the latter denounced price maintenance as unfair "price fixing".

This controversy pitched manufacturers and small retailers against large distributors and consumers.[2] In a series of legal cases, the two sides fought over whether RPM should be considered to be unfair competition and a restraint of trade or not. After the Sherman Antitrust Act of 1890, it was largely acknowledged that unfair competition should be prohibited, but, as Strasser notes, knowing what was unfair proved difficult and resulted in numerous Congressional hearings and court controversies. RPM favored small retailers who sought to add service value to the standard price charged by themselves and their competitors. Indeed, the practice of RPM also altered the relationship between independent grocers and brands. For a long time these retailers had seen branded products as a threat that bypassed their mediation by informing consumers directly about the quality of the product through their packages, thus weakening the retailers' power of substitution (Strasser, 1989). With RPM, however, trademarks rather became assets for the small retailers. They neutralized price competition and secured high markups, thus alleviating the competition from chain stores that favored more aggressive pricing strategies.

Two years after its launch, the *Progressive Grocer* joined the movement for a Federal law on RPM by engaging in two legislative projects. The first one was the Merritt Bill, introduced in 1924, aiming at "[making] it legal and possible for a manufacturer to establish a retail price and enter into contract with his distributors to respect that price" (1924, 03, 15). More precisely, the Bill had a triple aim: prevent price discrimination; make prices public; and protect goodwill. It was about entitling producers to set a standard price for their products and enabling them to maintain that price across the distributive

---

[2]   Even if some consumer activists saw price cutting strategies as mere baits, it proved difficult to convince consumers at large that retailers needed to be prevented by law from offering lower prices.

trades. The producer was offered the possibility to mark the resale price on the package or "otherwise make generally known the price":

> in any contract for the sale of articles of commerce to any dealer, wholesale or retail, by any grower, producer, manufacturer, or owner thereof, under trade-mark or special brand, hereinafter referred to as "vendor," who shall for the purpose of preventing discrimination and protecting his good will clearly mark on each salable unit of his product or the container thereof, or otherwise make generally known the price at which such unit shall be resold, it shall be lawful for such vendor [...] to prescribe the uniform prices and manners of settlement to all purchasers in like circumstances at which the different qualities and quantities of each article covered by such contract may be resold. (Merritt Bill project, quoted in 1924, 03, 52)

The second project was the Capper-Kelly Bill, also known as "The Fair Trade Act". This project was launched immediately after the 1929 crisis and was supported by The National Association of Retail Grocers (1930, 01, 38). It thus anticipated the massive deflation that was about to come. The Bill sought to make it legal for a manufacturer to refuse to sell to any dealer or distributor, to exchange information about price cutters, to sign contracts obliging wholesalers and jobbers to refuse to sell, and to prosecute price cutters as violators of their property rights.

While both these bills proved unsuccessful, they nonetheless illustrate the close link between the grocery trade and regulatory efforts. Eventually, it was the Great Depression and the Roosevelt Administration with its new interventionist approach that found the means to overcome the problem of price cutting: "From President Roosevelt on down, government officials told us that price-cutting must go" (1933, 10, 24). As we shall see, however, this did not mean that the solution was disconnected from the US grocery market.

A Plea for a New Deal against Price Cutting

In August, 1933, a project concerning a National Master Code of Fair Competition was filed with the Agricultural Adjustment Administration in Washington DC. The project was linked to the wider National Industrial Recovery Act and was prepared by the Food and Grocery Conference Committee, with the participation of seven trade associations, including The National-American Wholesale Grocers' Association, The National Chain Store Association, The National Association of Retail Grocers and the Associated Grocery Manufacturers of America (1933, 09, 14–15). The text included several provisions against what was considered "uneconomic and unfair trade practices". Many of these were aimed at preventing mass distributors from exerting excessive pressures upon manufacturers and small retailers:

> No grocery manufacturer or wholesale grocer shall pay a trade buyer, and no trade buyer shall request a grocery manufacturer or wholesale grocer to pay for a special advertising or distribution service by such buyer [...] No grocery manufacturer or wholesale or retail grocer shall offer or give, and no wholesale or retail grocer shall request or accept a free deal. The term "free deal," as used in this paragraph, means the gift of a product or any special deal discount (other than a regular quantity discount) or allowance to a trade buyer or consumer conditioned upon the purchase of a product [...] No grocery manufacturer or wholesale or retail grocer shall require a buyer to purchase one product in order to purchase another. (Project of Master Food Code, quoted in 1933, 09, 19)

Among these practices, those pertaining to prices were of course central. The Master Code project introduced, for the first time, a principle of "Open price competition", meaning that manufacturers and wholesalers must sell at "open prices" uniform to "all trade buyers of the same quantity under the same conditions" (1933, 09, 17). The requirement of open prices was made to avoid discrimination between large and small businesses in order to protect the latter. It should be noted, however, that this openness of prices was restricted to the transactions between businesses and did not apply to consumers. Hence, while displaying retail prices was not made mandatory, the subsequent ban on price discrimination of consumers suggested that prices had to be uniformly set at store level and not be negotiable on an individual basis.

The "hottest" measure against price cutting was the prohibition of "leaders", or more specifically what the Master Food Code project called "loss leaders", that is, products sold below their cost in order to attract customers. To prevent this practice, the architects behind the initiative did not hesitate to interfere with the management of business operations by proposing minimum markups. It was suggested that wholesalers should be required to sell their merchandise at a price at least 2.5 percent above their purchasing price, while retailers would have to use a minimum markup of 7.5 percent. Goods that retailers bought directly from manufacturers would have a minimum markup of 10 percent (1933, 09, 14). These measures proved highly contentious during the Congressional hearings in October 1933 (1933, 10, 24). On the one side, 300 leaders of the food industry supported them almost unanimously (1933, 11, 79), even if chains asked to have them confined to branded merchandise (1933, 11, 28). On the other side, mail-order houses and consumer groups vigorously opposed the "price-fixing" feature of the Code (1933, 10, 25). The strongest opponents were consumer organizations and The Consumers' Division of the recovery administration (which the *Progressive Grocer* suspected to be full of economists blinded by their theoretical approach and dogma in favor of pure price competition) (1933, 10, 82).

After fierce debates, The Code of Fair Competition for Retail Food and Grocery Distributors was signed by President Roosevelt on 30 December 1933, and became immediately effective. The Code was to be administered by the National Recovery Administration (NRA), under the supervision of a special Authority consisting of representatives from all the major national food trade associations. The *Progressive Grocer* labeled this regulation the "most revolutionary change in the history of food and grocery merchandizing". It stressed that the Code would rule the conduct of "half a million different food and grocery business establishments" and would do so by "outlawing many of the practices that have distressed food distribution since the dawn of history" (1934, 01, 14).

The Code enacted the philosophy of open price competition and adopted several provisions from earlier bills. For instance, it banned price discrimination between businesses ...

> Discrimination in prices or terms of sale against purchases of the same quantity under the same conditions of delivery and in credit services for the same class of buyers [...] is prohibited. (Wholesale Food and Grocery Distributor's Code, Article VII, Trade Practices, Section 2, Price Discrimination, quoted in 1934, 01, 17)

... but also, more audaciously, between retail customers – even if it did not go as far as to prescribe mandatory price display, which would have been a logical corollary of the prohibition:

> No food and grocery retailer shall discriminate in price between customers. The term "discriminate in price" as used in this paragraph means directly or indirectly charging a different price for a commodity to purchasers of the same quantity who are located in the same competitive markets. (Wholesale Food and Grocery Distributor's Code, Article IX, Trade Practices, Section 1, Advertising and Selling Methods, quoted in 1934, 01, 62–3)

But the main measure, according to the *Progressive Grocer*, was the prohibition of loss leaders and the related markup clause. This had raised a heated controversy between business representatives, eager to find ways of getting rid of price cutting practices, and consumer advocates, for whom any "price fixing" policy was against the consumers' best interests.

It should be added that the Roosevelt Administration played an important role in settling the controversy and formulating a compromise between the sides. The government's main concern was not market but labor issues. Indeed, the Administration was seeking to advance wages and shorten working hours, according to the view that higher income and shared labor could be key ways to hasten the return of prosperity. But this view offered the means for a kind of trade-off. On the one hand, the Roosevelt Administration saw price regulation as a bargaining chip to make distributors improve labor conditions: "Because NRA wants wages increased and hours shortened in wholesale and retail establishments, NRA sees the necessity of giving the distributive trades some protection against predatory price-cutting" (1933, 10, 24).

On the other hand, distributors saw higher operating expenses as an acceptable means to get out of cutthroat price competition: "Most distributors were willing to go ahead even with this increase in operating expenses in the hope that shortly the distributor's code would afford them some protection against ruinous price-cutting" (1933, 10, 80).

With this compromise the final version of the Code was able not only to close the controversy, but also to combine the prohibition of loss leaders and the promotion of better labor conditions. The controversy was closed by abandoning the previously proposed markup rates. The link between the prohibition of loss leaders and the promotion of better labor conditions was established through the stipulation of a positive relationship between labor costs and selling prices, stressing that every price in the store should cover its part of labor costs, according to accounting rules set by an ad hoc authority:

> to prevent unfair competition against local merchants the use of the so-called "loss leader" is hereby declared to be an unfair trade practice [...] the selling price of articles to the consumer should include an allowance for actual wages of store labor, to be fixed and published from time to time by the Administrator and the members of the Code Authority appointed by the Administrator. (Retail Food Code, Article VIII, Loss Limitation Provision, Section 1, quoted in 1934, 01, 60)

Clearly then, the Code was about astutely renegotiating price formulas, that is, the series of operations that produce prices (Callon, 2013). It did so by disconnecting price adjustments from market interactions and instead linking them to operating costs and social concerns. In doing so, the US government anticipated Callon's call for socially conscious market design in two ways. First, it moved retailing away from a destructive "interface-market" logic, based on the shams of better prices without any concern for the underlying quality and social stakes. Second, it provided a new "market-agencement" for the grocery business by putting in place a complex web of power, technical and labor relationships to create a viable market setting (Callon, 2016).

The NRA thus reintroduced the visible hand of the Leviathan (in the shape of Uncle Sam; see Figure 3.9) to stop the visible hands of managers from playing the destructive game of market price cutting (making the "vicious price cutter" drop his knife). One would think that this development moved pricing practices away from the store, but this would be misleading, for at least

Source: *Progressive Grocer* (1933, 09, 15).

Figure 3.9   The Industrial Recovery Act and price cutting

two reasons. First, every store manager now had to follow the new rules of "administered price competition"; second, every existing technology for price display was still available; the era of open price competition proved difficult to reverse. Significantly, however, price tags for "specials" disappeared from the pages of the magazine, leaving only batch signs like "X quantity for Y price", even if these were sometimes referred to as "special", with a shy tribute to the days of loss leaders (1937, 02, 103).

* * *

The NRA policy proved successful ... for a while. Ironically, in the very same way that the Great Depression worked as an external force provoking and aggravating the effects of price cutting, World War II provided an external shock that triggered and eased price increases. Hence a new and opposite problem came to the fore: after having been committed to stop price cutting, the Administration was now forced to devise tools to control prices that spiraled dangerously upwards. Thus, the deflationist period we have focused on was followed by an era of inflation and the introduction of alternative strategies, regulations and devices. After World War II the political apparatus developed to avoid price cutting practices was reshaped to fight inflation, based on the enforcement of "price ceilings". This policy, far from being an abstract and remote regulation, took the form of new technical evolutions in price tags and price display practices. It is to these developments we turn in the next chapter.

4. Ruling prices: price ceiling policies

If the 1930s was the decade of deflation, the late 1940s and early 1950s saw several periods of high inflation (Ohanian, 1997; Schnidman, 2013). As a result, the era of managerial price cutting analyzed in Chapter 3 was followed by an era of governmental "Price ceiling" policies (Eichengreen and Garber, 1991; Letzler, 1954; Nelson, 1954). Market professionals seized this opportunity and government and market players joined forces to handle various problems associated with the price ceiling policy with tremendous consequences. The hybridization of Federal regulation and retail management contributed to reshape price setting in the retail market. The tension between price formulation and price competition (see Chapter 2) led market and government actors to collaborate to better control the market. The spread of what we term "stereoscopic prices" – the simultaneous display of offered price and reference price – gave rise to new forms of price competition. Finally, the bifurcated agency of price technologies reshaped product qualification and pricing processes.

PRICE CEILINGS: FROM INFLATION TO PRICE REGULATION

In contrast to the dramatic deflationary shifts of the preceding period – World War I and the interwar years (1915–39) – the US economy experienced repeated flashes of high inflation between 1940 and 1955 (see Figure 4.1). Before describing how the government and market professionals dealt with this, we will briefly present and explain this inflation phenomenon.

The first inflation peak occurred between 1941 and 1944 and was an effect of the war. Redirecting the productive forces towards the war effort and draining the labor market through the draft created an upward pressure on prices for raw materials, transportation and labor (1942, 07, 26–7). In this connection, the *Progressive Grocer* quoted George A. Eastwood, president of the meat-packing giant Armour and Co., who noted that: "government purchases for the armed forces and Lend-Lease are immense" and added that the army would absorb "40% of the output of pork during the remainder of the year and at least 60% of the output of lard" (1942, 09, 156). The Office of Price Administration (OPA) reported that one third of the production of canned foods could be available for civil consumption, implying that the remainder was going to the army (1942, 09, 162). The magazine further cited Roy F. Hendrickson from

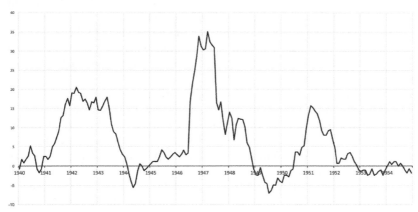

Source: US Bureau of Labor Statistics.

Figure 4.1   *US food inflation index (1940–55)*

the Agricultural Marketing Association, who expressed worries about coming shortages: "we will not have enough meat to supply all the civilian population with as much as they are ready to buy out of their high national income without equitable distribution of some kind" (1942, 09, 159). For the government, two strategies were available for alleviating the effects of inflation on the livelihoods of citizens: rationing or price regulation. In the following, we focus on the latter, given our specific interest in price formation.

On 18 May 1942, the OPA introduced the General Maximum Price Regulation (GMPR) (1942, 07, 128). This regulation was based on a new tool of price governance, so-called ceiling prices. These were maximum prices stipulated for some 1000 "cost-of-living items", including fresh beef, canned fruits, vegetables, juices, and other groceries (1942, 06, 38; 1942, 07, 45). Interestingly, the GMPR was a compromise between the free market and the interventionism of the Roosevelt Administration. The ceiling prices were not a list of uniform prices calculated and imposed by the government, but rather a frozen version of innumerable previous free market prices. A GMPR ceiling price meant the highest price charged for each included good by each individual retailer three months earlier, in March 1942 (1942, 07, 44). In other words, the idea was not to implement a universal standard price, but to rely on the previous pricing practices of the retailers themselves. In some respects, this solution anticipated current "libertarian paternalist" policies. In the same way that nudge theory (Thaler and Sunstein, 2008) seeks to preserve the free choice of economic actors (libertarian policy) while using appropriate devices to nudge them towards "better" conduct (paternalist policy), ceiling prices respected the retailers' previous pricing practices but trapped them in their previous decisions. As such, the GMPR ceiling price instrument reflects a "theorization of the relationship between the governing and the governed" (Lascoumes and Le Galès, 2007, 3): while retailers typically were to be trusted in their pricing decisions, the extraordinary times called for a temporary suspension of their pricing agency.

The new regulation was based on two pragmatic considerations covering the front- and back-office aspects of retail management, respectively. In terms of back-office, because the GMPR was based on existing local prices rather than a universally imposed uniform price, its success hinged on the authorities' ability to check retailer compliance. Therefore, the regulation required every retailer to keep a record of their prices relative to the March 1942 prices for all items subject to the policy. It further introduced two complementary requirements for this record: first, the record had to be filed with the nearest War Price and Rationing Board (1942, 06, 45; 1942, 07, 27). Second, the record had to be "kept in [the] store and made available for examination by any person during the retailer's ordinary business hours" (1942, 07, 27). This latter provision marked a transition between back-office and front-office logics. By loosely mentioning "any person", the regulation suggested that price control could be performed either by specialized officials or by ordinary customers.

Besides anticipating future policy ideas, as noted above, the GMPR also reenacted previous ones. The Code of Fair Competition for Retail Food and Grocery Distributors ("the NRA (National Recovery Administration) code") that had been passed in December 1933 to fight price cutting had also included a provision against price increases. One possible reason for this was the lengthy process of producing the code, which had been initiated right after the 1929 crisis (1930, 01, 38). By the time the code was issued, prices were increasing again, prompting the regulators to include a last-minute measure to fight inflation. This provision foreshadowed the price ceiling policy by tying price increases to a fixed previous date (1934, 01, 16). But the similarities went further: just like the GMPR, the NRA code required every merchant to "keep business records as may be necessary to determine compliance" (1933, 09, 14). Thus, when the GMPR was issued, it benefited from a philosophy and a set of proven tools for the regulation of prices. The major difference and novelty was the closer attention and greater role given to price display. When fighting the Depression, the NRA had faced a dilemma: promoting fair competition, which required price transparency, while avoiding the issue of price display, since this had proven to be one of the main drivers of deflation. Indeed, economic experts had identified the proliferation of new sales methods revolving around the display of prices in the 1920s and early 1930s, such as batch sales, leaders and specials, as one key contributor to the growing problems of the retail trade (1932, 02, 74). Faced with the challenge of inflation rather than deflation, the regulative authorities now embraced price display and price transparency as their new allies.

This front-office aspect of the GMPR was its key dimension. Significantly, the policy contained an abundance of practical details, indicating the importance attributed to the material aspect of prices and, implicitly, the importance of price display devices (1942, 07, 27). Displaying ceiling prices would contribute not only to their enforcement but also to a possible further reduction of prices by reactivating the price comparison and price competition mechanisms that had led to the "price cutting madness" of the 1930s (1933, 04, 76). To this end, retailers were required to post their ceiling prices. But this posting could not be done in any old way; prices had to be placed "on or near the merchandise, easily visible to customers" (1942, 07, 44). By stressing the spatial ("on", "near") and visual aspect of prices ("easily visible"), the GMPR attended – for the first time, to our knowledge – to the "mundane governance" (cf. Woolgar and Neyland, 2013) of prices, that is, to the local, material and technical details of price display.

Specifically, displaying a sign declaring that prices were in accordance with the GMPR was not sufficient; retailers had to *show* the ceiling price for each item covered by the regulation. If the retailer charged a lower price rather than the ceiling price, both prices had to be displayed side by side (1942, 06, 45). These requirements had two objectives: first, to inform consumers about the existence of the GMPR to ensure retailer compliance; controlling prices across the entire country presented a challenge beyond the capacity of existing inspection staff. In this respect, price display was an astute means of delegating inspections by transforming every consumer into a potential inspector. Remote central governance of prices was thus transformed into distributed mundane governance, carried out by the market actors themselves. The second objective was to introduce a new type of "dual" pricing, in the hope of turning the price freeze into a much more dynamic pricing regime.

We know that during the price cutting era dual pricing had been used to stress the lower price of batches and specials compared to regular prices. The GMPR invented a new version of this practice, where actual price was compared to the highest one allowed by the regulation. This engaged the retailer in a threefold competitive game. First, he was competing against himself: the ceiling price was not a standard one, but the price he had charged in March 1942. Second, he was competing against his competitors: being systematically displayed, ceiling prices could be compared. Third, the retailer was competing with the government: the ceiling price set by the GMPR acted as the regular price, challenging the retailer to do better than what the government required. Being a wartime regulation, the GMPR called on everyone, soldiers and civilians, including grocery retailers, to do their part. The GMPR offered a choice between two price display formulations: "Ceiling Price" or "our ceiling" (1942, 07, 44).

The first option emphasized a patriotic form of competition compliant with the regulation, while the second allowed the retailer to play a more aggressive game of price competition by suggesting that "his" ceiling was lower than that of other retailers. All in all, by addressing the material and discursive forms of price display and by imposing prices derived from former trade practices, the GMPR invented a hybrid form of "administered free competition".

The GMPR did not impose one specific method for price display, but offered alternatives that opened a space for complementary merchandizing strategies. The first option consisted in using a single placard for group displays listing brand names, sizes and prices (1942, 07, 44). This option, which could be seen as a minimum requirement, could attract retailers who did not rely on modern price tags or those who preferred not to direct too much attention to the new regulation (Figure 4.2). The second option, in contrast, linked to the use of modern price tags. It consisted in displaying the ceiling price beside the actual price for each individual good. As we will see, this option afforded a more pro-active use of the price ceiling regulation. The *Progressive Grocer* illustrated and suggested possible variants of both these options (Figure 4.3).

TYPEWRITTEN CARDS listing ceiling prices and present prices were placed on shelves in all departments at the United Farms Market, New York.

Source: Progressive Grocer (1942, 06, 38).

Figure 4.2   Typewritten ceiling price cards

FIG. 1. Ceiling price must be shown on all of your "cost-of-living" items.

FIG. 2. If present price is lower than the ceiling price, the ceiling price must still be shown, as above.

FIG. 3. This pricing technique may be used in floor and special displays.

FIG. 4. A single placard may be used for group displays provided names, brands, and sizes are listed.

Source: *Progressive Grocer* (1942, 07, 44–5, excerpts).

Figure 4.3   Displaying ceiling prices

THE HYBRID (PUBLIC–PRIVATE) MANAGEMENT OF PRICE CEILINGS

Enacting the Price Ceiling Regulation in Retailing

The illustrations in Figure 4.3 clearly show the hybrid character of the price ceiling regulation. The enactment of the ceiling price policy was both mandatory and competitive. It was mandatory in the sense that the ceiling price had to be displayed for all the goods subject to the GMPR ("ceiling price" is part of all the illustrations). But it was also competitive in the sense that there was more than one way of complying with the rules. Some of these ways were suggested in the GMPR itself: using price cards (Figure 4.3 lower part) or price tags (Figure 4.3 top). Others were recommended by the *Progressive Grocer*, which stressed the merchandizing potential of the new regulation by offering various reinterpretations of its rules. In the top right illustration, the enunciation of the rule ("If present price is lower than the ceiling price, the ceiling price must still be shown") was complemented with a recommended way of doing this: inserting a "now" ticket between the two prices. This ticket stressed the one-cent saving offered over the ceiling price. Moreover, it implied that prices may be more perishable than goods (cans) and thus that the offer should be seized immediately given that prices might rise in the future – a prospect that would have been familiar to most people in a context of inflation. In other words, price ceiling policies and strategies enacted the future through fictional expectations, a pattern well described by Beckert (2016). The lower left illustration also displays the rule by mentioning the ceiling price above the lower selling price, but here compliance with the rule was combined with the established practice of batch sales and specials.

However, offering advice does not mean changing behavior. Indeed, the magazine noted that "Merchants have been slow in compiling their records; slow in filing ceiling prices on cost-of-living items with the Office of Price Administration", that "retailers have been slow in posting ceiling prices on cost-of-living items", and that OPA officials had been "slow in cracking down on violators" and "when they did something, they did little" (1942, 07, 26). Last but not least, the magazine reported that when retailers complied with the regulation, they mostly chose the less engaging method:

> Methods of posting ceiling prices varied from store to store but most dealers were following the practice of placing a typewritten or handlettered card in each department listing the ceiling prices of cost-of-living items in the particular department. Some were listing both the ceiling price and the present selling price on the cards and their present prices in regular shelf position. (1942, 06, 38)

This comment hints at the old-fashioned character of grocery retailing at the time; grocers had just recently adopted open prices and relied more on handwritten signs than on printed price tags. But the slow adoption of ceiling prices and the preferred traditional method of display also signaled a technical difficulty: available price tags could display numbers and a few signs only. As such, they made it difficult, if not impossible, to discriminate between ceiling and regular prices at the shelf. It is worth noting that the magazine was very fast in establishing the retailers' sluggishness: the comment was made just one month after the regulation came into force. More importantly, if the retailers were (a little) slow in complying with the regulation, the price tag manufacturers were fast and responsive. And through their response, they offered the means to overcome the aforementioned sluggishness and difficulties.

The idea of having the retailer compete against himself, his competitors and the government via reference to frozen "ceiling prices" was imposed by the government and not by retailers or price tag manufacturers. While this may have constrained the retailer, it was an opportunity immediately seized by the price tag manufacturers, who tried to convince retailers that ceiling prices could be profitable for them as well. Less than two months after the GMPR was introduced, price tag manufacturers like Hopp Press and Charles George Co. offered new devices especially designed to support the new pricing policy (Figure 4.4). This quick reaction is noteworthy, given the time needed to design, produce and market these devices. The products advertised by the two companies offered solutions that faithfully implemented the two methods offered by the GMPR: the general price placard (see the "bulletin displays for meat department" offered by Hopp Press) and individual price tags (see the "ceiling price markers for grocery shelves" of Hopp Press and the "ceiling price tickets" qualified as "handy shelf moulding" of Charles George Co.). In other words, the price tag manufacturers sought to develop their business both through traditional hand- or typewritten boards for the more conservative retailers and through advanced price tickets for the more progressive users of shelf moldings. In so doing, they converted the citizenship logic of the GMPR into a business opportunity.

Indeed, price tag manufacturers seized the GMPR as an opportunity to (re) sell what they already sold, in the same way that present-day car manufacturers prompt car owners to switch to new models that comply with CO_2 requirements even if their current vehicle functions well. In Figure 4.5, Colonial's "ceiling price" plate on the right appears as a new item in a range of products including classic "wood mouldings" for which there are now "Ceiling Price tags" to complement signs like "¢", "doz", "for" or "↑" used for batch discounts and better display. The price tag manufacturers were thus assisting in the enforcement of the GMPR, sometimes even explicitly: "Comply with OPA regulations!" Hopp Press exhorted. More generally, they made the regulation visible and workable; they performed it, not only by showing the word (and numbers) of the law, but also by associating it with classic merchandizing and pricing strategies.

However, the price tag manufacturers did more. Not only did price ceiling tools supplement existing offers but they played a decisive role in the evolution of price tags towards the inclusion of more text and qualitative information. This is an ironic shift: while ceiling prices were squarely about prices, displaying them correctly required written text, at the very least the formulation "ceiling price" or "our ceiling". While this message was simple enough, it nonetheless required more than a purely numerical sign. As a consequence, price tags had to be redesigned from mere "calculative devices" (Callon and Muniesa, 2005) to "qualculative" ones, that is, signs combining qualitative and

Meet Requirements of
OPA CEILING PRICE REGULATIONS

HOPP PRESS BULLETIN DISPLAYS FOR MEAT DEPARTMENT

STURDY CONSTRUCTION FOR EXTRA LONG LIFE—Provision is made for additional items to be Ceiling-Priced later.

1 Bulletin Frame	With Wood Frame	$7.50
20 Celluloid Item Slides	With Metal Frame	$9.00
250 Celluloid Price Cards		

CEILING PRICE MARKERS FOR GROCERY SHELVES

ALL SIZES ... CELLULOID AND CARDBOARD
$3.50 per 1000 and up

Shew your SELLING PRICES as well as CEILING PRICES with HOPP PRESS Equipment

SAMPLES and FOLDER FC on Request

THE HOPP PRESS, Inc.
460 W. 34th St., New York, N.Y.

1400 CEILING PRICE
TICKETS $1.00 POSTPAID

Complete sets conforming to Gov't Regulations

Save time . . save money. Use these handy shelf moulding tickets to post Ceiling Prices. Printed in brilliant green on two sides of durable lite-weight cardboard. One side reads "Ceiling", other side "Price". Plenty of numerals, "2 for", "3 for", "Doz." etc.

● **HANDY INDEX BOX**
● **FULL INSTRUCTIONS INCLUDED**

ORDER NOW —from your jobber—or send $1.00, give name, address, town and state AND BE SURE TO IN-DICATE SIZE TICKET DESIRED: 1", 1¼" or 1½".

CHARLES GEORGE CO.
35 E. Wacker Drive   CHICAGO

Source: *Progressive Grocer* (left: 1942, 07, 101; right: 1942, 07, 129).

Figure 4.4   *Hopp Press and Charles George Co.'s ceiling price devices*

quantitative information. This change enabled consumers to make decisions based on both dimensions, that is, perform so-called qualculations (Cochoy, 2002, 207; Callon and Law, 2005; Cochoy, 2008a; Çalışkan and Callon, 2010, 29). Until then, there was a tacit and somewhat forced division of labor between manufacturers and retailers: the former controlled quality through information printed on packages, while the latter specialized in price display through numbers written on price tags. This division of labor was largely attributable to technical constraints: while printed labels could convey any type of message, from numbers to text and images, the small and equally sized

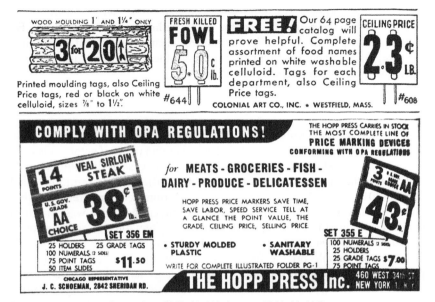

Source: *Progressive Grocer* (top: 1943, 01, 122; bottom: 1944, 04, 230).

Figure 4.5   Colonial and Hopp Press' ceiling price tags

price tickets and other simple signs available for shelf moldings effectively restricted retailers to price information.

At the introduction of ceiling prices, and partly as an outcome of Roosevelt's anti-Depression and wartime policies, other pieces of textual information had begun to spread, like the NRA Blue Eagle (1933, 11, 86), war stamps, rationing points, and quality grades (1941, 05, 52 et seq.; 1941, 07, 40–41). In parallel, new price display technologies appeared that offered greater possibilities to add qualitative information, like Colonial's plates (1937, 02, 192), copied first by Clamp-Swing (1938, 08, 59) and later by Hopp Press (1944, 04, 230). As shown in Figure 4.5, these were metal plates with preprinted messages equipped with stops for combining numerals for price display. While these devices clearly allowed the inclusion of more qualitative messages on price signs, they did so asymmetrically. The qualitative information was limited to preprinted words, whereas prices could be set through the combination of individual numerals. While these techniques were not created in response to the new price regulation, the latter clearly contributed to their spread. Besides ceiling prices, the regulation also introduced A, B, C grades and OPA rationing points, which added further display work for the retailers. Faced with such requirements, retailers could well see the appeal of "Hopp Press price markers" that would "save time, save labor, speed service", and moreover "tell at a glance the point of value, the grade, ceiling price, selling price". By making the display of "our ceiling" mandatory near any good that was subject to the regulation, the price tag regulation forced the adoption of "qualculative" price displays by all grocers.

From Freeze to Squeeze

Just as the price tags evolved, so did the economy and the related regulation. Markets are complex "agencements", that is, combinations of actors, rules and devices whose individual transformations lead to ceaseless reconfigurations of the web they form (Çalışkan and Callon, 2010). As Çalışkan (2009) and Callon (2013) have stressed, a price is always formulated in reference to other ones. In the particular case of ceiling prices, the current price was related to an older version of itself. The price of each given item must be equal or lower to that in March 1942, or, to put it in mathematical form: $P \leq P_{03/1942}$. This was an extremely simple pricing formula related only to the surface of market prices; in Çalışkan's and Callon's terms, it was a market-agencement based on a market interface approach. Contrary to the NRA regulation against price cutting, the GMPR paid no attention to costs, but relied on the outcome of previous market interactions, whatever their underlying structure. Even if truly market-based prices may never exist, the freeze assumed the existence of such a fiction thus "postforming" (rather than performing) the market. However, keeping prices calculated this way proved difficult: the freeze led to a squeeze.

The ceiling price regulation faced at least three problems. First, it did not account for the time lag between the announcement of new prices by the manufacturers and the display of prices in retail stores. Freezing all retail prices as of March 1942, so that the goods had to be sold at this level whatever the cost of restocking, could cause heavy losses for the retailers (1942, 09, 148). Second, manufacturers found it hard, if not impossible, to keep their prices at the 1942 level because their costs of labor and raw materials kept rising (1942, 09, 148). Third, large volume distributors were caught by their low margins; their business models made them more vulnerable to rising costs than other retailers. As a consequence, they refused to carry goods with low ceiling prices and instead offered other brands, which in turn affected the producers (1942, 09, 34). Of course, several goods and actors escaped the regulation, including products exempt by the GMPR (see below), as well as products and retailers that entered the market after March 1942 (1942, 10, 29; Letzler, 1954). But instead of mitigating the squeeze, this worsened inequalities. On the whole, the price ceiling regulation quickly proved unable to handle the situation, triggering calls for adjustments.

Amendments and New Trials

In fact, such adjustments were anticipated even before the squeeze. At face value, the prices regulated by the policy looked uniformly frozen, as if they escaped the fluctuation inherent to a market economy, at least in terms of upward movements. However, behind the scene, other price adjustments and fluctuations occurred. Instead of being negotiated at store level between grocers and their customers in the local market, prices were now negotiated at Federal level between trade associations and the government (1942, 07, 129). In fact, the OPA took a number of measures and issued innumerable exemptions to prevent a squeeze and handle concerns expressed by industry professionals. Providing the full list and the rationale behind these measures would be impossible, but a few examples can provide a sense of both their diversity and the intense discussions and lobbying that produced them: "Flour not subject to price ceilings includes wheat, rye, buckwheat, rice, corn, oats, barley, soy bean, and potato flour" (1942, 08, 114); "Cooked, frozen and smoked poultry and turkey are [...] exempt from the price ceiling. Canned and processed eggs and poultry are, however, subject to the price ceiling" (1942, 08, 116).

But preventive measures and multiplying ad hoc corrective adjustments proved unable to cure the squeezes that occurred as a result of the regulation. This prompted a general revision of the GMPR. In October 1942, the OPA adopted an amendment introducing a completely new approach to price control based on fixed markups rather than frozen prices. The new regulation was devised for 11 food categories for which current markups were considered abnormally low (1942, 11, 37). The amendment also categorized wholesalers and retailers into classes, based on their gross sales volumes and whether they were independent or belonged to a chain. A specific formula for calculating ceilings was then proposed for each type of product and class of distributor. This logic was completely at odds with the previous policy. Instead of starting with the retail "market price", at the risk of squeezing businesses if costs increased, the new formula started from production and wholesale prices. Indeed, the revised policy sought to put a completely new "market agencement" in place (Çalışkan and Callon, 2010; Callon, 2013), one that controlled prices by applying a maximum markup at each level in the distribution chain based on presumed cost differences. This agencement thus rested on a "planned economy" theory of the relation between the governing and the governed in which a calculating and governing center determined reasonable margins for different types of operations. For example:

> The formula by which canners will determine their ceiling prices for the 1942 pack is briefly as follows: 1. The canner calculates the weighted average price charged

per dozen for each kind, variety, style, and can size of fruits and berries during the first 60 days after he began to pack each fruit in 1941. 2. To this figure the canner adds 10% to cover all increased costs other than raw materials. 3 To this total the canner may add the average increase in his cost of the raw materials delivered to his factory by growers [...]. To his maximum price for the month of February 1942, instead of March 1942, the wholesaler adds the "permitted increase" as passed on to him by the canner. The sum of these two makes the wholesaler's maximum price [...]. The retailer uses as his base for the new price on canned fruits and berries his maximum price determined under the General Maximum Price Regulation and adds to that price for each can or container 1/12 of the "permitted increase" per dozen. (1942, 09, 154)

The accepted markups differed depending on which class a store belonged to. For instance, non-service stores were allowed a lower margin than service stores. In this way, the new regulation was expected to account for different cost structures and to preserve the business of small independent service stores. At the same time, it would also free mass distributors from the particularly fierce squeezes they suffered under the previous price ceiling (1942, 10, 29). However, the new approach also proved incapable of successfully framing market overflows. For instance, the largest service stores with sales of $250 000 or more soon suffered from a squeeze because their margins under the fixed markup formula were the same as the cash-and-carry supermarkets, despite their higher operating costs (1943, 03, 31). Fixing such problems led to several new ad hoc adjustments (1943, 06, 51), until inflation started to decrease, making further changes unnecessary. But as we saw in Figure 4.1, inflation resurfaced in full force a few years later, prompting a reactivation and renovation of previous arrangements.

The Next Floor's Ceiling and the Open Rooftop

Given our focus on price display, two subsequent developments are especially relevant. First, another inflation surge occurred in 1950–51 (Figure 4.1). Its causes were quite similar to those that provoked the inflation of the early 1940s: World War II caused the first episode and the Korean War triggered the second, with the same problems of privileged army supplies and related civilian shortages (Ohanian, 1997). These causes and effects were dealt with using the same methods as before: on 26 January 1951, the Office of Price Stabilization (OPS: the new name for the OPA) issued the General Ceiling Price Regulation (GCPR) that in many respects reactivated the tools, methods and provisions of the GMPR. Surprisingly, it was based on the frozen price logic of the early GMPR, without any consideration for the markup approach that was introduced to overcome its flaws (Letzler, 1954). Second, between the inflation flashes of 1941 and 1951, another inflation episode occurred in 1947.

This was by far the strongest of the three: food inflation reached as high as 35.1 percent in March 1947, that is, almost twice the level reached during the other episodes. Historian Evan Schnidman labels this episode "the 1947 wall" (Schnidman, 2013). Contrary to the other episodes, which were both connected to wartime conditions, the 1947 inflation peak occurred during peacetime, in a domestic and civilian context. It was a consequence of the highly accommo-dating monetary policy and the extremely low interest rates adopted to reduce the war-financing costs for the government. But despite its magnitude and contrary to the other two episodes, the wall did not lead the authorities to adopt price ceiling policies, due to strong disagreements between the Congress, which favored increased interest rates, and the Truman Administration and the Treasury, which supported the accommodating policy. As for the retail-ers, they did not express any particular concern about the situation, probably because rising prices meant higher profits for them, since their margins on existing stocks increased as time passed. If the GMPR set up the ceiling on the first floor and the GCPR the ceiling on the second floor of the regulation building, the response to the 1947 inflation was rather an open rooftop.

HOW CEILING PRICE TAGS DISCREETLY YET DECISIVELY CHANGED PRICE DISPLAY

Overall, the efforts to fight inflation in the US retail sector relied on a range of policies, devices and related market agencements. One approach was to work upstream on the financial costs by tuning interest rates as proposed by the Congress for the 1947 wall (even if this was never done). Another was to inter-vene downstream through ceiling price policies and price display techniques (like the regulations introduced in 1942 and 1951). The return of price ceilings in 1951 was indeed accompanied by a return of ceiling tags. Interestingly, just as the regulation was slightly adjusted (Letzler, 1954), the ceiling tags were subtly improved, along the pervasive logic that makes product innovation one of the key components of market competition (Callon, 2013). This evolution is clearly illustrated by a series of advertisements from the Shaw and Slavsky Co. (see Figure 4.6).

The system displayed in the upper left of Figure 4.6 uses the solution intro-duced by Colonial Art Co. in the late 1930s: a metallic plate which could hold embossed cards and tags. As already mentioned, this technology is asymmetric in that it offers a limited choice of preprinted qualitative messages and a set of simple numerals allowing innumerable price combinations. In this case, the technology was simply adapted to the new objective of price ceiling display. The large plate, with its preprinted "Ceiling price" and "Today's price", sug-gested a shift from the mandatory/regulatory display of ceiling prices ("to help you post ceiling prices under general ceiling price regulations issued January

Source: Progressive Grocer (upper left: 1951, 04, 13; upper right: 1951, 06, 16; lower left: 1951, 07, 6; lower right: 1951, 11, 7).

Figure 4.6   Shaw and Slavsky's ceiling price tags

26th, 1951") to a voluntary/managerial "dual pricing" strategy. According to this logic, the maximum price had to be cut, as with the "specials" of yester-year. Moreover, the old logic was not just reactivated, but improved: the price cut was emphasized by colored numerals and asymmetric sizes, in sharp contrast to the modest 1 cent (2.3 percent) rebate proposed. Finally, the company also offered a more flexible choice consisting of two smaller, independent plates (see below the large plate). These could be shown side by side to replay the "ceiling price cutting" game, or they could be used separately, allowing the retailer to display the regulated price only. By offering such a choice, the Shaw and Slavsky Co. was covering all bases/business opportunities. In the subsequent months, the company refined, improved and strengthened its offer further by devising the means to migrate the ceiling price onto classic price moldings and by emphasizing the merchandizing logic through an appropriately catchy name – "double duty ceiling price tags" (1951, 11, 6) – and an accompanying commercial rhetoric.

Shaw and Slavsky improved its equipment in the hope that grocers would adopt it, or upgrade and replace their current equipment, as the other ads show. The upper right ad in Figure 4.6 apparently displays the same system as the upper left. But a closer look shows that it introduces two innovations. First, it uses removable flags instead of simple tags to present qualitative dimensions. With these, the system turned "ceiling price" into just another quality dimension, comparable to "good grade". Second, the plate and its tags were inserted into metallic shelf-moldings. Such moldings had been introduced by Shaw and Slavsky a few years earlier (1947, 07, 28; 1949, 02, 0) as a sanitary and durable improvement over previous wooden devices (top of Figure 4.5). By migrating onto the shelves, the plates solved one of the main problems of price tags: their failure to ensure a clear correspondence between prices and goods. Indeed, until now, shelf moldings had been capable of displaying prices only through the combination of single numerals and simple signs. To be meaningful, these prices had to be put exactly under or above the product they referred to. This was challenging, since goods and price tags were often misplaced, leading to confusion over prices. By contrast, the new device from Shaw and Slavsky helped individualizing "qualculative" information by repeating the product's name on the price tag, thus attributing the price to the right product, whether properly located or not (see Figure 4.7).

These technical refinements could be presented as optional and incremental improvements over existing solutions: "The wise food merchant never loses a sale", the ad said. But once adapted to ceiling prices, the offer also benefited from the mandatory aspect of "price ceiling" display. Of course, retailers were free to use other means to meet the regulatory requirements, but Shaw and Slavsky worked hard to present their solution as an "obligatory passage point" (Callon, 1986). The company explored numerous means to extend its business: it devised "qualculative" plates and moldings, new "price ceiling" signs for retailers who had already adopted the company's metallic moldings, and so on.

This work was both technical and rhetorical, as illustrated by the caption that went with the lower right ad in Figure 4.6:

> Yes, you can eliminate price resistance ... ring up more sales — and comply 100% with O.P.S. regulations at the same time! Price your meats to show both the legal ceiling price plus your feature "Today's Price" as well. Alert, salesminded merchants can cash by providing customers with a frank, hard-hitting comparison of the ceiling price vs. *their actual selling price!* Everytime you sell at lower than ceiling, *pound the fact* home by using DOUBLE DUTY CEILING PRICE TAGS! Let customers see the plain, truthful price facts! Let them know what you are doing to help keep prices down — and mister — you've gained good will and repeat business you just couldn't buy at any price, or get in any other way. See the *customers'* side ... AND

Source: *Progressive Grocer* (1949, 02, 0).

Figure 4.7   Shaw and Slavsky's new price tag system

THEY'LL COME TO SEE YOU! Get extra business … extra profits — with Shaw & Slavsky DOUBLE DUTY CEILING PRICE TAGS! (1951, 11, 6)

The ad proposed a means to "comply 100% with O.P.S. regulation". But far from presenting this compliance at its main objective, this was a secondary effect ("at the same time") of another more important goal: eliminating "price resistance" and "ring[ing] up more sales". The method was carefully explained: the trick was "providing customers with a frank, hard-hitting comparison of the ceiling price vs. *[the] actual selling price*". The copywriter could have added that highlighting "today's price" without providing any clue about tomorrow's price called on customers to seize a guaranteed bargain rather than risk paying an inflated price later (reiterating the trick of "now", see above). The new price tag devices were presented as endowed with almost magical powers. Indeed, they supposedly turned the regulation upside down: ceiling prices, which previously were a cause of financial losses because of the squeeze they introduced between fixed prices and rising costs, were now presented as a means to "Get extra business ... extra profits". In other words, by combining the administered economy with free market competition, shifting the price ceiling obligation into a price cutting tool, the price tag manufacturer sought to turn a mandatory and costly constraint into a voluntary and profitable strategy and ... into an occasion to increase its own business.

ON THE "POLYSCOPIC" CHARACTER OF PRICES

The comparison between the offered price and the ceiling price reflects a "dual" or "stereoscopic" price strategy that is intimately connected to price display devices. With this strategy, prices always appear in pairs, with one being a bargain compared to the other. The reference price could be the "item" price for batch sales, the "regular" price for specials, or the "ceiling" price under price control. Each time, competition is framed differently. One competes primarily with oneself in the case of batch sales, with other grocery retailers in the case of specials, or with the government in the case of "our ceiling". The dual pricing strategy and its variants show that price competition, far from being a one-dimensional market force, is plural and enacted through managerial decisions and material means.

This observation can be used to complement Çalışkan's and Callon's previous contributions on the economic sociology of prices. Çalışkan (2007; 2009) shows how prices are made in different places and how they are connected: a price set at one point in the market is both an actual price (it leads to a real transaction) and a prosthetic price, serving as a reference for future transactions. "Stereoscopic prices" involve the use of such "prosthetic prices" in that one of the two prices (the ceiling price) is used to assess the other (the offered price). This said, our account differs from and complements Çalışkan's in two respects. First, whereas Çalışkan focuses on centralized price setting arrangements based on negotiations between professional buyers and sellers, we show that a similar price setting mechanism was enacted in a distributed fashion in innumerable retail market locations and directed at end consumers. Second, whereas Çalışkan's prosthetic prices are conceived as a conceptual equipment, our account demonstrates that the material shaping of price references plays a decisive role in the performativity of price proposals. More precisely, by materializing both the offered price and a prosthetic price, price tag technologies shift prices from negotiable values to relative offers. The mechanism of price formation via negotiation is replaced by a strategy of price display set up in a "take it or leave it" fashion. In other words, flexible prices shift into rigid ultimatums, to borrow a term from game theory (Güth et al., 1982; see Chapter 2). However, the simultaneous presence of the ceiling price entices the retailer to lower the offered price to "nudge" the consumer, thereby implicitly espousing the logic behind the nudge, whether this is the government's fight against inflation, the profit-through-volume logic of batch sales, or the instant bargain of today's special. Price tag devices thus promote not only prices but also underlying worldviews and even ideologies.

Our findings about price cutting strategies and price ceiling policies reported in the previous and the present chapters allow us to extend Çalışkan and Callon's (2010) argument that prices are less the result of a spontaneous adjustment mechanism than the expression of complex managerial formulas that relate any given price to other prices (see also Callon, 2013). Through price display, prices become connected not only to internal price structures, but also to external prices. In other words, price interrelations are both vertical and lateral. Vertically, as discussed by Çalışkan and Callon, prices are connected to other prices via underlying cost structures, profit rules, and business strategies. Laterally, prices are connected to other prices via various types of references. However, these references are not one-dimensional and inescapable "market prices", but managerially enacted references chosen depending on the circumstances. Such price references are repeatedly activated and renewed: the batches, specials and ceilings that we focus on here have since then been joined by others, such as special discounts for loyalty card holders, flash sales, and so on. In other words, price formulation refers to both the prices beneath (markups) and the prices beside (references). Our account shows that external price interrelations are largely attributable to the development of appropriate price display technologies and that these technologies are themselves largely indebted to the price ceiling regulation that encouraged their systematic use.

A last prominent, yet curiously overlooked, consequence of the price ceiling policy is that it not only acknowledged the practice of price display but also imposed it, at least partially and indirectly. Without saying so, the ceiling price regulation made price display mandatory for a large number of essential goods. During the Great Depression, the NRA had made a first, discreet, and maybe involuntary move in the same direction by banning price discrimination between consumers. Price ceiling regulations pushed this idea further, by performing it in technological terms. Indeed, the price ceiling policy was largely about "price seeing".

In addition to the study of price cutting strategies reported in the previous chapter, the analysis of price ceiling policies further contributes to our understanding of the interaction between economy and society by overcoming the opposition between the economists' view of price competition and Çalışkan's and Callon's view of "price formulation". For economists, a market price is the aggregate effect of the meeting of supply and demand. For Çalışkan and Callon, however, prices are "formulated": any price is always calculated with reference to other (previous) prices, as illustrated by the basic equation "price = cost + markup" (Chapter 2). The price ceiling case demonstrates that governing prices is a compromise between two logics: managerial and political efforts are aimed at controlling and calculating prices, but such calculations are always endangered by the emerging effects of price competition, thus leading to revised price formulations (and the other way round). We propose to handle this by viewing prices as dependent on other prices not only vertically but also laterally.

Then, related to the point above about lateral dependence, our study reveals the "polyscopic" character of prices in retail settings. Contrary to the common wisdom that a given good in a given market has a single price, as in the famous "law of one price" (Isard, 1977; Baffes, 1991), our study supports and complements Çalışkan's insistence on the multiplicity of prices. We saw that price display often combines two prices, such as the unit price and the package price for a given bundle, the special price and the regular price for a given promotion, or the ceiling price and the actual price in our particular case. Each of these prices works as a prosthetic price acting as a reference to appreciate the offered price. However, the fact that both prices are presented simultaneously using the same material device contributes both to spread the logic of the prosthesis and the acceptability of the offered price: the logic of price display overshadows that of price setting. Price display is thus stereoscopic at the shelf level – the price offered + a reference price to which the former can be compared – and polyscopic at the global level, given the multiplicity of references that can be selected to stage such price "duos". At first sight, this observation just accounts for the mundane details of price display. But on second thoughts, it has tremendous implications, by unveiling that prices are not one-dimensional. Until recently, the multidimensional nature of the economy was associated with the multiplicity of different "orders of worth" along which goods can be "valued", suggesting that the market and its price dimension was just one possible such order (Boltanski and Thévenot, 2006; Stark, 2009). Our study supports Çalışkan's intuition that the price itself is multidimensional. This means that different types of price competition and, indeed, different economies are enacted depending on which reference prices market actors use.

* * *

The history of ceiling prices discloses a kind of "bifurcated agency" of price display and its consequences. Of course, as a technology, price display seems to rely on one single agency: that of the actor who designs, controls and fixes the price. A price tag tells what one asks it to tell, and nothing else. However, we observed that in order to display a given price, for instance a "ceiling price", it was necessary to reshape the device. Notably, price tag manufacturers had to reconfigure their devices to afford written information, such as "ceiling", to complement the traditional price tickets. This introduced the "bifurcated agency": while faithfully conveying the inscribed messages, the price tags proved able to do other things as well, like introducing qualitative dimensions into price qualification, thus shifting price tags from mere calculative devices to more sophisticated qualculative tools. Similarly, by spreading the practice of pricing each item, ceiling price tags also paved the way for the subsequent practice of item pricing. The next two chapters precisely address the further extension and implications of these two developments.

5. Printing, sticking, and stamping prices: rebalancing power between manufacturers and retailers

The development of branded goods and the technical constraints concerning in-store printed communication in the first decades of the twentieth century had supported the development of a discreet yet decisive division of labor between manufacturers and retailers. Manufacturers gradually assumed control over the description of qualities by adding printed information to their packages, while grocers focused on managing the prices on their shelves. The latter task was in part cemented by authorities contesting the right of manufacturers to print fixed prices on their goods.[1] As we will see, this division of labor was first reinforced by the introduction of self-service devices and price tags inside the shop, but was later counteracted by the development of in-store pre-packaging and other novel techniques that began to give grocers more control over the overall labeling process. The development of price printing technologies further extended the "numberization" discussed in Chapters 1 and 2: price tags allowed prices to be displayed throughout the store; price printing disseminated them further and merged price and quality dimensions.

PRICE TAGS AS DIVIDERS BETWEEN PRODUCT QUALIFICATION AND PRODUCT VALUATION

The particular design of early price tags strengthened the quality–price, manufacturer–grocer division. Early price tag systems consisted of a set of cards that could be combined to display any given price and a device that could hold these cards appropriately, so that prices were firmly fixed yet easily removed (see Chapter 2). The system was astute, since it sped up but also standardized pricing operations, thus removing two of the main flaws of handwritten price cards. But the system also had obvious and important limitations. The combination of price cards of the same size on rails nailed onto wooden shelves could only display prices, since writing something else using the same logic, like the product's name and other qualities, would require too

---

[1]   We allude to the long-lasting battle for resale price maintenance (see Chapter 3).

many cards, too much effort of combination, and much more space than the rails could offer. As a consequence, the first generation of price tags deepened and locked-in – both in the material and figurative sense (David, 1985) – the division between quality-oriented packages and price-oriented shelves, and the underlying distribution of tasks and labeling power between manufacturers and retailers.

One could say that the development of price tags favored the view of prices in economics over that in economic sociology. While price is often seen as one quality among others in economic sociology, it has a particular status in economics. While other qualities are inseparable from a product conceived as a bundle of characteristics (Lancaster, 1966), prices remain detached from it and fully flexible. With price tags, the world dreamed by economists was made true, along a largely involuntary performation (Callon, 1998). Products became fully and exclusively qualitative, whereas prices were physically detached from the goods, and made public and largely flexible, thanks to a system easing quick and cheap price display and adjustment. However, even if prices were detached from the goods, they did not float around like abstract aggregate expressions produced by the price mechanism. In this sense, the performation of economics was partial and in appearance only. Prices worked as material labels and could not only be managed, but also multiplied, and enriched with quality information by virtue of new innovations in terms of item pricing and in-store pre-packaging. As we will see, these innovations helped grocers regain control over product qualification.

The grocers' loss of control over product qualification was largely due to the development of packaged goods and self-service devices. These features transferred most of the labeling power to manufacturers, leaving only price labeling to the retailers. In this respect, it is no wonder that it was through new developments in service operations and service technologies that grocers eventually managed to regain part of the lost territory.

PRE-PACKAGING AS COUNTER-LABELING

Pre-packaging is a practice that hybridizes self-service and service. On the one hand, pre-packaged goods are displayed according to the self-service logic; they are packaged and labeled so that consumers may help themselves. As such, the practice of pre-packaging was about serving self-service, so to speak. On the other hand, pre-packaging operations require the retailer's intervention and thus function as a new type of service. This intervention re-empowered the retailer; packaging products in-store offered the possibility to label them, not only in terms of price but also in terms of quality. However, the link between pre-packaging and product labeling developed gradually as a side effect of innovative technologies, rather than as the result of conscious efforts on behalf of retailers to regain lost ground. Indeed, the adoption of in-store pre-packaging acknowledged the retailers' surrender to self-service by extending this logic to the last products they still fully controlled: fresh meat and vegetables.

Before the advent of branded packaged goods, grocers had been used to wrapping goods as part of their service. But wrapped goods are not labeled goods. When wrapped, the products totally disappear under an opaque sheet of paper made hermetic with appropriate string, so that no label is visible anymore, be it the manufacturers' qualitative labels, or the grocer's price labels (most of the time abandoned on the shelves). However, the replacement of string by tape surreptitiously offered the possibility of a discreet, but important and innovative strategy.

Consider the devices advertised by the Nashua Package Sealing Co. on the left and in the middle of Figure 5.1. As its name suggests, the main purpose of the Nashua package sealer is to promote a new way of wrapping products, not of labeling them. However, this way is that of a continuous tape instead of a long string, and this changes everything. The tape, contrary to the string, is not a thin and round braid made of vegetal threads, but a wide and flat paper ribbon. It can be printed on and thus turned into a labeling device allowing the name of the grocer to be placed front-stage (the wrapped package), in front of the brand of the product being packaged: "Hammer home your Store personality", the ad says, "Advertised brands dominate in nearly every line. Don't let your store be dominated—impress your store name—everyday in every way".

Source: *Progressive Grocer* (left: 1927, 06, 104; middle: 1930, 07, 105; right: 1935, 05, 129).

Figure 5.1   Nashua package sealer and Scotch cellulose tape

Still, the Nashua package sealer was primarily a packaging tool rather than a labeling machine. Its poor labeling power was due to two limitations. First, the continuous paper strip could only repeat the same word, thus restricting its use to advertising the shop's name, and excluding a more varied and specific quality labeling. Second, the labeling strip was made of gummed paper that needed moistening to be glued. Even if the package sealer was made to ease such operations, it could not overcome all its flaws, like imperfect adherence, lack of convenience, and so on. These limitations had to be removed to fully link wrapping and labeling.

The required improvements came from two innovations developed outside the retail business, but soon applied in it. The first was Cellophane, a material developed by the Dupont Co. in 1924 based on an invention patented in 1912 by the Swiss chemist Jacques E. Brandenberger (Carlisle, 2004). From the point of view of our contemporary plastic culture (Hawkins, 2010), Cellophane looks like a mundane, old-fashioned, insignificant and imperfect innovation. We see it as a cracking, noisy and humidity sensitive ancestor to our modern soft, silent and hermetic plastics. But from the point of view of twentieth-century grocers and consumers, Cellophane was a dramatic, revolutionary, almost magical breakthrough: it succeeded in creating an equivalent to soft glass, a goal that twenty-first-century engineers are still pursuing when trying to invent flexible computer screens. As such, Cellophane joined and furthered the logic of open display and turned it towards self-service: instead of displaying goods behind fragile windowed showcases, one could now have the goods both glassed and manipulable. Thanks to this transparent skin of commerce (Hawkins, 2018), safe sanitation, open exposition and risk-free manipulation became for the first time compatible. The final obstacles on the road towards full consumer access to goods was overcome, their hands having previously been restricted to handling opaque and solid cans and packages.

The second innovation is Scotch tape, based on the combination of Cellophane and new pressure-sensitive adhesives. Initially, Scotch tape was not developed for retailing, but for car painting. In 1925 Richard Drew, a young lab assistant of the Minnesota Mining and Manufacturing Co. (3M), had noticed that auto painters struggled to cleanly paint cars in two colors as was the trend at that time (Saxon, 1980; Hanson, 2016). In order to help them overcome these difficulties, he had the idea of combining the new Cellophane material with new pressure-sensitive adhesives (see Drew's 1931 patent, USPTO, Patent no. 2,331,894). By doing so, Drew invented an adhesive yet removable tape that permitted painting zones to be temporarily delineated. But thanks to the marketing skills of his company, Drew's invention soon found other applications, particularly in the retailing business.

The advertisement to the right in Figure 5.1 shows the very first appearance of the Scotch tape in the grocery world, as staged by *Progressive Grocer*. In this ad, the Scotch tape appears exactly as we know it today, with its familiar tape roll, desktop dispenser and handy cutting device. But despite this modern appearance, the use of the tape is modestly presented as an improvement over its competitor, the Nashua package sealer. The staged purpose is just about closing a plain paper wrap ("[the tape] instantly becomes part of the package"). The claimed advantages systematically address and allude to Nashua's weaknesses: unlike Nashua, Scotch is fully transparent; unlike Nashua, Scotch needs no moistening and relative tedious operations ("slight pressure seals it"). But the ad evokes no other use than sealing packages. Scotch tape simply improves on Nashua's solution, but nothing else. Ironically, it actually does less, since its full transparency prevents advertising your brand name!

Three years later, however, 3M had transformed Scotch tape from a mere sealing tool to a new and powerful labeling device. The advertisement reproduced in Figure 5.2 articulates two uses of Cellophane: the Cellophane bag and Cellophane tape. 3M also created another device, the Scotch paper label, liable to multiply and redefine the usefulness of the first two. Instead of sealing an opaque paper package, Scotch tape could now seal a transparent one when combined with a transparent bag. And this changed everything. Previously, the Cellophane bag could show the goods in full transparency, but at the expense of removing the writing space of the package or the can that worked as a labeling surface. Moreover, the closing of the Cellophane bag remained uncertain. By combining Scotch tape and Cellophane bag with a paper label, one could easily seal the bag, but also freely adjust its transparency and writing space, either by inserting the label inside the bag and closing it with the tape ("Scotch Bag Label placed inside bag"), or by placing the label over the bag and sticking it with the tape ("Scotch Bag Label tucked under flap"). Just as Eastman Kodak invented photo albums to develop the use of its cameras (Jenkins, 1975), Scotch developed the paper label and enrolled the Cellophane bag to increase the market for its tape. As a result, the tape went from a product sold as a back-office tool for retailers into a good for everyone sold by the same retailers (1948, 04, 36–7; 1951, 05, 26–7; 1951, 09, 180–81; etc.).

But as we will see, the means gradually became a goal in itself. By putting product labeling into the grocers' hand, the 3M paper label challenged the previous division between quality-oriented manufacturers and price-oriented retailers and opened new opportunities for qualifying products from the grocer's perspective. However, these opportunities had still to be seized, and the Scotch device was just opening a road that others would have to travel to fulfill its promises. Like Nashua's device, the Scotch label and tape still had their limitations. If the Scotch system helped overcoming the impossible choice between Cellophane transparency and paper literacy, it did so by juxtaposing, rather than merging the two. Indeed, it is important to note that the Scotch label and the Scotch tape were two articulated, yet independent innovations. The

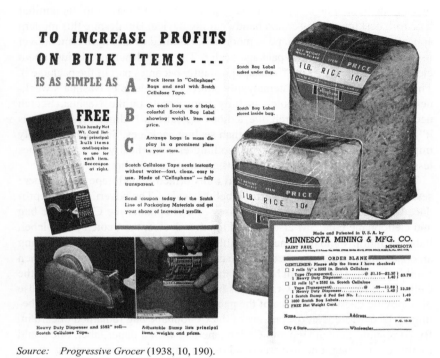

Source: Progressive Grocer (1938, 10, 190).

Figure 5.2   3M Scotch bag labels

paper-tape label was still to be invented. Moreover, a close look at the Scotch label shows that its promises were largely deceptive. Of course, the label helped the grocer to qualify the good. But this qualification was still mostly price- rather than quality-oriented, since it was really workable for the display of quantities and prices only. Indeed, and apart from the self-advertisement for Cellophane printed on the label, the only available quality liable to be labeled by the grocer was that of the generic product name. And even the availability of this name was open to question. The advertisement shows an adjustable rubber stamper (left) meant to allow the printing of product names along with prices and quantities. But a closer look at the adjustable stamper reveals that the available product names were probably about a dozen – a mere fraction of the items carried by even the smallest grocery store.

ITEM PRICING

Despite its limitations, the adjustable stamper offered a partial answer to other unexpected consequences of the new self-service arrangements. With self-service, more and more goods were sold, while customer choice and subsequent payment were physically separated. As a consequence, the clerks in charge of checking and charging for the chosen items at the checkout had more and more prices to memorize, as the posted prices of goods remained attached to the shelves. Several companies quickly recognized this new burden as a business opportunity. They devised special marking devices designed to support the new practice of item pricing and thus contributed to a better-functioning price competition: price pens, stamping pens, price stamps, and price label printers.

The first proposed technique was that of simple marking pens. The price pen, introduced by the Listo company in 1941, is the simplest device: it looks like an ordinary pen, but uses a special ink that works on any kind of surface ("Tin, glass, cellophane or waxpaper cartons", Figure 5.3). But, as previously with price cards, the tediousness and messiness of handwriting prices on innumerable products led to the development of more sophisticated devices.

The stamping pens appeared a decade later (1951, 08, 115). They looked like the price pen, but instead of writing the price on each item, they enabled stamping the price faster and more clearly, through the repetition of standardized rubber-inked characters rather than variable and often confusing handwritten signs. These stamping pens were sold in collections that consisted of a large number of pens covering a wide range of specific prices (see Figure 5.4).

A third technique, the price stamps, worked similarly to the stamping pens, that is, price marking by applying ink in a repetitive procedure (see the solutions proposed by the Kwikmark Co. and Stewart and Co., Inc and other similar tools subsequently proposed by other companies: Des Moines: 1952, 10, 351; Garvey: 1954, 01, 98; Jos. Freeman and Co., Inc.: 1954, 04, 80; etc.). However, compared to the stamping pens, the price stamps allowed greater flexibility, because the same device could be used to print different prices. This was made possible by the use of adjustable rubber wheels that allowed you to combine different digits into a specific price that could be duplicated on the products in much the same way as the 3M stamper shown in Figure 5.2 (see Figure 5.5 for two examples).

However, both stamping pens and price stampers restricted the types of surface that prices could be applied to as well as the legibility of those prices (stamped prices had a tendency to smear). More importantly, the resulting prices were too durable, since it was difficult to modify a price once it had been stamped on a product. Providers of other price marking devices were quick to

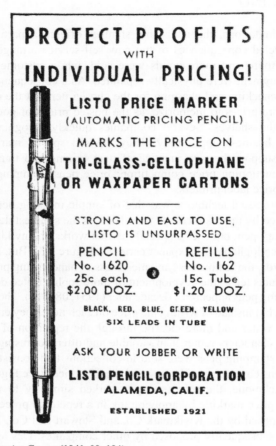

Source: *Progressive Grocer* (1941, 09, 194).

Figure 5.3   Listo price pen

point this out, stressing the ability to change prices as one central argument in favor of their devices. This issue was partly solved by the price label printer, a fourth type of device that enabled more flexibility in terms of the surfaces that prices could be attached to as well as increased opportunities to change prices. One example of such a device was Kimball's "Stamp-It", which combined "Zip-Strip" labels with a price stamp for applying the price on each label (Figure 5.6).

All of these devices were in a sense less ambitious but more realistic than the 3M ones. Indeed, they were limited to what was really workable with dialing

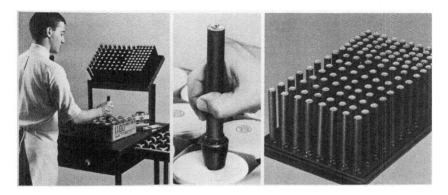

Source: *Progressive Grocer* (1968, 02, 99).

Figure 5.4   *Garvey Multimarx stamping pen*

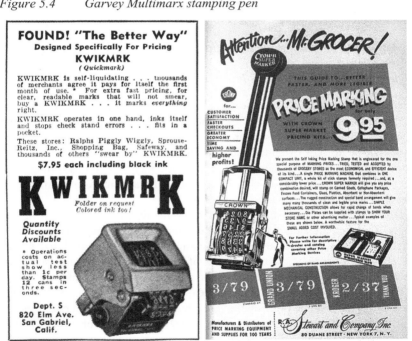

Source: *Progressive Grocer* (left: 1950, 07, 214; right: 1952, 06, 109).

Figure 5.5   *Price stampers*

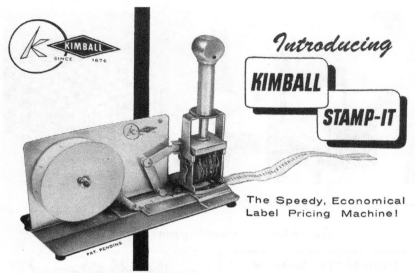

Source: *Progressive Grocer* (1958, 11, 203).

Figure 5.6   Kimball Stamp-It with Zip-Strip labels

wheels in the retail context: the wheels offered price dialing only and thus excluded the use of the letters of the alphabet, with exception of special signs like "/", "$" and "¢", that is, characters that were price related only. In other words, these devices extended and reinforced a logic introduced by the shelf price tags by transferring them on to the products themselves. In so doing, they strengthened the division of labor between quality labeling for manufacturers and price labeling for retailers.

However, the dramatic improvement of another feature introduced in the 3M paper labels soon changed the game. Remember: the 3M paper label offered fixed qualitative terms that could be complemented and singularized with the stamped ones. The main drawback of this solution was the dissociation between a label that was writable but not stickable on the one hand, and a tape that was stickable but not writable on the other. Stewart and Co., Inc., by contrast, proposed a single price marking machine that combined, in one compact unit, a whole kit of *stick stamps* (1952, 06, 109). Like 3M before with its paper label, the Stewart stamper relied on another innovation, that of adhesive labels. These labels merged the 3M paper label and the 3M sticking tape. In so doing, they considerably eased and generalized item pricing: sealing was no longer necessary and the price stickers could be attached to any surface. As a consequence, the retailer could now label every item in the store. Additionally, the adhesive stamps, like the paper labels, offered the possibility to display short qualitative messages: "Die plates can be supplied with stamps to SHOW YOUR STORE NAME or other advertising matter" (see the three samples at the bottom right of Figure 5.5). However and as before, progress came with flaws. The main flaw of the Stewart system was that … it was a system! Instead of being a single integrated device, it articulated adhesive stamps on the one side, the stamper on the other, and this new dissociation probably significantly slowed down the speed of labeling operations. A last and significant advantage of stickers over previous price pens and price stampers was their greater readability compared to the often smearing inked messages – a well-known problem addressed both in cartoons and in advertisements for competing price markers to stress the superiority of their solutions (see Figure 5.7).

A closer look at the innovations introduced by the Monarch Company reveals how quality labeling was gradually merged with price labeling. In 1958, Monarch (see Figure 5.8, left ad) launched a dispenser that could stamp individual adhesive labels. Once again, the genius of the innovation was to merge solutions that were present but separated. The Nashua tape discussed above was a continuous ribbon provided by a dispenser, but its gluing system was imperfect and the ribbon could display one message only. The Stewart adhesive stamps were discontinuous and could display different messages and prices, but being separated from the stamper, their use required time-consuming operations: sticking the stamps, stamping them, and so on. Kimball's Stamp-It made label stamping continuous, but then the labels needed to be separated before stamping them. In contrast, Monarch's machine could continuously stamp and deliver adhesive labels in one operation, thus considerably easing and speeding up price labeling and therefore encouraging the practice of item pricing further.

THE QUALITIZATION, DIGITALIZATION, AND PAPERIZATION OF GROCERY LABELS

However, the Monarch company did much more: it paved the way for rebalancing prices and qualities on item labels, reunifying the scattered languages of manufactured qualities (on product packaging) and retail prices (on store shelves), and thus re-agencing product labeling in favor of the grocers. This development took several decades and relied on a number of innovations to come fully into fruition, along a complex process of qualitization, digitalization, and paperization of shelf labels.

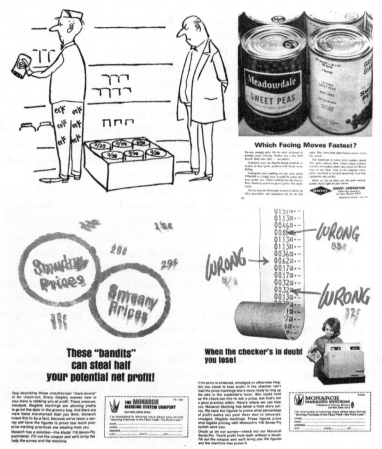

Source: Progressive Grocer (upper left: 1957, 01, 149; upper right: 1967, 05, 150; lower left: 1968, 10, 051; lower right: 1969, 05, 197).

Figure 5.7   Smearing ink problems and competing solutions

Qualitization

The first part of this development was linked to improvements in the devices pioneered by Monarch and their competitors. A first improvement was introduced in 1962, with the Monarch's shift from heavy desk dispensers used in back-office storage rooms to light portable price "guns" usable in the store aisles (see Figure 5.8, middle ad). Compared to its predecessors, the major advantage of the price gun was that it printed the price and applied the label

Source: *Progressive Grocer* (left: 1958, 05, 220; middle: 1962, 10, 209; right: 1972, 05,131).

Figure 5.8   Monarch labeling devices and red hot motivators

to the product in a single operation. Thus, price guns enabled price marking at a high speed ("at the speed of rubber stamping") but with the legibility and flexibility of the label printers ("prints a 6-character price line neatly, legibly") (1962, 10, 209). This innovation became to labeling machines what the Kodak pocket camera was to photography (Jenkins, 1975): it spread the use of the device to a scale previously unseen.

A second improvement was the continuous diversification of Monarch adhesive stamps, as illustrated in the advertisement for Monarch's "Red hot motivators" (Figure 5.8, right ad). This advertisement is amazingly paradoxical: it advertises price labels by showing ... no prices whatsoever! A closer look shows that the tactic is far from nonsensical. The idea is to sell a space where prices can be printed, but most importantly to show the distinctive features and advantages of this space. What matters is the information that may surround the prices and give them another dimension, another flavor, another *quality*. Take the label in the upper left corner: "OUR LOW PRICE", it says. At first sight, this means almost nothing; it seems fully indexical, connected to a given unknown encrypted context, as ethnomethodologists would say. But in fact it tells a lot to every grocer. This microscopic phrasing suggests that the price that will occupy the blank space, whatever its face value, will be different from "their" price. No matter to whom the pronouns refer, this opposition enacts an immemorial anthropological scheme whereby a social identity emerges from the opposition between itself and an external group (Mead, 1934).

Most of the other proposed labels added information that was either fully price-oriented ("WEEK END SPECIAL", "TODAY'S SPECIAL", "SPECIAL", "REDUCED" ...) or generic and somewhat superfluous ("PRODUCE", "BAKERY", "MEAT"). However, while the price-oriented formulations outlined the grocer's power in terms of price management, the quality-oriented messages extended this power to quality control. Indeed, "THICK SLICED", "BONELESS", "FRESH DAILY" or "AS ADVERTISED" clearly referred to the grocer's choice about what qualities to emphasize. They hinted at the grocer's distinctive contribution to the production (and not only distribution) of qualities, in terms of proper slicing, delivery or promotion. The available quality dimensions were not only numerous but indeed infinite, since the grocer could customize his price label: "Die cut in a variety of shapes, styles and sizes ... colorful fluorescent red or bright white ... pressure sensitive ... easy to use. Available with stock messages or *buy them blank and print your own with a low-cost Monarch imprinter*" (1972, 05, 131, emphasis added).

In other words, Monarch's Red hot motivators introduced a qualitization of price labels, allowing the grocer to recover some of the lost qualification power by complementing price labeling with quality labeling. The implications of this innovation were considerable. Until now, quality had been given, based on information made available on the packaging, while price was a purely quantitative valuation added to the periphery of the good, as a fully independent and adjustable dimension. Every good received a market price, just as in economic textbooks. With the new price stickers, prices could be accompanied by new qualitative dimensions. Quality was redefined at the same time as the good was priced. Price tags were not simply price tags anymore. First, the added information turned price tags into price-quality tags; the calculative device was converted into a qualculative one (Cochoy, 2002; 2008a). Second, the tags shifted from fixed cards on a shelf detached from the good to stickers firmly attached to the product packaging. The price-quality stickers thus became part of the product, complementing or potentially challenging the manufacturer's labels. Of course, Monarch's stickers were just a start on the road towards recovery of the grocers' qualification power.

Indeed, the Monarch system remained old-fashioned and asymmetrical: qualities were preprinted, and only prices could be easily adjusted. If we exclude the additional purchase of a Monarch Imprinter (a device whose working and performance was obscure), the list of available quality dimensions was rather limited, in sharp contrast to the fully adjustable prices. This said, whatever its limitation, Monarch devices created a market for quality-price labels. Although imperfectly, Monarch labelers complemented numerals with letters, and thus reopened a qualification war. Only the price was qualified ... but at least it was. Thanks to Monarch's adhesive labels, there was not just the price as with previous price tags, but also several diversely qualified prices for every item. In other words, the price label was labeled; prices received qualities. This opened the door for further labeling games, providing one could find the means to overcome the everlasting difficulty of combining or dialing a long range of letters rather than just a small set of numerals.

The solution to this came in the late 1970s, as a result of the growing sophistication of pre-packaging machines that progressively integrated scaling, calculating, wrapping and printing functions. These devices looked more and more like complex automated chains of production that made the grocery store look like a car factory (see the 1966 Toledo Valuematic II system to the left in Figure 5.9). Of course, with the new pre-packaging devices, labels still came as preprinted forms with colored predefined zones and messages, just like on the original Monarch ticket. As can be seen in the ad for the fifth generation of the Toledo Valuematic Scale launched in 1979 (Figure 5.9, right), every ticket had invariant preprinted parts: a yellow label with a white field in the lower right hand corner and text preprinted in red: "Thank you – Pre-packaged for your convenience", "net wt.", "price per lb.", "total value".

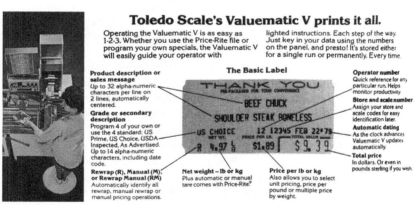

Source: *Progressive Grocer* (left: 1966, 10, 164; right: 1979, 08, 72).

Figure 5.9   *Toledo Valuematic V scale*

This preprinted framework deepened the shift from price to quality labeling. On the Valuematic V ticket, the price now came as the final piece of information provided when reading from top left to bottom right, following a long and varied list of other information. Furthermore, the price was now confined to a peripheral and tiny box, in sharp contrast with the big, central and single price that dominated the first price tag moldings. Obviously, quality information was gaining ground over mere price information, even if previous labels and former techniques, far from disappearing, often coexisted with the new ones.[2] But the biggest change introduced by the new machines lay elsewhere, beyond, or rather inside, the preprinted framework, with a shift from the stamping to the printing logic.

Contrary to the previous scheme, where letters had to be preprinted because of the dialing limitations of stamping systems, the inclusion of printing devices into the scale machines opened the possibility to write anything on pre-packaging labels, from the quantitative price information available before, to new fully qualitative, literary-like messages. Numerical information still mattered, and could even be enriched: thanks to the inclusion of an electronic calculator, the machine was now able to provide not only the item price but also the unit price. Yet several of these numerals, despite appearances, had a fully qualitative dimension. The date, for instance, functions as a sign of freshness and thus quality. It is also the case for other numbers whose role was surprisingly regressive. Indeed, many of these numbers were not consumer-oriented messages following the self-service logic but instead grocer-oriented information, following a back-office logic. What was being coded was different from before though: it was not the product's value, as when the full service grocers used cryptic systems to hide prices from customers, but the name of the operator and the identifier of the store and the scale used. Here again, a number worked as a tracer of identity and thus quality.

More specifically, the Valuematic V introduced a more dramatic shift on the side of alpha rather than numeric information: on the new label, the grocer could now print (rather than dial) any kind of messages. These could be rather generic, like the product's name ("beef chuck" "shoulder steak") but could also convey qualitative information about this product ("boneless"). Most importantly, for the first time, the grocer could decide to use the label (of paper) to circulate a label (of quality), like "US choice". The first category worked like a narrow version of contemporary tweets, with "up to 32 alpha-numeric characters per line on 2 lines"; the second offered the choice between a tailor-made secondary description of up to 14 characters, or four preset standards: "US Prime", "US Choice", "USDA Inspected", "As advertised". The consequences of this innovation were dramatic: for the first time, the grocer could produce labels with customized numbers and letters that looked like package infor-

---

[2]   For a striking illustration of the coexistence of novel and ancient techniques, and an analysis of the issues such coexistence may raise, see the recent case of Electronic Shelf Labels that have to compromise with paper signs in contemporary supermarkets (Soutjis et al., 2017).

mation, and thus compete with the manufacturers using the same approach to product description. They could complement the price-quality information either related to the grocery world (see "boneless") or to external third-party quality schemes (see "US choice"). Both implicitly underlined that producers were both judge and judged, that other perspectives could matter, that quality was a complex, political matter that could be handled differently by a multiplicity of market players, instead of being monopolized by the manufacturers.

Digitalization

The new alphanumerical tools were not enough to ensure a full recovery of the grocer's labeling and qualifying power. The next step was taken with the process of digitalization. To a certain extent, digital developments were already embedded in the previous Toledo machines (and others) with built-in calculators assisting weighing, computing and dialing operations. But these digital devices were hidden, internal, removed from the sight of consumers and professionals. Everything changed in the late 1970s with the spread of the Universal Product Code (UPC) in the retail business (an innovation we discuss in greater depth in the next chapter). This innovation amazingly radicalized archaism and modernity. It obviously strengthened modernity, by making public the new power of machines to read information, connecting it to large remote databases, guaranteeing correspondence between a given item and its price, keeping record of every transaction, and so on. It could also fight the high costs attached to paper item pricing,[3] both in terms of labor and potential frauds, for instance when consumers moved stickers with lower prices onto higher priced boxes – two problems that are (involuntarily?) addressed in the ad for the Bell Food Distribution digital system (Figure 5.10).

But as incredible as it may seem, the UPC also invigorated archaism. We saw above that some of the numbers printed on a label could have a meaning for grocers only. But since such numbers appeared as ordinary numerals, customers might not even notice them. The barcode, by contrast, used a hitherto unseen and spectacular graphic language that was more or less unintelligible. As such, it represented a comeback of the old practice of grocer-coded information (see Chapter 1). This ambivalent archaic-futurist barcode was first added to branded products but soon colonized pre-packaging labels, thus helping grocers stay in the qualification race by giving them the means to benefit from the same advantages as the manufacturers.

---

[3] Provided State laws accept the full replacement of paper item pricing by UPC codes, which proved not to be guaranteed; see Chapter 6.

What goes up should be profits.

A typical store with the normal grocery inventory makes 250 to 400 price changes every week. Any delay in the process can shrink profits, and may even result in selling some items at a loss.

Price change notification by mail or company truck, the usual method, is labor-intensive and time-consuming.

The problem is information management. The solution belongs to Bell.

Applying our knowledge of information management to the management of price changes, we can design, install and maintain a simple system to link your computer center and data bases to all your stores.

Our unique combination of Dataspeed terminals and COMM-STOR data communications storage units can speed price changes, improve the scheduling of labor, and expedite administrative messages dealing with promotions, product recalls, merchandising. You can use the same system to complement your direct store delivery information management system and keep personnel files current.

Your system is backed by Bell technology, and is designed to grow with your growing sales.

A call to your Bell Food Distribution Account Executive can put our knowledge of information management to work for you.

The knowledge business

Registered trademark of Sykes Datatronics, Inc.

Source: Progressive Grocer (1982, 09, 93).

Figure 5.10   Bell Food Corporation: what goes up should be profits

The effect of the introduction of barcodes on pre-package labels is as ambivalent as the codes themselves. On the one hand, the encrypted and largely meaningless code blatantly reactivated the impression of hidden back-stage control by occupying a large portion of the display surface. On the other hand, thanks to its digital compatibility, the same code worked as a key for accessing new product characteristics and thus further the transformation from calculative price labels to qualculative price-quality labels. Indeed, the barcode provided a means for connecting the good with remote databases. As such, it offered grocers a choice about what information to display from a long list

Source: *Progressive Grocer* (1986, 07, 201).

Figure 5.11   Barcode qualculative label

of product characteristics stored in the database. Once again, the effect is an ambivalent combination of opacity and transparency. The grocer decided what to show (or hide), but in so doing could provide access to qualities that had never been visible before: the label printed with the 960 UPC Pre-Pac Scale of the Franklin Electric Co. (see Figure 5.11) gives the means, thanks to its UPC feature, to print for the first time in pre-packaging settings, nutritional facts about calories, fat, cholesterol and other nutrients in the weighed product. It does so thanks to an "eight line, 432 character message printout [that] allows any store owner to expand his nutritional information program and segment his market with Nutri-Facts standard graphics such as 'Gourmet,' 'Barbecue,' or 'Cents-Off'" (1986, 07, 201). In other words, thanks to the UPC, the label was further qualified and, if the grocers wished, it could work as a true certificate of quality, as in the meaning of the French word *label*.

Thus, the new alphanumeric printable and UPC equipped labels gave quality management control back to retailers. But in so doing, did the labels help the retailers to really compete with their suppliers in terms of quality? Not really. We should not overlook the fact that the new labels were effectively applicable only to pre-packaged food products. As such, they compete against … nothing! They are equipped with all the proper weapons, but they don't target any adversary. The competition is misplaced: instead of juxtaposing packages and setting off a qualification war concerning how to label goods properly, they rather filled a void, along a complementary rather than competing logic. Pre-packaging labels did not challenge existing packaged products, but introduced a new package-logic for goods without a package, that is, all the generic products like meat and vegetables that grocers buy in bulk.

Paperization

Surprisingly, for more than 30 years, grocery-printed paper labels remained attached to pre-packaged goods; it is only in the early 1980s that they started to migrate to the shelves.

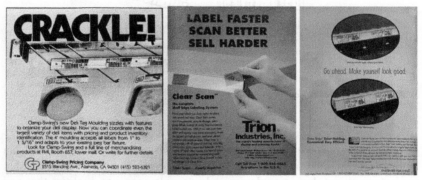

Source: *Progressive Grocer* (left: 1981, 05, 95; middle: 1998, 01, 89; right: 1998, 10, 56).

Figure 5.12   Paper price tags

Hence a puzzling question: why did it take so long for the grocers to extend the logic of grocery labeling to the other aisles and products packaged by the manufacturers? This lag is hard to understand from a contemporary point of view; the mundane adhesive paper labels appear simple enough to be easily transferable anywhere. But if we step back in time and try to assume the point of view of the involved actors in their historical settings, and pay close attention to the technologies they were using, two partial and complementary explanations come to the fore. The first is that of path dependency. Price tags were not just individual bits of information, but part of a complex and sophisticated infrastructure that came as the result of decades of effort and investment in store design and equipment (this infrastructure will be described in full detail in Chapter 6). In the very same way that train characteristics have always been dependent on rail gauge standards (Puffert, 2002), item labels were inseparable from shelf moldings, along the now classic framework of path dependency linking the successful technologies less to their inner merits than to the networks they are part of (David, 1985). The second explanation complements the first and is even more technical. Path dependency indeed could not explain everything. In fact nothing prevented price tag companies from proposing labels that could be simply stuck on existing moldings (see the left image in Figure 5.12). But what is simple is not necessarily workable. As the upper part of the image to the right in Figure 5.12 attempts to show, adhesive labels were easily damaged, difficult to remove and thus badly superimposed. And it took years to get appropriate plastics and, based on them, invent a flexible screen that could avoid the use of adhesive labels and facilitate both their proper protection and easy removal (see the middle and lower right images in Figure 5.12).[4] It is this innovation (invisible by design!) that helped realize the full paperization of store labeling and thus extend the retailers' qualculative power – that is, their ability to combine price and quality labeling (Cochoy, 2002; 2008a) – to any kind of product. From there, the renewal and improvement of shelf labels went on, with new changes based on multiplying paper labels, or shifting paperized labels into digitized ones.

* * *

If grocer-controlled labels were initially reduced to speak the language of price only, they gradually gained the ability to speak about quality, at the risk of introducing a language war between manufacturers and retailers. Such transformations were both the result of managerial efforts (getting control over market information) and contingent innovations like the invention of price tags and the subsequent introduction of new materials like Cellophane, and new devices like printing technologies and Scotch tape. Eventually, the unexpected articulation and agency of these solutions reshaped the power relationship in grocery settings. The lesson is clear: one should not restrict quality labels and price tags to abstract signs, irrespective of how powerful such signs may be. The material dimension of such devices matters as much, and maybe more: what is displayed depends to a high degree on the affordances of display technologies. Our story shows that gluing, sticking and displaying devices had the power to rebalance power relationships between manufacturers and retailers in terms of product qualification and valuation. Moreover, it suggests a way of accounting also for more recent developments in that abstract quality schemes (labels as certificates of quality) cannot be separated from the tools used to circulate them (labels as material devices). Our history of labeling, centered

---

[4]   Early attempts have been proposed, see the Patent no. 2,451,581 filed in June 1947 by the Shaw and Slavsky Co. about a "Price tag molding having a slide held tag and a transparent cover strip". But significantly and to our knowledge, the company has not advertised any product based on this patent, probably because the system was not workable.

on the technical modalities of labeling (an actor-network theory version of Howard Becker's labeling theory; see Becker, 1963), unveils interesting clues about the importance of the stickiness, in the material sense, of economic information, be it qualitative or quantitative. Product information sticks to shelves and boxes, to particular actors, and thus to the economy at large. These two scenes – the local, material and mundane settings of the grocery store, and the global, abstract and sophisticated realm of the economic system – are connected through hidden but essential infrastructures, as we will see in the next chapter.

6. Infrastructuring prices: from paper to digital price systems

As we have seen in previous chapters, the history of price tags is partly one of gradual accumulation of individual devices. Most of these devices were conceived separately by independent and even competing providers of store equipment. And if they ended up being articulated, it was the result of erratic and emergent adjustments rather than collective and coordinated efforts. Moreover, price tags are static and one-dimensional devices. They display the price of a good near them, but the connection between the one and the other is lost, or at least endangered, when the good leaves the shelf, joins a customer's basket, and moves towards the checkout. Prices are part of a wider, more dynamic environment, and the self-service arrangement can work only if prices circulate with the goods and customers, and do it correctly. Prices move with the goods, are summed up, and thus need to be displayed repeatedly and differently. In order to ensure such circulation and operations, new price devices were needed. Just as carrying one's voice from one phone to the other relies on the hidden work of "repeaters" all along the network (Latour, 1987), having prices correctly and efficiently handled in the store environment needs the mediation of an ad hoc infrastructure (Chakrabarti et al., 2016; Pflueger et al., 2019), and more precisely information infrastructures (e.g., Star and Ruhleder, 1996; Star, 1999; Bowker and Star, 1999; Bowker et al., 2010; Edwards et al., 2013; Larkin, 2013).[1]

Prices thus became part of a wider integrated technical system, at the crossroads of local initiatives focused on developing new devices and more general efforts aimed at selling infrastructural solutions as new products on the market for price display and price control. As we will show, the building of this price infrastructure went along a two-step, twofold development. In the early period, improvements in scales and cash registers worked discretely to connect price

---

[1]   We are thus concerned with the enactment of infrastructure *for* a market, in this case the grocery retail market, and with the markets related to this infrastructure. Such market infrastructures may well include elements that fit the classic understanding of infrastructure. For instance, Burr (2014) describes how the development of use-environments (roads, etc.) had a supportive influence on the early development of the market for bicycles.

tags to price tickets. Later, the pre-packaging and item pricing we met in Chapter 4 further bridged shelf and checkout price display, first with ink marks and printed tickets and later with the introduction of electronic devices. The Universal Product Code (UPC) started this movement in the 1970s and was followed by the subsequent spread of point-of-sale barcode scanning and the development of various digital solutions for grocery stores.

SCALES AND CASH REGISTERS: INTEGRATING PRICE DISPLAY INTO A PRICE INFRASTRUCTURE

Source: Progressive Grocer (1926, 10, 115).

Figure 6.1   A traditional-transitional service store interior

Up to this point, we have focused on price display on shelves and prices printed on goods. But from the very beginning, other devices played a discreet yet decisive role in spreading price display and articulating prices in the retail environment. Figure 6.1 shows a traditional store of the mid-1920s equipped with two scales and a magnificent cash register. By being aligned like picket fences on the counter, by working as service devices whose operation is the grocer's privilege, and by facing the grocer, with no information displayed to the customer, these devices largely locked-in the counter-service system and gave customers no other choice but to trust the retailer each time they wanted to complete a transaction. This said, at the time, the sparkling cash register was a new and costly device which was part of the movement from traditional to modern management (Spellman, 2009). The new desk scales with price per pound indexes, porcelain finish, electric lighting and other features (1925, 01, 91) were replacing the Roman scales of the past (1924, 07, 102). In fact, in the coming years, producers of scales and cash registers (sometimes the same: see the case of the Dayton Company) joined the endeavors of other equipment providers to reshape the trust relationships around price display in grocery stores in several ways.

Their first contribution was to improve calculation and measurement. Prices had to be correctly summed up; weights had to be accurately measured. Indeed, scales and cash registers are quantitative trust devices. They complement the qualitative evaluation of products obtained through sensorial experience, grocer's advice, and/or product information, with the corresponding weight evaluation and price assessment. This said, early cash registers were not oriented towards price display, but rather conceived as preventative tools aimed at fighting thefts by employees (they were designed as safes). In fact, cash registers and adding machines remained separate entities until the Sustrand Company proudly presented a novel device that merged the two (1923, 04, 77). From then on, these machines performed several tasks, such as avoiding the risks associated with mental and manual calculations (e.g., Burrough's Cash Machines, 1932, 08, 71) and providing sophisticated means to monitor the sales per clerk, department, and product category (e.g., National Cash Register (NCR), 1930, 02, 78–9). Burrough's also introduced price tickets listing all prices paid and the sum total, which gave customers a means to verify the accuracy of the sum charged (1932, 08, 71). Several years later, NCR provided new features like the possibility for grocers to dial the tare and automatically adjust price information accordingly (1955, 09, 2) as well as automatic display of both the total amount paid and how much change the customer should receive (1955, 06, 185). These innovations contributed to increase the actors' overall trust in the numbers manipulated inside the store (Porter, 1995). Possibly, it also led them to "decalculate", that is, relax their calculation efforts by delegating them to available devices and consequently comply with the price ultimatum regime enforced in and by the new retail environment.

In the very same way that cash registers had to calculate the correct sum, scales had to measure the correct weight and thus operate a delicate conversion of a unit price displayed on a price tag into the specific price that the consumer should pay. The issue was delicate, depending on who benefited from possible errors. Several advertisements for scales presented the issue in a deliberately *unbalanced* way, based on the implicit idea that the device would sell better if presented as a way to avoid losses for the grocer. The trick was to convince grocers that the new scales were better than existing devices. Toledo claimed that its scales were "saving time, preventing errors and stopping losses" (1926, 07, 120). Stimpson argued "It doesn't take long for half ounce errors to become tons of losses" (1928, 06, 88). However, scale manufacturers soon found ways to present the issue of fair and exact price as one of ensuring customer trust and thus grocers' profits.

It is no wonder that the balance is the symbol of justice. An advertisement from Toledo claimed that "the scale determines how much money the merchant gets for his goods" (1926, 07, 120) while another ad from the same company balanced this argument by asserting that "the scales determine how much the customers get for their money" (1925, 07, 103). Moreover, anticipating that the grocer could consider the two assertions to be dissimilar, Toledo re-equilibrated them by adding that scales "[could] do more than any other one thing in the store to make or break customer-confidence" (1925, 07, 103). Linking scales and customer trust was a very subtle rhetoric, aimed at showing that fair price – the "Honest Weight" as a "Protection for both sides of the counter" (1930, 04, 120) – was not about splitting the benefits equally between the grocer and the customer. Rather, it favored the grocer's interest more by fostering trust, goodwill and loyalty, and therefore increased sales. Thus, while the grocers were embracing the logic of profit through volume, magically allowing them to earn more by selling more cheaply (Tedlow, 1990), Toledo scales renewed the wonders of the old Smithian idea of profit through honest trade.

The second contribution of cash registers and scales was improved display. As early as 1929, Remington cash registers had proposed two ways of improving price information (1929, 04, 128). First, they suggested enhancing the homogeneity of price display throughout the store, by extending the graphic appearance of price tags to the cash register. Second, they proposed improving price handling by increasing the visibility of prices – "visible from all angles" (see Figure 6.2, left ad). Scale manufacturers took a similar path, introducing two features aimed at improving price visibility. First, scales were increasingly equipped with cylinder indexes easing the identification of the correct price per pound. For instance, the Dayton Company – the branch of IBM specialized in retail equipment – launched "Easyread": "a specially colored, fast-reading computing chart that has more prices per pound than any cylinder scale has ever had—46 in total—which means 38,976 individual price computations in this most efficient of all computing scales" (1927, 04, 62–3). Second, the Toledo Company improved this system further through the addition of a lens that magnified the price to "twice the usual size" (see Figure 6.2, right ad). Their "Safety Lens" would "protect profits when they *start*—and that is on your Computing Scale. If marks are small and dim, carelessness, rush or poor eyesight may lose for you, that few cents which are your profit" (1932, 06, 76). This said, Dayton's and Toledo's visual improvements were restricted to the perspective of the service professional just as the "all angles" view of the Remington cash register (above) was limited to the 180° facing the grocer. Thus, while the grocer saw prices better and from everywhere on his cash register or scale, the customer still saw nothing. If prices had begun to appear here and there on price cards in the window or price tags inside the shop, they had not spread to the counter yet. The advertisements were business-to-business oriented; they were about the grocer trusting the new devices; they presented arguments for replacing older models with more sophisticated ones, but largely overlooked the question of customer information.

Source: *Progressive Grocer* (left: 1929, 04, 128; right: 1932, 06, 76).

Figure 6.2   Remington giant indication and Toledo Safety Lens

However, other companies soon addressed this problem, leading to a third contribution in the form of two-sided price displays. For the first time, price display was extended to the cash register and scale. The NCR was the first manufacturer to display the price on both sides of the machine (Figure 6.3, left ad). While the advertisement still implicitly acknowledged counter service as an "obligatory passage point" (Callon, 1986) for grocery transactions, it extended the perspective from the grocer-oriented 180° angle to a more universal 360° angle that included, for the first time, the customer's view. Dayton adopted the same logic for its scales. In 1932, the company launched its "Customeread" model: "A scale with a computing chart on the customer's side!" This functionality was so new that it came with a sign inviting customers to pay attention: "Please read weight and money value of your purchase", it said. Even more interesting is the way customer interest was presented as coincidental to grocer interest:

> This scale makes a direct appeal to the customer. That is why it appeals to the merchant. Here is a scale that is positive evidence of a merchant's determination to give his customers a square deal. Every customer can read the exact money value of each purchase. There is no chance for error ... no possibilities for ill-will because of mistakes in reading computations. (1932, 09, 58–9)

The argument was an explicit enactment of the aforementioned B2B2C logic according to which what "makes a direct appeal to the customer ... appeals to the merchant". The new device implicitly presented transparency and double-checking as ways to prevent errors and thus foster customer trust, grocer reputation, and ultimately generate profits:

> This DAYTON CUSTOMEREAD builds good-will. It establishes customer confidence. It attracts and adds new customers ... and holds old ones. It becomes a business builder for every merchant using it. It permits customers to read their own computed values as well as the weight. It renders a protection that shoppers appreciate—and they respond with increased patronage. It will not only bring you new customers but will win you greater favor with your present trade. (1932, 09, 58–9)

Toledo scales elegantly solved Adam Smith's problem of (supposed) incompatibility between a subject's self-interest and ability to adopt the view of an impartial spectator and look at things from the perspective of the other (Hirschman, 2002). Indeed, Toledo devices promised grocers they would earn more by adopting their customers' point of view.

The last but most significant contribution of scales and cash registers was to ensure consistency in the prices displayed and circulated in the new self-service economy. On the one hand, both devices contributed to enhance grocers' confidence that it was in their best interest to adopt open prices and spread them in the store. On the other hand, the two devices did so in very different ways, to the point of pushing the development in opposite directions. Scales were immemorial devices closely associated with the traditional service scheme of selling bulk goods over the counter. The new scales were a means to modernize service rather than omit it. In contrast, while the cash register started as a service device, it also eased the transformation to cash-and-carry and self-service. Indeed, the cash register favored quick summing up rather than extended price negotiations and credit book entries. These opposite contributions led to a bifurcation. While originally sharing the same counter, scales moved to the back of the store, confined to specialized "service departments", while cash registers travelled to the front of the store to assist in completing the self-service transaction at the checkout. In the process, the old counter was

Source: *Progressive Grocer* (left: 1930, 08, 44–5; right: 1932, 11, 67).

Figure 6.3   Price display on both sides of an NCR cash register and a Dayton scale

removed, or rather reduced and split in two: in the service department scales topped smaller furniture; at the store exit, cash registers took center stage on brand new "check stands". And in between, self-service fixtures proliferated.

This spatial separation raised a major issue: that of the durability and robustness of the price chain. With prices scattered throughout the store, the correspondence between displayed price and charged price became uncertain. Cash register manufacturers soon realized that their fate was linked to the quality of the price chain since errors would be easier to spot during payment than anywhere else in the store. Chances were thus great that cash registers would be considered responsible. As a consequence, these companies made considerable efforts to promote clear price display and price accuracy not only through the design of the cash register itself, but also in the store at large. To ensure a robust price chain through the entire store, the NCR first introduced pen-like price stampers like the ones we met in Chapter 5 (1951, 08, 115). This innovation was not only about diversifying their product range but also evidenced the company's concern for price accuracy inside the store. It amounted to forging the missing link between shelf price and cash register or, in other words, building a first price infrastructure. Conversely, improvements in the reliability of cash registers allowed grocers to extend the distance between goods and payment, thus easing the spread of the price display economy.

The NCR system consisted in a spatial and temporal extension of the cash register inside the store. NCR not only advertised the clarity of its price display but enrolled the customer as part of its larger system, thanks to the two-sided scales and cash registers introduced a few years earlier. In the middle of the left ad in Figure 6.4, it is not a technical device but the consumer who constitutes the link that ensures price accuracy. Dujarier (2016) recently outlined to what extent self-service put the customer to work by making her accept that she had to perform tasks that were previously handled by grocery professionals. Here, we see that the delegation of work can be pushed further if we supplement physical work with cognitive work. Or rather, NCR invents a new kind of double-entry bookkeeping, where the cashier's price and the consumer's price are confronted to ensure they are one and the same. NCR explicitly presents its overall conception of an efficient price infrastructure: the company draws the arrow indicating a complete price chain, from the price printed on the box with an NCR pen-stamp, to the price displayed on the NCR cash register, to the price printed on the consumer's ticket, to the cash deposited in the drawer of the cash register. Just as in science, NCR constructs price display and price accounting as a chain of inscriptions in which price is an "immutable mobile" (Latour and Woolgar, 1979) that fosters customer trust and loyalty as well as grocer efficiency and profits.

Scale manufacturers also played a part in building the price infrastructure by contributing to the development of pre-packaged goods and product labeling (1955, 05, 213). We noted above that the scales migrated to the back of the store. In fact, they went even further, disappearing from the open store space into the back room. In the process, the scales changed. The small, elegant porcelain scales used on the counter were replaced by massive, floor mounted back-office units (see the Toledo Valueprint system in Figure 6.4, right ad). These scales were not used to calculate prices for individual customers but rather to prepare series of pre-packaged goods, thus allowing bulk commodities to enter the age of self-service. This required them to be more than just scales. We saw in Chapter 5 that three other features were added: the Cellophane film that extended the packaged logic to fresh products, the printer that gave grocers the means to price the product quickly, and the new glues and paper stickers that allowed price information to be attached to the goods. The price ticket stuck on the product complemented and improved the price infrastructure, by guaranteeing that shelf price and checkout price were one and the same.

Despite their benefits, the systems were far from perfect. NCR price stamps could be blurred; price stickers could be destroyed, removed or replaced. Trusting numbers in supermarkets remained a concern for customers just as trusting customers remained a concern for grocers. To handle these difficulties, new devices and strategies were devised in the subsequent years. Among these devices, the UPC certainly played the role of a disruptive innovation,

Source: *Progressive Grocer* (1951, 07, 128; 1955, 05, 213).

Figure 6.4   NCR pricing systems and Toledo Valueprint system

liable to bring into play an entirely new and powerful price infrastructure. More precisely, the formation of this infrastructure involved three phases. The first phase revolved around the development of the UPC barcode and scanners. The second phase revolved around the implementation of checkout scanning and its integration into in-store information systems. The third and final phase revolved around the transformation of these systems into a global retail market infrastructure.

DEVELOPING THE UPC, BARCODES, AND SCANNERS (1967–78)

The UPC barcode was originally intended to provide a unique identifier for individual goods and, as such, its spread had a structuring influence on the upstream grocery markets. Barcode scanning, on the other hand, purported to improve the efficiency of retail operations, primarily by improving the precision and speed of checkouts. But the success and continued spread of barcodes to virtually every product sold in grocery stores meant that they could be appropriated for other uses, such as loyalty programs, tracking of purchasing behavior, consumer analytics, and targeted marketing. More recently, third parties have also enacted product barcodes as a market infra-structure for the digitalization of retailing. One example of this is the use of the UPC (or its European counterpart, the European Article Number code) for consumer-oriented product information apps and purchasing guides, such as GoodGuide or Yuka (Soutjis, 2020). Thus, through expanded intercon-nections, the altered market infrastructure increasingly served to equip and stipulate managerial as well as consumer abilities in the market.

The creation of the UPC code, the barcode symbol, and electronic scanners capable of reading the barcodes actually started with the scanners. In the late 1960s two suppliers of retail equipment – Monarch Marking Systems (owned by Pitney Bowes) and IBM – engaged in a joint project with the Minneapolis-based wholesaler and voluntary retail chain Super Valu (1968, 12, S33–S40). The aim was to develop a program for "Customized Profit Improvement" relying on optical scanning and computerization to simplify retail operations. This is the first account in *Progressive Grocer* of an effort to make goods and prices legible not only by humans but also by computers (see Figure 6.5). While there were several alternative technologies for achieving this, like magnetic ink (1961, 02, 204) and mechanical and audio recognition (1972, 01, 94), optical scanning seems to have been the primary solution pursued.

This program primarily focused on back-stage operations – aiming to make reordering and restocking more effective. In short, it sought to improve the retailers' capacity to link production and consumption by rendering their business-to-business relations more efficient. A similar project called COSMOS focused on computer usage as part of retail operations and involved manufacturers, distributors as well as several retailers, for example, Jewel, Marsh Foods, Winn-Dixie and Ralphs (1969, 12, 48–50). In both cases, focus was on internal operations and supplier relations rather than consumer relations.

But there were also ideas on how electronic scanning could possibly improve front end operations already in the late 1960s. As noted in the pre-vious section, a long-standing and growing challenge for retailers was how to ensure correct ring-ups at the checkout. As supermarkets grew, it became increasingly difficult to maintain a strong link between the prices displayed at the shelves and the prices charged at the checkout (e.g., 1966, 07, 24). Hence, the grocer's ability to charge the correct prices was reduced. In a futuristic vision of how grocery retailing would work in 1975, published by *Progressive Grocer* in 1969, electronic scanning had solved this problem (1969, 12, 42–4; Figure 6.6). A key challenge was the code itself – to really make scanning feasible, a uniform code would be needed, the innovators said, and in the envis-aged scenario this was still not in place. However, prompted by the possibilities

Computer also prints shelf labels which, with individually printed dials for optical-scanner ordering, are placed on shelf holders below each item. Indications for facings and depth of rows are penciled in by hand during reset. Colored "dots" indicate backroom stock.

Source: *Progressive Grocer* (1968, 12, S33–S40).

Figure 6.5   *The scanner (top) and scanner symbol (bottom) developed as part of Super Valu's "Customized Profit Improvement" program*

linked to front end automation, manufacturers, retailers, and grocery trade and industry organizations had started to discuss a joint code and symbol.

Work on a uniform code picked up speed in late 1970 after major grocery producers, wholesalers, retailers and trade organizations joined together to form the Ad Hoc (UPC) committee to develop a common code. Half of the 16 members of this committee represented retailers and distributors and half represented manufacturers (1973, 02, 68). A first report commissioned by

Source: *Progressive Grocer* (1969, 12, 43).

Figure 6.6   *"Computers will become an integral part of food store*
                     operations in the 1970s. As this three-part illustration
                     shows, an optical scanning check-stand (this model at far left
                     features a tunnel; others may simply have slots) is connected
                     to an in-store computer (center) which immediately looks
                     up price, records the sale and prepares the reorder for
                     automatic transmission later to the central computer (right)."

the committee from McKinsey & Co. in 1971 saw considerable potential in
a universal code:

> The food industry is moving slowly but surely toward realisation of the long-time
> dream of fully automated front end operations. […] the study finds that the problem
> of universal price coding, the key to electronic checkouts, is feasible and practical
> and that the combination of electronic scanning and price-coded merchandise can
> bring benefits to the industry. (1971, 08, 6)

Things then progressed quickly: by early 1972 the UPC committee had secured
the support of all major US retail trade associations (Grocery Manufacturers
of America, Super Market Institute; Cooperative Food Dealers of America;
National-American Wholesale Grocers Association; National Association of
Food Chains; National Association of Retail Grocers; and National Association
of Convenience Stores). Moreover, the committee had successfully negotiated
a ten-digit numeric code system as a compromise that both manufacturers and
retailers could agree on. Based on this, the committee established a timeline for
the work ahead, which suggested that a final decision on a machine-readable
symbol would be taken by April 1973 (1972, 01, 90–94).

Some equipment manufacturers, such as RCA and Zellweger, had already
initiated tests of automated checkouts with retailers (1970, 06, 160; 1972, 01,
94). By 1972, McKinsey & Co. reported that at least 24 potential equipment
suppliers were developing and/or evaluating hardware for automatic checkouts
(1972, 01, 92), including IBM, Pitney Bowes, and RCA. Towards the end
of 1972, initial results from in-store tests were showing that the technology
worked in terms of being able to scan product codes and link those to a product

and price database (1972, 12, 36). In terms of the potential for rationalization, the results were less impressive, although some timesaving was noted (Figure 6.7).

Throughout this process, the recognized benefits of scanning primarily concerned the retailer, for example, "eliminate ring-up errors", "provide instant sales audits by item", and provide "a monumental new resource in marketing intelligence" (1972, 06, 36). On the customer side, the primary benefit was said to be to "provide the shopper with the first tell-all register tape" (1972, 06, 36). In effect then, scanning would move the retail sector away from decades of price-only information on receipts towards combined qualitative and quantitative information, allowing customers to link their shopping lists to prices paid. Potentially then, the new barcode-based infrastructure could have a significant cognitive effect.

While the UPC committee invited any firm to submit a symbol proposal for evaluation, some firms, such as Norand, did not wait for the decision on a standard symbol, but developed their own solutions (1972, 12, 59). During spring of 1973 the committee evaluated seven proposed optical symbols (Figure 6.8, right). Six of these were part of complete scanner systems and were being tested in stores at the time, while IBM submitted a simulation-based proposal. Three months later the UPC committee announced the winning code as an improved version of IBM's proposal (1973, 06, 13). In the year following this decision, several manufacturers presented cash registers with an optical scanning capacity. Pitney Bowes had been one of the scanning pioneers and had proposed a scanner symbol similar to IBM's to the UPC committee (see Figure 6.8, left). It was thus not surprising that the company was very quick in launching a complete scanning system (1973, 05, 7). Other firms, such as MSI and Bunker Ramo, advertised systems offering the possibility to upgrade to scanning "when it gets here" (1974, 01, 13; 1974, 04, 228).

In order for scanning to "get here", source marking was considered a critical issue that *Progressive Grocer* gave a lot of attention in the years directly following the decision on the barcode symbol. Once again this brought the back-stage vs front-stage of retail operations to the fore. Obviously, the benefit of checkout scanning would increase for customers, clerks, and retailers if more items had barcodes. The question was, who should put them there? A large number of manufacturers quickly joined the new UPC council (1973, 12, 56). Some were also quick to print the symbol on their product packages and tell the retailers about it, including manufacturers as diverse as Miller beer (1974, 05, 100), InterHarvest (1975, 03, 58), and the Sioux Honey Association (1975, 09, 113). But retailers also had to apply codes to a lot of goods themselves. Various devices were introduced to help them do so, including special barcode printers (1974, 12, 98) as well as both stationary and hand-held labelers capable of printing UPC code (1974, 02, 33; 1974, 11,

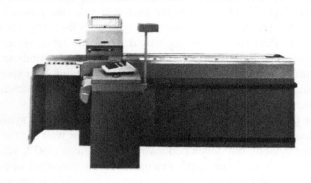

APOSS
Technical Triumph,
Economic Question Mark

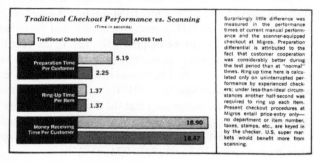

Traditional Checkout Performance vs. Scanning
(Time in seconds)

| | Traditional Checkstand | | APOSS Test | |

Preparation Time Per Customer	5.19
	2.25
Ring-Up Time Per Item	1.37
	1.37
Money Receiving Time Per Customer	18.90
	18.47

Surprisingly little difference was measured in the performance times of current manual performance and the scanner-equipped checkout at Migros. Preparation differential is attributed to the fact that customer cooperation was considerably better during the test period than at "normal" times. Ring-up time here is calculated only on uninterrupted performance by experienced checkers; under less-than-ideal circumstances another half-second was required to ring up each item. Present checkout procedures at Migros entail price-entry only—no department or item number, taxes, stamps, etc., are keyed in by the checker. U.S. super markets would benefit more from scanning.

Source: *Progressive Grocer* (1972, 12, 36–8).

Figure 6.7   Excerpt from a report on one of the early scanner tests

117). Despite the considerable work that would be required to put barcodes on all items, projections at the end of 1974 suggested that 75 percent of packaged goods might be source marked with barcodes by 1975 (1974, 12, 66). For this to become reality, however, a lot of technical details had to be worked out, as indicated in the following quote: "The Symbol Technical Advisory Committee [...] established improved guidelines for location of the UPC symbol on cans, glass, plastic, and other cylindrical containers; issued guidelines in relation to highly reflective package surfaces and developed print specifications for in-store symbol printers" (1974, 12, 67).

Note: To the left, Pitney Bowes advertisement for their CODABAR system. To the right, the seven symbols tested by the UPC committee.
Source: Progressive Grocer (left: 1973, 02, 53; right: 1973, 02, 69).

Figure 6.8   UPC scanner symbols and evaluations in 1973

In the meantime, store tests showed less impressive results regarding source marking. At Marsh's – one of the scanning pioneers – only 27 percent of the goods were found to be source marked (1975, 03, 61). Still, the views were generally positive about the prospects: "UPC, soon on a product near you!" However, despite technically working, despite a few pioneering installations of automated checkouts, despite increased source marking, and despite optimistic views about growth, scanning did not take off. Why?

It seems the entire US grocery industry was caught off guard by a massive resistance from consumerist organizations, labor unions, and politicians. Indeed, there was actual picketing outside stores converting to scanning in the mid-1970s (1975, 05, 39). Essentially the controversy was about the non transparency of barcode scanning. A key advantage of the barcode was that prices could be updated without having to engage in costly remarking of all individual items. The critics, however, demanded item pricing, that is, prices printed on each good rather than only on the shelves, to prevent retailers from misleading their customers (1974, 10, 12). In a senate hearing on the matter, one retailer was quoted saying: "If the price is left off the merchandise, the opportunity to rip off the American public will be the greatest in history" (1976, 01, 25).

Initially, both the UPC council and the grocery industry disqualified these demands and mobilized to counteract the development, for example the grocer's association in California was able to get a 2 year moratorium to prove that scanning did not reduce consumers' price-awareness (1975, 09, 30). But the problem did not go away and some individual states actually legislated to make item prices mandatory, including Connecticut, Rhode Island and California (1975, 12, 47). In reaction to this, the grocery industry sponsored studies to show they were right (1975, 11, 52; 1975, 12, 58; 1976, 12, 33). The result of a study performed by researchers at the University of Michigan, however, showed that they weren't: consumers proved much less knowledgeable about prices without item prices (1976, 05, 40). In response to this, retailer and scanning pioneer Robert Wegman, the chairman of the UPC subcommittee admitted, "some consumers today apparently have problems shopping in a 'prices off' environment" (1976, 05, 40). This led the grocery industry to back down from its staunch line and, by doing so, remove a central reason for introducing scanning: the avoidance of costly price marking (1976, 05, 95–6). By this time, some retailers like Ralphs had already started to use price labelers modified to print both barcodes and prices (1975, 09, 30).

Producers and retailers now refocused their efforts on informing the public about the benefits of scanning (1976, 12, 27). The results of these efforts were mixed, but awareness did seem to increase (1977, 10, 16; 1977, 12, 58). Besides making various suggestions on how to sway customers towards scanning, the *Progressive Grocer* also sought to explain why consumers were so critical. Among the main reasons, the magazine argued that the high inflation was making people price sensitive and that various current developments involving the United States, such as Watergate and the Vietnam War, had made Americans cynical (1978, 03, 58). As a result of this, US customers had to be convinced that the barcodes were not there to confuse them and/or disguise prices.

This takes us to the end of the first phase in the development of barcode scanning, which could be summarized as the creation of a technology struggling for acceptance. By 1977–78, there were working scanner systems and an established optical symbol, but few working applications of this technology. The UPC, barcodes and scanning had yet to become part of the US retail infrastructure; they were still very much a topic for stores and customers alike in the sense that they were noted, discussed, and actively worked on (Star, 1999).

During this first phase, the primary focus was on store operations – making scanning work for the retailers and the clerks – which may have led to overly optimistic views about the ease of introduction. During the introduction of scanning, poor timing and lack of trust appear to have been two key issues slowing down the process. As a result, consumer and labor organizations questioned the grocery industry's motives for introducing scanning.

TOWARDS CHECKOUT SCANNING AND STOREWIDE INFORMATION SYSTEMS (1975–90)

The second phase in creating a digital market infrastructure in grocery retailing concerns the continued efforts to implement scanning by the grocery industry, including equipment manufacturers, producers and retailers. The controversy over item prices and the resulting slow growth of scanning caused several pioneering scanner producers to drop out. The ones that remained focused on improving the technology and making it work internally for the retailer during the late 1970s and early 1980s (e.g., 1976, 09, 105; 1978, 04, 2; 1978, 04, 163; 1981, 04, 45). In particular, efforts were made to reduce scanner costs, make the technology and hence the investments modular, and improve scanner performance. Related to the latter issue, the *Progressive Grocer* noted, "each time a UPC code can't be read, and must be rescanned or manually keyed into the register, it creates a barrier to scanning productivity" (1985, 03, 93). This prompted some major grocery producers like Procter & Gamble and Kraft to try to improve the readability of their preprinted barcodes (1985, 05, 7; 1986, 11B, 35).

In parallel, a number of complementary products were developed to fit into a scanning environment (Figure 6.9). This included store equipment, such as checkout counters (1975, 05, 159) and shopping carts (1975, 05, 171). According to the Folding Carrier corporation, carts had to become bigger and higher to fit a scanning environment. Specifically, their new "U Com-70 Model 109" cart had "the capacity and maneuverability to stimulate superstore volume/profit essential for full benefits of electronic POS [Point Of Sale] front end equipment" and fit "the trend to high checkout counters for scanning where shopper unloads and checker scans" (1975, 05, 171). Other in-store adjustments required more work, like agreeing on a scanner code for products sold by weight in the store, for example fresh meat (1979, 02, 39). This led to the development of UPC-compatible scales and connected label printers (1980, 02, 36; Figure 6.9, right). These and other developments of add-ons illustrate the gradual adjustment/formation of a more comprehensive in-store infrastructure around the barcodes and scanners.

There were also efforts more directly aimed at easing the transition to front end scanning. These included specialized staff education (1979, 04, 31), offers

Note: Left: scanner-compatible checkouts; center: UPC/scanning-compatible shopping carts; right: UPC-compatible scales.
Source: *Progressive Grocer* (left: 1975, 05, 159; center: 1975, 05, 171; right: 1980, 02, 36).

Figure 6.9   *Development of scanner-compatible auxiliary equipment in the mid to late 1970s*

of complementary equipment needed to manage in-store barcoding (1980, 05A, 72; 1980, 12, 36), and ways to build customer credibility and confidence (1979, 09, 29; 1981, 12, 38). Given the controversy around price marking, it is not surprising that retailers focused on the latter issue. The *Progressive Grocer* reported on and discussed various solutions to this, including advertising campaigns prior to introducing scanning (1979, 09, 29), using technical devices to inform about prices at the checkout (1981, 12, 38), and improving routines to ensure price correspondence between shelf and checkout (1980, 02, 96–8; 1983, 11, 95). Several equipment suppliers promoted the latter type of solution offering hand-held scanners for checking correspondence between shelf price and scanner-generated price (1981, 12, 67; 1983, 11, 95–100; 1982, 12, 106).

In parallel to seeking external acceptance for scanning, there were also efforts to improve the performance and accounting of back-stage operations using the barcode standard for ordering and delivering goods. Indeed, some commentators in the magazine argued that this was the central issue. "It's ridiculous to put scanning in unless our systems are in place first. It really has to be put into a company that already is systems-oriented, that has people who know how to analyse systems and use information" (1979, 04, 192). This suggests that what was considered proper use of scanning was still under development. But in order for retailers to make better use of its potential, more standardization was required, this time of communications. So, in the late 1970s six trade associations jointly engaged to develop a Uniform Communication System adopting a similar approach to that which so successfully had generated the

UPC (1980, 12, 12). The envisaged digital information systems would connect several in-store systems as well as link the store to headquarters and suppliers in what was known as Direct Store Delivery or DSD systems. This, in turn, would allow stores to realize major savings in terms of reduced inventories due to reduced order processing and execution time (1980, 12, 12). As a result of the increased communication needs, telephone operators such as AT&T started to develop offers tailored to grocery retailers (1986, 10, 43). Through the increased integration of various market devices, then, new (types of) actors were able to tap into the market and further refine the workings of the barcode system and develop the market for the new market infrastructure.

During the 1980s the *Progressive Grocer* also initiated discussions about what to do with the data generated by the new scanner systems. Generally, commentators considered the potential to be huge: "[electronic checkouts] is the most important tool *ever* developed in marketing research" (1983, 02, 63). Initially, the focus was on internal uses, such as managing the assortment and making in-store merchandizing decisions (1982, 05, 173; 1983, 05, 187). With this use came the argument that in-store scanner data could give the retailer a much more accurate image of their particular market situation than data available to producers and market analysts. As a result, the power balance started to shift not only between producers and retailers but also between marketing research firms and retailers (1987, 05, 11–12). At the same time, the prospect of selling the data was also raised and several market research firms initiated scanner data projects (1983, 02, 64). The relatively modest share of scanner sales at the time made it difficult to generate representative market figures directly from in-store scanner data. This led some marketing research firms to initiate projects in which participating individuals were equipped with their own scanners so that they could scan their purchased products at home. This setup would also allow the linking of scanner data to individual and social variables. Besides triggering new forms of market research, the barcodes also allowed for new retail marketing aids such as barcoded and hence scannable manufacturer coupons (1985, 07, 68–9; 1987, 05, 14–15). These developments represent the first examples of barcodes being used for other purposes and by other actors than those who originally put them in place. As we will see below, this trend would be further emphasized in the years to come, notably through the introduction of various types of retailer loyalty schemes.

In terms of uptake there had been some signs of scanning taking off already at the end of the 1970s (1979, 12, 49). And indeed, the number of stores using scanning grew each year throughout the 1980s, as did the number of items that were being scanned. By the end of the 1980s it was estimated that 62 percent of US grocery sales were made via scanners (1989, 10, 55).

To summarize: by the late 1980s the UPC, the barcode symbol, and optical scanning were increasingly becoming parts of storewide information systems covering both back-stage and front end operations, some even extending beyond the stores. From the late 1970s, the number of stores using scanners grew steadily and quite rapidly, although the degree of system integration varied. For newcomers (retailers, clerks and customers), scanning and barcodes were still topical, presenting them with new issues to handle, but for a growing number of clerks and customers who relied on them daily in scanner-equipped stores, barcode scanning was starting to fade into the background. In parallel, various third parties were exploiting opportunities and developing novel uses of the barcode and scanning data.

AN EMERGING BARCODE-BASED RETAIL INFRASTRUCTURE (1987–2020)

This takes us to the third phase, during which the development of novel uses of the barcode came to the fore along with more refined, integrated systems. A first example of a retailer taking scanning one step further was a joint project undertaken by a Virginia-based grocery retailer called Ukrop and Citicorp POS Information Services to exploit available digital information about sales to increase customer loyalty (1987, 05, 133–6). In short, Ukrop launched a Valued Customer Card, which Citicorp explicitly modeled on the successful loyalty programs operated by the airlines (see Araujo and Kjellberg, 2015; 2016). Having introduced scannable coupons in 1986 (see previous section), Ukrop was able to create a customer program that offered members digital coupons and stored their purchase data. This setup would allow Ukrop to target their marketing to specific members and/or groups of members.

Several firms engaged in the area of "electronic marketing" during the late 1980s. Essentially, there were two types of applications: (1) loyalty card systems (often involving cooperation with one of the major banks), and (2) aggregated analyses of scanner data performed by third-party market consultants such as AC Nielsen (1987, 04A, 13; 1989, 11, 45) and Arbitron (1990, 05, 101). Given these efforts and the growth of scanning, the *Progressive Grocer* asked (1990, 01, 30): "Will the 1990s be the decade that scan data finally pays off?" A few years later, however, the magazine noted that the promise of data was still largely unfulfilled (1994, 07, S04): "Two decades on, scanners are still under-used. The first commercial scan took place 20 years ago last month. Scanner marketing, however, is just getting started." It proved to be a gradual and slow process to actually make use of the scanner-generated data. Nonetheless, the use of scanner data linked to frequent shopper cards grew steadily throughout the 1990s (1995, 02, 14). In parallel, the major third-party analyst, AC Nielsen, further developed their ECR (Efficient Consumer Response) offering by creating Nielsen Solution Partners together with key actors in the US scanner market (1994, 07, 42).

An extension of this idea was to make the stores even more data driven, both at the front end (sales and checkout) and at the back door (purchasing and delivery). In the cartoons from 1989 shown in Figure 6.10 the storewide information system is telling both the retailer and his customer what to buy. Actual development in this direction was quicker at the back door than at the front end. Building on the collective investments made into the Uniform Communication System (see previous section) as well as initiatives by suppliers of scanners and systems (1990, 05, 38), systems integration reached back to suppliers and wholesalers and coupled with in-store computer systems. One article described the setup at Easter Foods in Des Moines, Iowa:

> The back door has a Norand 2200 radio data system with two-way FM hand-held terminals, a transceiver base station and a multiplexer which lets eight hand-helds run independently to either receive or do price verification. […] The PC also holds the item/price file and communicates directly with the store's Casio scanners. In addition, it provides the ability to print out shelf labels. Price changes made here hit the registers at once. (1990, 04, 105–106)

Although complete automation was still a future dream, these more pedestrian developments certainly contributed to alter the purchasing agency of the retailers, supposedly making them more competent purchasers.

Despite the fact that scanner use had grown steadily, the issue of correspondence between shelf price and system price kept coming back. Not all retailers had the level of sophistication attributed to Easter Foods in the article quoted above. In 1993, the ABC news show *PrimeTime Live* compared shelf and scanner prices in 39 stores with quite embarrassing results for the studied retailers: more than half of the stores either charged too much or too little (1993, 05, 13). Over the years, repeated efforts had been made to solve this issue, including the introduction of new devices for comparing shelf prices against scanner prices aka price verification (1987, 01, 41; 1990, 04, 105) and suggested routines for ensuring up-to-date prices (1988, 03, 100–101). In some cases collective measures were taken, such as the scanning certification program of the Pennsylvania Food Merchants Association, which offered customers the good for free if the scanned price was higher than the shelf price (1993, 06, 106). Here, then, the trade association proactively sought to turn a back-stage operational problem into a front-stage marketing argument. In other states, such as Michigan, legislative measures were instead considered in order to "put some teeth" in the penalties for overcharging (1994, 07, 8). Various technical devices were presented as solutions to the price consistency problem, including Electronic Shelf Labels (1985, 11, 54) and radio transmitting price tags (1994, 06, 10). The former were held out as particularly promising, although later developments proved that the path from promise to realization can be long and arduous (see Chapter 7).

Source: *Progressive Grocer* (top: 1989, 05, 94–5; bottom: 1989, 05, 96).

*Figure 6.10   An in-store information system supporting retailer and
                  customer activities alike*

In the 1990s, barcodes and scanning were increasingly seen as business as usual for clerks and customers. While there were continual changes underneath the surface of the scanner systems, these could now go without notice for users: "To you [the owner of retail store], it provides comprehensive reports on inventory, cashiers, and now, your shoppers. To Betsy [a checkout clerk], it's business as usual" (1992, 06, 95). In parallel, others developed entirely new uses of barcodes, such as Epoch's hand-held gaming console "Barcode Battler"[2] from 1991 that used barcodes to give game characters new abilities. The game encouraged players to find "which supermarket product boasted the most powerful barcode",[3] allegedly causing Japanese retailers to guard their product packages so that the part where the barcode was printed was not removed.[4] When you think about it, the battler was actually not so different from the overall story of the introduction of barcodes in retailing – in one case you seek to alter the agency of in-game characters, in the other, that of retailers and their customers.

Back inside the grocery stores, the increased use of checkout scanners was starting to trigger discussions about potential negative consequences, notably the risk of "cumulative trauma injuries" (1994, 01, 67–74). Once again the hands and fingers of retail staff came into view. In short, the issue concerned the strain caused by the repetitive bodily movements required of clerks when scanning products at the checkout. Besides various training programs devised to counteract these effects, retailers soon recognized that parts of the new barcode infrastructure could afford an alternative solution. Indeed, by simply handing over the scanners to the customers (1994, 07, 12), Dutch retailer Albert Heijn saw a number of potential positive effects. In terms of retail operations, the primary benefit would be to rationalize the time-consuming and therefore costly checkout procedure. For the customers, the move would not only reduce the distance between shelf and checkout, so to speak, but also increase their agency inside the store. With a scanner of their own, customers could more easily detect errors between shelf price and scanner price as well as keep track of the sum total of their purchases. The end benefit for the retailer is ambivalent. On the one hand, consumer barcode scanning would save labor costs by putting the consumers to work (Dujarier, 2016); on the other hand, it would reintroduce into shopping practice the budgetary constraint that had largely been replaced by the volumetric constraint of the shopping cart (Cochoy, 2008a).

---

2   See https://en.wikipedia.org/wiki/Barcode_Battler.
3   See http://www.pocketgamer.co.uk/r/Multiformat/Handheld+Classics.
4   Svenska Hemdatornytt (1993, 9).

Finally, we fast-forward 15 years to glimpse the start of yet another reap-propriation of the barcode infrastructure (2009, 04, 18). At this point in time, self-scanning had become routine to many customers and had also been extended with self-checkout enabled by the barcode infrastructure (2020, 08, 76–9). However, it had also paved the way for further developments. Specifically, the emergence of smartphones and other mobile computing technologies allowed yet other actors, like competitors and third parties, to appropriate the established barcode infrastructure. Examples include white goods manufacturers developing automated shopping list generators linked to home refrigerators (2009, 03, 56) and a wide variety of price comparison and sustainability apps that use barcode scanning (2014, 05, 49) (Hansson, 2017). Here, then, we see third parties, notably consumer advocates, leveraging the barcode to ensure their own (virtual) presence inside grocery stores (Soutjis, 2020). While the claim that this would make the consumer "Commander of the Shopping Experience" (2009, 04, 18) seems overly exaggerated given the various interests behind these efforts, it does highlight the changing power relations over time even within a single market infrastructure.

Once in place, then, barcode scanning allowed other actors to develop new uses of the existing barcodes and scanners. Some of these were clearly related to the retail market, such as using scanner-generated data to improve retail marketing and purchasing, while others were seemingly disconnected. A decade later, new actors put the same barcode infrastructure to entirely new uses by exploiting its possibility for product identification and qualification in combination with the rapidly developing communication infrastructure offered by smartphones.

WEB-BASED SMARTPHONE APPS: THE EMERGENCE OF CONSUMER-BASED ALTERNATIVE INFRASTRUCTURES FOR PRICE AND QUALITY DISPLAY

Until recently, digitalization modernized rather than revolutionized the price infrastructure. All the systems we reviewed so far, and even the Electronic Shelf Labels that we will address in the next chapter, are based on the same one-sided communication scheme, from grocer to consumer. During the past 20 years or so, however, new interactive devices like self-scanners and consumer-oriented barcode and QR-code reading apps have started to chal-lenge this scheme. These innovations further develop the "qualitization and "digitalization" of price tags (see Chapter 5) by offering the possibility to extend and enrich the information on the goods and in the store (2020, 01, 48–9). Beyond that, they also introduce the possibility of interactive commu-nication. They do so by adjusting offers to the consumers' profile (when for instance consumers use loyalty cards and agree to share their sales record and personal information), or by helping consumers to select the information they need (in displaying information organized along treelike menus, rather than all at once). Last but not least, digital interactive labeling devices renew the competition for consumer attention between manufacturers and retailers. In particular, the UPC works as a single key that may be used to offer multiple qualifications, depending on the reading apps and the underlying databases, be they connected to the manufacturer, the retailer, or to some third party who may engage the manufacturer and the retailer in a game much as the cat did with the rabbit and the weasel.[5]

Indeed, the two main breakthroughs of the new portable UPC or QR-code readers are their interactive character and their capacity to connect a given code to distinct databases. These features allow the database owners to hide, select or disclose information according to their interests: for instance, a manufacturer can insist on his brand, while a retailer may prefer to stress nutrition facts (or any kind of information that he believes will increase his goodwill and/or profits). In this respect, the UPC raises again the issue of information transparency in marketing channels, by replacing the old-fashioned coding of prices with a similar game now focused on quality (2020, 04, 80–81; 2020, 11, 98). Electronic interactive labels may thus appear as deceptive rather than informative since the competing presentations of the same products reveal the arbitrary choices of those who inform their customers about the products.

But the UPC also gives the means to reverse this power and arbitrariness. Recently, consumer activists engaged in what could be called a "wikization" of product codes. They developed smartphone apps that use the UPC to connect any given product to an alternative database. This database is organized according to an open data, wiki-like logic. It allows consumers to perform instant comparisons but also to add or access information that is missing on

---

[5]   "A Rabbit left his home one day for a dinner of clover. But he forgot to latch the door of his house and while he was gone a Weasel walked in and calmly made himself at home. When the Rabbit returned, there was the Weasel's nose sticking out of the Rabbit's own doorway, sniffing the fine air. The Rabbit was quite angry— for a Rabbit—, and requested the Weasel to move out. But the Weasel was perfectly content. He was settled down for good. A wise old Cat heard the dispute and offered to settle it. 'Come close to me,' said the Cat, 'I am very deaf. Put your mouths close to my ears while you tell me the facts.' The unsuspecting pair did as they were told and in an instant the Cat had them both under her claws. No one could deny that the dispute had been definitely settled. The strong are apt to settle questions to their own advantage." (*Aesop for Children*, translator unknown, 1919, available online at: http://www .gutenberg.org/files/19994/19994-h/19994-h.htm#Page_55).

the product package, such as consumer reviews or ratings,[6] or the traffic light grading of foods based on nutritional facts that French manufacturers fight so hard at the political level[7] (Soutjis, 2020). In France, far from being anecdotal, these apps now play a major role in retailing. A few years ago, we would have presented these systems as weak and fragile, almost powerless in comparison with the industry, hampered by the work required of the consumers to access the information. However, the situation has changed quickly. The leading app, "Yuka", has been downloaded by more than 13 million consumers and is used monthly by 5.5 million of them. This shift of market power has forced manufacturers to adapt their strategy and public authorities to adjust their regulation. It is significant, for instance, that the French Senate, despite its conservative and pro-supply side orientation, passed a law in March 2020 aimed at making it compulsory for manufacturers to have data on food products available as open data.[8] Today, price and quality information infrastructures are beginning to incorporate the voice of the consumers themselves, and thus to further "re-agence" the price and quality display system.

* * *

Overall, this chapter has shown how the US retail price infrastructure gradually emerged, then was digitalized over a 40-year period through investments made by a wide variety of actors including trade organizations, equipment manufacturers, retailers, wholesalers, producers, and legislators. While (market) infrastructures are at times conceived and indeed attempted to be realized as systems developed from a single, onetime plan (Démurger, 2001), there is no obvious such "infrastructurer" in our case. Of course, there are several actors who plan for particular futures, but apart from the UPC and UCS committees, they do so as independent companies, developing the markets for their own devices. These devices compete on the same market, but also connect to each other – a property that is used as a commercial argument. This leads to the development of a single infrastructure by multiple actors, including manufacturers, wholesalers and retailers, but also equipment suppliers and major consulting firms. The new market infrastructure is thus a product sold

---

[6]   See "Open label", http://www.triplepundit.com/2012/04/bar-codes-apps-allow -socially-conscious-consumers-make-informed-choices/.

[7]   See Open Food Facts, http://world.openfoodfacts.org/.

[8]   Cabanel, Henri et Loisier, Anne-Catherine, Rapport no. 341, Sénat, séssion ordinaire de 2019–2020 20 février 2020, Rapport fait au nom de la commission des affaires économiques sur la proposition de loi adoptée par l'Assemblée nationale, relative à la transparence de l'information sur les produits agricoles et alimentaires, Procédure de législation en commission en application de l'article 47 ter du Règlement, https://www .senat.fr/rap/l19-341/l19-3411.pdf.

on multiple markets. Similar to more traditional notions of infrastructure, the material dimension has a formative role in this process; technological constraints and material conditions are central to the enacted infrastructure, for example machine-readable symbols, communication standards, barcode printers, barcoded packages, and so on. Among these tools, Electronic Shelf Labels could play a central role but were slow to do it, for reasons that we will discover in the next chapter.

7. Digitalizing prices: the long history of Electronic Shelf Labels

One of the most striking developments affecting contemporary markets is their digitalization (Hagberg et al., 2016; Cochoy et al., 2017; MacKenzie, 2017; Chimenti, 2020; Duffy et al., 2020; Hagberg and Kjellberg, 2020; Mellet and Beauvisage, 2020). During the past decades digitalization has spread like a technological plague: computerized networks and other IT infrastructures, big data, wearable electronic devices, digital platforms, artificial intelligence. The signs of digitalization show up everywhere, in high-frequency trading in financial markets (MacKenzie, 2017), in RFID (radio-frequency identification) chips inside products and product packaging (Simakova and Neyland, 2008), and in phone apps in mundane consumer settings (Fuentes et al., 2017). As we saw in the previous chapter, retail price tags have not escaped this process, indeed, they were an early example of it. The influence of digitization is further evidenced by the long history of Electronic Shelf Labels (ESLs) that we focus on in this chapter.

Against the backdrop of the previous chapters, it is easy to see that digitalized price tags would be alluring. They could give consumers access to more reliable price information and provide grocers with a means to instantly adjust prices in response to changed market conditions. Yet, the trajectory for ESLs is puzzling. On the one hand, ESLs represent one of the latest and most sophisticated incarnations of price tag technology. On the other hand, their presence is still marginal, particularly in the United States. In a 2016 post on the *Progressive Grocer* website, journalist John Karolefski noted the discrepancy between the European and US markets:

> Grocers around the world are enjoying [the] benefits [of ESLs] for store performance, coupled with an improved shopper experience. In the United States, ESLs have been talked about for a long time, and while a few pilots have been staged over the years, no widespread deployment has taken place. (Karolefski, 2016)

While ESLs have indeed been more widely used in other countries, there are indications that they do not fully replace but rather coexist with previous technologies, like paper labels, in the stores where they are introduced (Soutjis et al., 2017). In this chapter, we continue our historical exploration of price tag technologies in the US grocery sector by focusing on the development and use of ESLs. This allows us to further develop our argument that *digitalization* is better understood if one takes all facets of its etymology into account. Among contemporary retail practitioners and researchers alike, digitalization is primarily associated with *computerizing*. However, as we have shown in previous chapters, it is also linked to *indexing* and *numberizing*, and in this respect the history of ESLs is no different from previous generations of price display technology.

To map the history of ESLs, we review their introduction in the United States based on articles and advertisements appearing in the *Progressive Grocer*. This helps us illustrate the promises attached to the technology since its inception, the many problems encountered during its 35-year (and counting) introduction into US grocery retailing, and its modest use so far. This leads us to argue that knowing the history of price display technologies matters for understanding the fate of ESLs. We show that the digitalization of markets, far from being reducible to the radical novelty of electronic displays, should be conceived of as a dynamic agencement of combinable technologies that have evolved at different paces; in some cases, the apparent modernity of the most recent devices even hides a return to old technological features and practices.

THE INTRODUCTION OF ESLs IN US RETAILING

How were ESLs introduced in the US grocery retail market, and to what effect? As noted in the previous chapter the attention to computerized devices and digital gadgetry in the *Progressive Grocer* grew from the 1970s onward in terms of both articles and advertisements. The articles chronicle innovations ranging from major ones such as electronic cash registers and checkout scanners, computerized store management systems, and data centers, to less well-known tools such as fingerprint recognition (2000, 04, 90 et seq.; 2002, 02, 20; 2004, 15, 34 et seq.), shopping cart assistants, store directories (2001, 01, 58), and RFID tags (2004, 16, 62). Paradoxically, however, the digitalization (in the sense of computerization) of retail price display, that is, the digitalization of the most important information about goods from an economics perspective, occurred as a relatively late and marginal evolution. Indeed, it occurred after the digitalization of the retail environment (e.g., cash registers, scales, and scanners) and after the digitalization of the elements surrounding prices: barcodes were closely linked to prices, but as we saw in Chapter 6, the displayed prices remained in their "paperized" state also when barcodes entered the store. Finally, the uptake of ESL technology has remained sluggish, as illustrated by numerous pictures of store interiors from the magazine throughout the past four decades that contain no traces whatsoever of ESLs. For these reasons, ESLs occupy a central yet puzzling position: central because with them the price becomes (further) digitalized, but puzzling because this digitalization has so far been marginal, slow and discrete.

Arguably the most innovative product of the year is an electronic price display system that ensures 100% consistency between shelf price and scanners. In test in a Loblaw supermarket, the shelf tags provide unit display prices or other information—i.e."salt free"— at the touch of a finger. (Telepanel, Inc., 245 Riviera Dr., Markham, Ontario L3R 5JR, 416/477-7877.)

Source: *Progressive Grocer* (1985, 11, 54).

Figure 7.1   Electronic price display, Telepanel, Inc.

ESLs first appeared in the magazine in 1985 in a small follow-up that presented them as "Arguably the most innovative product of the year" (Figure 7.1). Four things are worth emphasizing about this introduction: first, it attached to ESLs a promise to solve one of the pressing problems associated with the new barcode-based infrastructure that was developing inside retail stores at the time (see Chapter 6): "an electronic price display system that ensures 100% consistency between shelf price and scanners", the text says. Second, the new device was shown to be aligned with the trend of the time of combining digitally legible information (see the permanent barcode in the lower left corner of the display frame) and printed text (see the top left and lower right parts of the display frame) as discussed in Chapter 5. Third, positioned between these well-known features is the real novelty: an LCD display capable of presenting not only a changeable price, but also other brief bits of information about the product in accordance with the gradual recovery of communicative ground on the part of the retailers mentioned in previous chapters. Fourth and finally, as suggested by the text, this additional information was available to the customer "at the touch of a finger", testifying once again to the close link between digital as in computerized and digital as in fingers-based.

While the magazine did not report much on the development of ESLs during the remainder of the 1980s, several suppliers were developing ESL solutions in parallel so that by 1990 there were at least six competing solutions available (1990, 01, 61–6). In a comparison made by the magazine the key function was described:

> The basic concept is simple. Instead of using paper tags, retailers put small liquid crystal display (LCD) labels on the edge of the shelf. These labels–either battery powered or wired–can display new prices instantly on command. Because price changes are sent to the front end and the labels at the same time, price integrity between shelf and scanner is ensured. (1990, 01, 61)

At this point, the primary advantage of ESLs was seen to be their ability to perform price fixing in the third sense of the term, that is, their ability to display *adjustable* prices. By linking the labels and the cash registers to the same price database, the system would also allow retailers to resolve the price integrity issue that they had grappled with since the introduction of posted prices and that had become increasingly topical with the introduction of scanning. With this clear link to a persistent and pressing concern among grocery retailers and with scattered reports of pioneering ESL tests underway, it is not surprising to find the magazine stating in 1993: "ESLs are moving from a stage of testing by a few pioneering retailers to acceptance by more mainstream supermarket users. This trend is typical of supermarket technology cycles" (1993, 12, 23). However, as we will show, the actual development of ESLs since their introduction until today proved to be anything but typical.

BACK TO THE FUTURE: THE HISTORICAL ANCHORING OF ESL TECHNOLOGY

Against the backdrop of previous chapters, the development of ESLs represents yet another step in the long history of price display technology development. These chapters suggest that innovative price display is more about technical agencement than technological progress: what matters is to find the proper means and solutions to build compromises between an eternal concern – that of fixing prices by setting, posting and adjusting them – and contemporary retail conditions, such as available technological resources, cost constraints, and existing legal and material retail environments. In other words, price display solutions cannot be isolated from the available technologies and market surroundings. In this respect, an electronic price display is just one element among many in the socio-technical system that is the grocery store. Whether this element represents the future is far from certain and due to its selective links to the past, its place in the present can be contested and riddled with practical problems.

At first glance, digital price displays present all the characteristics of a world in and of itself: disconnected and isolated, as if they had nothing to do with previous price tag technologies. Telepanel (Figure 7.1) and its early competitors were outsiders in the price tag business and their solutions seemed to introduce a radical shift, a disruptive innovation, and a technological revolution in price display. But on closer inspection, there is also continuity to be found. One recurrent theme in the development of price tag technologies has been how to fix price tickets in holders or rails and the holders or rails on the shelves. In other words, it has been focused on addressing the fundamental dilemma we met in Chapter 2: prices should be easily changeable when needed (to implement pricing decisions and save grocers' time, effort and money) and firmly attached once applied (to avoid them being removed or displaced accidentally or by indelicate consumers, notably children; see Chapter 2). This pertains to one of the digital aspects of price tags: because price tags can be manipulated with fingers, it becomes of utmost importance to discriminate between the fingers of consumers (that must remain powerless) and the fingers of market professionals (that should be able to adjust prices as smoothly and quickly as possible). As we saw above, the introduction of ESLs did not change this.

Many of the technical solutions proposed for price display in the past century relied on the same way of displaying prices: you selected cards with preprinted single numerals and combined them laterally in a rail or holder. In other words, modern price display was always fully digital: selecting digits among ten discrete possibilities and placing them – with one's fingers – in the proper order to display a desired price. But this dominant card-combination approach drastically limited how goods could be qualified at the shelf. The sets of cards focused on prices, offering only a few possibilities to add qualitative information. Indeed, writing other information with the same system would require too many cards – there are ten digits but 26 letters – and, more importantly, too much space on the shelf – in most cases, writing a word would require more space than the width of the allotted shelf space. Consequently, the

technology of card-combination supported a division of labor between manufacturers and grocers (see Chapters 4 and 5); whereas the former dealt with the
qualities of goods by printing information on the product's package, the latter
dealt with product prices only. This division of labor can be traced back to one
of the very first price tag solutions, introduced by The Hopp Press Company
in the 1920s: the sectional price ticket holder (see Chapter 2). In hindsight
this was a milestone in price tag history, so successful that the device became
a generic and dominant price display technology until the 1980s. Hopp Press'
solution introduced both price ticket combination and the insertion of price
tickets into an appropriate holder. As a consequence, price displays ended up
displaying prices only.

Paradoxically, despite the huge temporal gap – some 60 years – the first
ESL from 1985 had strong similarities to this solution. Instead of leading
towards the future, it seemed to bring retailing back to the past, because with
the segmented technology display constraints of early liquid crystal displays,
the only changeable information was essentially numerals, just like The Hopp
Press tickets introduced in the 1920s. Moreover, the readability of LCDs was
far behind that of both the elegant fonts of the early twentieth century and the
standardized preprinted tickets. Of course, the new device was more sophisticated than Hopp Press' price ticket holder, since it complemented the adjustable numbers with stable qualitative information. However, it is important to
stress that the first ESLs partly reiterated the division of labor between qualitative and quantitative information described in Chapter 5. On the one hand, the
grocer could now adjust prices electronically and complement them with some
qualitative information. On the other hand, the control of price and quality
information was still asymmetric: while prices could be adjusted swiftly and
easily, many qualities would remain fixed at the periphery or displayed with
classic paper stickers beside the new electronic label. Needless to say, (re)
placing such information took much more time and effort. Consequently, the
new solution proposed that grocery management should focus on prices and
leave other qualities to the manufacturers.

In relative terms, this meant that with the use of ESLs, control over information about product quality would be handed back to the manufacturers. This
was due to a development that had taken place between the introduction of
the sectional price ticket holder by Hopp Press and the introduction of ESLs
by Telepanel: the replacement of price tags by paper stickers (see Chapter 5).
The introduction and spread of these stickers had allowed retailers to gradually expand their control of in-store communications. One important step in
this process was the development of in-store pre-packaging, which gave the
retailers control over both quality and price information, thanks to the use of
labels printed in the store that described the goods as well as their prices. In
the 1980s, these labels migrated from the departments where goods were being

pre-packaged to all aisles of the store, replacing classic number-only price tags. In their first incarnation, ESLs threatened to partially ruin this advance by reintroducing an asymmetry between instant price changes and delayed or impoverished quality information. While later versions, such as "electronic paper labels", solve this particular issue, their cost remains problematic as does their black and white appearance, which fits poorly with the colorful environment of contemporary supermarkets. In this environment, ESLs have to compete for attention with paper labels, which are not only cheaper, but also more attractive, legible, and flexible in terms of size and design. Indeed, the continuous presence of paper labels compromises one of the main advantages of ESLs: the possibility of adjusting prices quickly. When prices are duplicated throughout the store, electronically but also on paper, the speed of a price change must adjust to the slowest media (paper labels) (Figure 7.2 and Soutjis et al., 2017).

Source: © Franck Cochoy.

Figure 7.2   **Paper price labels, New York, April 2016**

AN ETERNALLY FUTURISTIC TECHNOLOGY

From their introduction onward, ESLs were continuously presented and discussed in positive and promising terms, such as "ESL up and running" (1993, 12, 23–4), "one of the most important new technologies out there" (1994, 08, 136), "ESLs roll on" (1995, 07, 12). Later reports said, "Connectivity is about to change the way retailers think about customer relationships" (2002, 02, 14) and "Every time we think there is nothing else to improve, there is additional data for digitizing the store" (2015, 12, 26). Many of the reports had future-oriented titles or subtitles, describing ESLs as a "technology that will be driving your store – and your customers – within the next five years" (2002, 02, 13). Indeed, as late as 2015 ESLs were said to be part of the "Supermarket of the future" (2015, 12, 22 et seq.) and 2 years later "they will be the future of grocery shelving" (2017, 09, 119). In this chapter, then, we are focusing on a solution and technology for price display that has had a place in futuristic visions of grocery retailing for more than 35 years.

Three contributions of ESLs were recurrently proposed in support of this positive view. First, the promoters of ESLs stressed the device's ability to improve shopper experiences. ESLs were supposed to meet this objective through a combination of in-store tags and data-mining methods: "Shelving technologies can help brands and retailers drive customer engagement and loyalty" (2016, 01, 98). New technologies of information would "bring back to retailers what massification of marketing took away" (2002, 02, 13). Here, then, the *Progressive Grocer* connects ESLs to shifts in the conceptualization of marketing including the advent of relationship and collaborative marketing based on the figure of the postmodern consumer (Cova and Cova, 2012). In short, ESLs would improve consumer satisfaction by being easier to read; they would be more securely attached than paper labels and "cleaner looking" (1994, 08, 136); and they would allow for changing prices several times a day, hence adjusting instantly to market fluctuations and retail price competition (i.e., 1993, 12, 23; 1991, 07, 100). ESLs would further improve the transparency of product information (i.e., 1991, 07, 102; 1990, 01, 66) and thus allow the retail sector to address growing consumer concerns about fairness, sustainability (Dubuisson-Quellier, 2013) and food safety (Frohlich, 2017). By being adjustable, ESLs could provide more information to consumers (1991, 07, 102; 1990, 01, 66), show time-sensitive promotions (1991, 07, 102), and enhance consumer–product interactions (1991, 07, 102; 1994, 08, 136; 1995, 12, 14). These possibilities were further emphasized in connection with the advent of ESLs based on "electronic paper", which promised much richer visuals. While the latter technology might appear to be recent, it had already made its first appearance in the *Progressive Grocer* in 2002: "Electronic papers, shelf labels, and plasma signage bring to the shelves promotional and pricing power never before imagined" (2002, 02, 14).

Second, ESLs were presented as a means to simplify logistical operations in the store (in particular, through the coupling of ESLs and RFID technology) and to dramatically increase the speed of inventory management and checkout services. This was tightly linked to the idea that ESLs would solve two long-lasting issues in grocery retail. First, they would reduce the time and cost of price changes (1971, 06, 5) – ESLs are about "displaying price instantly on command" (1990, 01, 61). Second, they would solve the old problem of price discrepancies between shelf price and checkout price – the device "ensures 100% consistency between shelf price and scanners" (1985, 11, 54), "price integrity between shelf and scanner is assured" (1990, 01, 62), and "people came to the [equipped] store because they believe prices to be right" (1994,

08, 135). Taken together, these features would allow an ESL-equipped store to streamline several costly retail operations.

Third, and related, the different testimonies gathered and reported in the magazine outline the idea of a continuous interconnectivity between all in-store technologies. In this respect, the fate of ESLs clearly depends on their coupling with other in-store innovations. One early example was the view of ESLs as extensions of the use of computerized databases in the retailing sector (1990, 01, 61; 1993, 06, 18; 1995, 07, 12). A more recent articulation between ESLs and wider market infrastructures is their possible coupling with smartphones: the *Progressive Grocer* reported that ESLs could connect to the customers' smartphones via Bluetooth beacons to provide real-time and targeted promotions as well as help them navigate the store (2016, 01, 96). On the logistics side, coupling ESLs with wireless communication technologies could provide store staff with digital planograms for the store and even alert about restocking needs. This latter link between price display technology and restocking was not new, as we saw in Chapter 6. Another link mentioned already when ESLs made their first appearance (see Figure 7.1) was their capacity to convey additional information stored in a central database. Initially, the additional information was limited primarily to unit prices due to the display constraints discussed above. In contrast, contemporary second-screen technologies afford the display of much more diverse information (e.g., nutritional data, allergens, manufacturing conditions). Through this coupling with in-store (or chain-wide) databases, ESLs are presented as the missing link that affords fully connected stores. This tight link to other in-store technologies means that while other issues dominated over ESLs in the 1990s, the success of such technologies may well render ESLs more interesting by articulating potential technological combinations.

In parallel to these optimistic views, however, ESLs were also repeatedly put forward as a source of concern by the *Progressive Grocer*. This was first visible in questioning titles chosen by the magazine: "Will supermarkets play electronic tags?" (1991, 07, 99 et seq.) and "Are ESLs worth it?" (1994, 08, 135). As suggested by the latter title, the high cost of ESLs was noted early on – "Despite their many advantages, electronic shelf tags cost too much for supermarkets to take them seriously" (1991, 07, 99, see also 1993, 06, 18) – and repeated in relation to subsequent generations of the technology – "an affordable [color] ESL is still years away" (2013, 09, 145). Doubts about ESLs were also nurtured by reflections "questioning technology's promises" (2002, 02, 52): "How often will labels that aren't hard-wired require battery changes and will that create havoc? Don't LCD units wear out in five years anyway? What happens to hard-wired systems when a shelf is damaged or becomes embedded with syrup, for example? Are hard-wired systems cumbersome to install and operate?" (1990, 01, 62). This final question raises the issue of implementation, which was also highlighted as a potential concern. During the early days, the lead time required to get a system up and running and the amount of work that the retailer would have to put into this were brought up as important factors to consider as part of the investment decision (1993, 12C, 24). Installation was described as "hard and long" (1994, 08, 136). This, in turn, favored the retail chains over independent stores, since the former could expect future installations to benefit from the learning generated during (more cumbersome and expensive) pilot projects.

This decidedly more skeptic view of ESLs was partly fueled by some troubling facts. The competition among ESL suppliers in the early 1990s offered one such indication: out of six key suppliers presented by the *Progressive Grocer* in 1990 (1990, 01, 61 et seq.), three were noted to have "bowed out" 1 year later (1991, 07, 99 et seq.). A second indication was given by customer assessments from the retailers that did test ESLs: there were several early reports of chains deciding not to roll them out after the initial trial run. A supermarket in New Jersey, for instance, decided to pull its ESLs after having tested them in 1988 (1990, 01, 63). In 2002, a survey showed that most retailers were unsatisfied with the available in-store technologies: "In general technology overpromises and underdelivers", stated a chief executive (2002, 02, 52). Given this, it is not surprising that ESLs met with lukewarm interest despite their promises: "Electronic shelf labels have been lurking on the sidelines for more than 30 years" (2013, 09, 145); "ESLs have been slow to take hold" (2017, 09, 119).

How can we explain these skeptical discourses and practical difficulties? A first contributing factor was the application of item-pricing laws in the United States, which required retailers to stick the price on each product. This kind of law was first introduced in Massachusetts in 1970 to counteract discrepancies between shelf prices and checkout prices. Several states followed suit in the mid-1970s as a reaction to the introduction of barcodes and scanners (see Chapter 6). In 1991, item-pricing regulations were applied in eight states: Connecticut, Minnesota, Michigan, Massachusetts, Rhode Island, North Dakota, California, and New York (1991, 07, 100). ESLs were initially presented as a way to fight this regulation, using the argument that they could eliminate price discrepancies by electronically linking shelf price and checkout price. While this could be an attractive development to the grocery retail sector at large, we may still suspect that the individual retailers operating in these eight states had little interest in implementing ESLs as long as they still had to stick prices manually on every product. As late as 2008, among the states with item-pricing laws, only Connecticut exempted retailers equipped with ESLs from marking every item (Bergen et al., 2008). Meanwhile, the investment in ESLs would have been seen as risky to retailers in other states, given the threat of a possible item-pricing ruling or possibly the introduction of such a law.

A second, more generally applicable explanation seems to be the gap between the promises of the technology and what it was able to deliver in practical use. As with any new device, early ESLs had technical flaws: "Some of the early failures of electronic shelf labels have been almost comical. There were labels that exploded upon impact with shopping carts, labels that attached themselves to the bottom of skids not to be found for months, labels that displayed test patterns seemingly at whim" (1990, 01, 61). Because of these failures, the *Progressive Grocer* ranked ESLs twenty-seventh on a list of the new retail technologies in terms of CEO satisfaction, with only 20.2 percent of the few users who had tried the technology considering it to be "satisfying" or "very satisfying" (2002, 02, 52). As noted, one main argument against the technology was its cost and the resulting relatively long payback time: in 1991, the unit cost was around $10 and the expected payback time for investing in a complete system was at least 2.5 years. The case for an investment was made more problematic by the fact that it might be entirely unnecessary; after all, retailers could "get along with paper labels" (1990, 07, 102).

The final comment directs attention to a third, interrelated set of explanations for the slow uptake of ESLs: the alternative solutions available, their compatibility with the existing store infrastructure, and the prioritized issues related to this infrastructure. While ESLs might be much more advanced than and offer several benefits over a paper label, the two placed very different requirements on the context. ESLs required new forms of interconnectivity in the store: "[Electronic labels] may yet prove to be the missing link that brings together all the other high-tech systems in the store" (1990, 07, 102). Paper labels, on the other hand, relied on well-established conduits for their performance: store staff and printers transferred information from one system to another and adhesives ensured the association of this information with the goods. This allowed paper labels to float on top of the existing retail infrastructure rather than be hardwired into it.

Between 1990 and 2010, many retailers saw innovations such as electronic payments, POS (point-of-sale) software, and back-office applications as more urgent matters (1994, 07, 104). The lack of a robust and standardized communication network also seems to have weakened retailers' confidence in ESLs (1995, 12, 14; 2002, 02, 14). From 2005 to 2009, *Progressive Grocer* published an annual survey that is useful for contextualizing ESLs among other available technologies. The magazine reported the results of a poll among top executives of companies operating up to ten supermarkets about how they envisioned the future of digital technologies. Table 7.1 compiles the results of this survey (2005, 02, 52; 2006, 01, 63; 2007, 01, 86; 2008, 02, 65; 2009, 02, 83). For 2005–2008, the table reports the percentage of respondents who rated each technology as the most or second-most promising (on a scale of 1 to 5). For 2009, it reports how respondents use or view the same technologies

Table 7.1 Independent retail executives' view of key digital retail technologies

	2005		2006		2007		2008		2009			
	In next year	In next 3 years	In next year	In next 3 years	In next year	In next 3 years	In next year	In next 3 years	Using/ rolling out now	High priority/ important	Unsure/ not interested	Don't know
POS hardware/software	67	76	60	66	52	60	48	48	72	13	12	3
Back-office applications	52	61	54	62	47	50	49	51	71	13	13	3
Mobile/wireless applications	39	46	42	44	33	42	28	33	56	13	28	3
Internet-hosted applications	36	49	32	36	28	37	23	30	47	14	35	4
Loyalty programs	28	33	35	35	30	35	25	25	31	18	47	4
Electronic shelf labels	**18**	**25**	**23**	**26**	**18**	**28**						
RFID	15	22	18	21	11	17						
Fuel automation	13	19	20	23	22	24	11	10	14	14	61	11
Self-checkout	6	17	10	23	12	19						
Electronic payments					57	61	59	62	71	12	17	0
Shopper information kiosks							15	20	9	25	56	10
Big screen multimedia/displays							11	19				
Merchandizing									45	20	28	7
Loss prevention									43	26	27	4
Demand planning and ordering									16	21	54	9
In-store quick-service restaurants									9	15	40	36

Source: *Progressive Grocer* (2005–2009) (2005, 02, 52; 2006, 01, 63; 2007, 01, 86; 2008, 02, 65; 2009, 02, 83).

(row total = 100%). The resulting compilation provides an overview of how the store technology priorities of US grocery retailers developed during these years, which helps situate ESLs in the wider context of digital devices and promises. Despite that it only covers a period of 5 years, the table shows the tension between a statistical approach that requires stable categories, and the monitoring of innovations where new entities constantly enter the picture. The lower part of the table contains items that were added over the years while the absent values in the columns for 2009 represent technologies that no longer were considered key digital retail technologies.

Among the top-ranked innovations, we find "POS hardware/software", "back-office applications", "mobile/wireless applications" and "electronic payments" (which was included for the first time in the survey in 2007). In contrast, ESLs are repeatedly found in the lower half of the ranking, along with "RFID", "fuel automation" and "self-checkout". Clearly, the responding retailers did not consider ESLs to be among the most promising and interesting technologies. Indeed, in 2009, ESLs were removed from the list of digital retail technologies, indicating they were considered insignificant, pushed aside by new promising topics such as the use of digital solutions for merchandizing, loss prevention, and so on.

Despite this marginalization, though, experimentation with ESLs continued and evolved. In December 2015 under the heading "Supermarket of the future", the *Progressive Grocer* reported on a Kroger store in which a more elaborate and articulated ESL system had been put in place (2015, 12, 22–8). The store was described as "a laboratory to deploy and study the latest in-store technologies" in which Kroger had created an "ecosystem" blending "shopper-facing hardware" with "sophisticated technology behind the scene" (2015, 12, 22). This included hand-held scanners and ESLs, but also an IT system architecture called Retail Site Intelligence linking all the digital tools. The project lead for the shelf technologies explained that the system integration made it possible to replace paper labels with ESLs. According to him, ESLs rendered prices bigger and brighter, and facilitated shelf management via digital planograms. In terms of price display, another project lead actually stressed the hand-held scanners rather than the ESLs, linking "the running tally" kept by the scanner to "the savvy budget customers". Kroger had assumed a pioneering role before when it came to price display technologies, notably in the adoption of barcodes by installing a cash register equipped with a scanner as early as 1967, well before the development of the Universal Product Code in 1974 (Kato et al., 2010). Given that ESLs were first introduced in the mid-1980s, their launch of this ESL-equipped store in 2015 does not appear to be particularly pioneering as such. But this would be to disregard the systemic character of their effort; this was an attempt to build a "fully digitalized" retail environment. Here, then, the ESLs were made part of a wider retail machine together with self-scanning, shelf motion videos, and integrated planogram functions (2015, 12, 22 et seq.).

The attention paid to other technologies, and specifically the recognized interdependencies between such technologies and ESLs, suggests that ESLs and their fate must be understood as part of a wider retail-technological system. The way in which ESLs are discussed in the articles invites retailers to think about them not only as independent entities, but as part of an overall market "agencement": "a form of arrangement [made of various human and non-human resources] that acts and at the same time imposes a certain format on the action" (Callon, 2016). As we have seen in previous chapters, this system is typically the result of a gradual development in which traditional devices are combined over time with new ones that in some cases replace older solutions and in others are added on top of what is already in place. Recognizing this, the *Progressive Grocer* had directed a lot of attention to other digital technologies within the retail store system, such as electronic paper, electronic signage, in-store plasma screens, hand-held scanners, data mining, POS, self-checkout systems, mobile phones, wireless communication programs, smartcards, fingerprint payments, and Bluetooth and RFID beacons (2002, 02, 52). In later years, the focus was primarily on the link between ESLs and smartphones, depicted as "the linchpin of most in-store technologies" (2016, 01, 96), especially if coupled with other devices, loyalty programs, and big data. This focus was also reflected in various retail initiatives, such as mobilizing customers' smartphones via apps used for digitalizing loyalty programs, collecting data, sending targeted marketing campaigns, providing further product information (allergens, nutritional data, provenance, carbon footprint, etc.), and dealing with virtual coupons and recipes. Despite this, it seems clear that only in a few special cases were grocery stores subjected to the kind of wholesale technology shift that was described in the case of the Kroger experimental store, above.

All in all, the introduction of ESLs in the United States is clearly marked by an oscillation between hype and skepticism: ESLs and their promises are praised, then fail to deliver on these promises, improvements and additional innovations ensue, and the optimistic discourse is reactivated in an updated form. A striking pattern is the repeated formulation of hopeful comments after the expression of disappointments. In 2002, the magazine noted that, despite previous difficulties "there is life in ESLs" (2002, 02, 14). Fourteen years later, similar statements were reiterated: "[ESLs] might not become standard fare in US grocery stores any time soon, but the pace at which technology is advancing suggests that even such futuristic scenarios may be plausible one day" (2016, 01, 99); "no widespread deployment has taken place. That may change soon" (Karolefski, 2016). In other words, while ESL manufacturers presented the device as a "path to the future" (1993, 12, 22), the development towards this future has been an ever delayed one, announced and then postponed, as if the future was always escaping but deserving another chance. This is clearly visible in Table 7.1 where, year after year, a quite stable group of informants (18–28 percent) expressed confidence that ESLs would be an important topic for the next year and an even more valuable one in the next 3 years. For retailers, then, ESLs seem to work like the proverbial carrot dangling in front of the donkey: with each step forward, it moves a step into the future.

This makes ESLs stand out in comparison to most price display technologies of yesteryear. While there had been uncertainties linked to the profitability of investing in equipment such as price moldings, price guns and scanners, this did not prevent retailers from taking them on board. In this sense, the technologies discussed in previous chapters put their mark on retail operations. In some cases, this process took some time (e.g., for scanners), in others, the mark left by the technology proved quite temporary (e.g., for price stamps). With ESLs, however, we observe a new pattern: a technology seemingly stuck in a perpetual state of offering attractive prospects for the future but never (thus far) leaving more than a modest mark on actual retail operations.

FIXING ARGUMENTS TO ENSURE CONTINUED RELEVANCE

With ESLs remaining a prospective technology for more than 35 years, it is not surprising that some arguments presented in its favor changed. The retail context into which this promising innovation was first proposed in 1985 (see Figure 7.1) obviously differed in many ways from the US grocery retail context in 2020. Despite this, there are also several arguments that have remained remarkably stable throughout the course of the process. In a sense then, we can apply our preferred notion of "fixing" also to this part of our historical exposé: on the one hand, some arguments in favor of ESLs have been fixed in the sense of remaining stable for the duration of the period, on the other hand, some have been fixed in the sense of having been adjusted to fit the contemporary retail context.

ESLs were first introduced with a promise of "100% consistency between shelf price and scanners" (1985, 11, 54). As we saw in Chapter 6, this was a contextually relevant argument at the time, given that the introduction of scanning was well under way and that retailers were actively seeking to increase customer confidence in scanning. Delivering on this promise, however, hinged on having or putting in place an integrated storewide information system that could link the ESLs with checkout scanners, cash registers, and back-stage delivery systems. At the time of the introduction, such systems were not typically available in US grocery stores, which made the decision to invest in ESLs a much more encompassing one for the retailers. Even more so as the major alternative solution to price consistency relied on continued use of paper labels (requiring no investment), possibly in combination with a hand-held electronic scanner operated manually to compare the label price with the price in the "master pricing file" (see Figure 7.3, 1997, 02, 49). This kind of equipment had been available since the 1970s for reordering purposes (e.g., 1968, 12, 39; 1975, 01, 03; 1977, 05, 180), and as scanning started to grow in the early 1980s, price checking functionality was added to assist retailers in ensuring "price integrity" (1982, 06, 65–6). At that time, the main driver was said to be the "potentially hostile political forces in the marketplace" and the

Who Pays The Price When The Price Isn't Right?

You do. When the prices on your shelves don't match those at your POS register, you can lose in a lot of ways. Your money, your customer, or usually both. And, there's always the risk of legal action and costly fines.

Telxon has the most accurate and cost-effective solution in retailing today. A wireless price integrity system that allows your employees to verify and update prices from anywhere in the store and communicate the information,

in real time, to your master pricing file. Result: the price on the shelf and the price in the register always match. Your costs plummet and customer satisfaction soars.

Telxon's "Wireless Store" concept provides a host of mobile computing and wireless networking solutions that work from your back door through your point-of-sale to help increase productivity, strengthen your bottom line and enhance customer satisfaction. Call 1-800-800-8008 and check us out.

TELX⦀N.

See us at MARKETECHNICS '97 Booth #805

Source: Progressive Grocer (1997, 02, 49).

Figure 7.3   Competing against ESLs

associated "need to establish pricing credibility". Presumably, the hand-held scanner solution worked best if you updated the "master pricing file" to reflect the price at the shelf, since changes in the other direction would require printing a new paper label. Either way, the solution remained highly reliant on the fingers of the store staff to operate the scanner, print, and replace price labels.

The fact that the scanner-based solutions still required manual labor was picked up and used as a further argument in favor of switching to ESLs. "Replacing paper shelf labels, electronic price tags are linked to the store POS computer, ensuring consistency between shelf price and scanner price. The labels also reduce labor and printing costs, improve margins and supplement store applications such as shelf management and computer-assisted ordering" (1993, 06, 18). In particular, emphasis was put on price changes, which were costly to effectuate in a paper-based system: "One of the major benefits of ESLs is eliminating the labor required to post price changes on paper shelf labels" (1994, 08, 136). The price integrity and laborsaving effects of ESLs were repeated throughout the 1990s and early 2000s, but did not result in any major breakthrough for the technology. This is perhaps not that surprising since the period from 1991 to 2006 was one of relative price stability in the US food sector, with annual food inflation rates varying between 1.2 percent (1992) and 3.4 percent (2004). While grocery retailers still engaged in price fixing, in the sense of adjusting their prices, the external pressure to do so during the period was low compared to earlier periods (see Chapters 3 and 4). In the relatively stable US retail market of the 1990s and early 2000s, then, the savings from investing in ESLs were reduced.

By 2010, and with little real growth in ESL use, new arguments were starting to appear in favor of the technology. "In addition to the solution's paperless sustainability benefits, it's also expected to offer significant customer service and product knowledge potential–including promotional information. [...] another step toward better serving our customers with current, best-available prices and the most up-to-date product information" (2009, 11–12, 108). While the basic functionality of ESLs remained largely unchanged, an updated contextualization allowed for new arguments related to both sustainability and customer service. One specific sustainability argument beyond using less paper was that ESLs would allow retailers to "easily and quickly mark down perishable stock to reduce food wastage" (2016, 09, 151). The customer service argument consisted of a whole range of arguments for ESLs in the era of e-commerce and smartphones: "Electronic shelf talkers [...] interact with customers by way of customer-specific and relevant content at the point of decision" (2013, 09, 145); "New digital in-store technologies improve the customer shopping experience and help the retailers better compete against e-commerce" (2016, 09, 150). Here, ESLs and other shelf technologies are linked to the appearance of a new type of challenge for grocery retailers: the advent of e-commerce. In this connection, we also see the addition of new functionalities linked to electronic shelf technologies: "The Powershelf Mobile Network allows retailers to push timely and relevant content to consumers' mobile devices" (2016, 09, 150); "Grocery shelves fitted with wirelessly controlled electronic labels are delivering more real-time product information, the latest prices and personalized information to engaged shoppers' smartphones" (2016, 09, 151). Once again, the interconnections with other in-store technologies and systems are presented as keys to success.

By 2014, a new alternative to investments in store-specific digital signage had entered the scene. Exclusive reliance on paper labels was no longer the only substitute to ESLs since most retail customers now had access to much better screens at the tip of their fingers via their smartphones (2014, 09, 170). Instead of requiring investment in thousands of store-specific miniature screens with limited communication skills, the new solutions sought to make use of the investments that customers had already made, for instance through Bluetooth beacons providing real-time and targeted promotions (2016, 01, 96). Here, then, we see yet another example of the infrastructurization of commercial technology that we saw in Chapter 6, although this time, the original investments were made by the retail customers. While some of the proposed solutions to exploit customers' smartphones inside the retail store were combined with ESLs, many were not. Indeed, this development seems to have resulted in a return to very familiar issues concerning digital (as in fingers-based) shelf display (see Figure 7.4).

Source: *Progressive Grocer* (2014, 09, 170).

Figure 7.4   *Back to the future in shelf labeling*

This revisit of previous issues and/or arguments was not an isolated case. In fact, in 2018, the magazine returned full circle to the original argument for ESLs by noting that the problem of price integrity was still alive and kicking:

> Improving pricing and promotional strategy is a top strategic priority for retailers, [a representative of an ESL provider] notes, but the inability to price match in real time is cited as a contributor to losing customers in-store. "We believe that ESLs can bridge that gap", [he] asserts. "Our solution enables the centralized management of any number of ESLs across any number of stores in seconds. Our ESLs can display product, price, promotion, nutritional information, reviews, stock levels, and much more information that's important to shoppers and store associates." (2018, 12, 85)

While the first argument about price integrity is very familiar, we can also note that some things have changed. First, the price integrity issue is no longer confined to a single store but framed as a problem when operating multiple stores. Second, the original limitation of ESLs when it came to the display of information other than price, which we noted above, seems to have been thoroughly dealt with. Indeed, the development follows a familiar path observable across previous generations of price display technology: in the beginning these featured price cards only, while the advent of label printers allowed the display of much more information (see Chapter 6). Similarly, early LCD-equipped ESLs displayed numbers only whereas recent, matrix-like ESL screens allow the display of much richer information – hence reasserting some measure of retailer control also over quality-related matters. With these developments and improvements, then, ESLs once again seems poised as a price display technology that we will see much more of in the years to come.

* * *

The desire of both equipment suppliers and grocery retailers to engineer fast and easy-to-use price displaying devices has been part of our account from the 1920s up until the latest developments related to ESLs, one century later. Our account also shows that the attempts made to address this issue have followed a quite erratic trajectory. Many innovative solutions have shown little concern for preceding solutions, except for the path-dependent reproduction of certain basic features, such as price tickets and shelf moldings. In this development, we have seen that the digital, in the sense of computerized, was preceded by – and remains accompanied by – the digital, in the sense of numerals (digits) manipulated by fingers (*digitus*). This strengthens our assertion that price display cannot be reduced to electronic signals, not even in the case of ESLs; prices remain defined, manipulated and visualized in a finger-dependent material environment featuring numerals but also other qualitative signs.

Our account of the (still) ongoing introduction of ESLs highlights that the success of an innovation is a problem of both timing and environmental fit. Technologies rarely appear in isolation, or stand alone, but must fit with the wider contexts, systems and infrastructures – or "market agencements" (Callon, 2009; 2016). Innovation, then, is more the expression of a material web than a matter of single inventions. Novelties become successful when they fit with previous solutions and push them further. Consequently, we should abandon the linear progressive conception of technological development. ESLs can be presented both as an alternative to paper price tags or as a development ensuring their continued proliferation, as the widespread use of paper stickers in US supermarkets during the 2000s shows. New technologies do not simply replace old ones, but rather combine with existing ones to gather resources but also constraints. ESLs further articulate certain historical solutions, for instance, they reinforce the value of barcodes and data centers at the shelf level (see Chapter 6). At the same time, other solutions of yesteryear remain, like the paper stickers, which so far have succeeded in hampering the spread of ESLs, perhaps performed better than them, and so on.

More precisely, our findings show that the spread of price tags takes the dual form of *path dependency* and what we propose calling an *interlocking pattern*. New features paradoxically recycle and reinforce previous schemes (see how the introduction of easy price-locking systems reinforced classic price tags and price tag moldings). Our anamnesis of ESLs also unveiled instances of amnesia. Indeed, history proved to be less a matter of cognitive memory than a matter of material traces. The temporal links between technologies do not primarily reside in some form of neural network but in much more concrete machineries. Whereas neural networks are like flexible webs of embedded immaterial relationships, the retail machineries we have described are more like jigsaw puzzles into which new components must fit exactly and interlock with other tangible entities. These interlocks concern entities from the past but also contemporary devices. It is in the retailers' best interest to associate the different tools at their disposal to get the most out of them. In this respect, innovation is a sideways movement: the current in-store digitalization and the peripheral innovations that gradually invade the retail sector (smartphones, beacons, POS systems, etc.) influence the retailers' interest in ESLs, provided that what interlocks with recent additions to the technical infrastructure also fits with what is already in place. But this is neither self-evident nor easily achieved.

The jigsaw puzzle of price display technologies is a complex and dynamic one, made of pieces whose nature and shape evolve constantly and in relation to each other. As we have seen throughout our account, the involved actors evaluate these technologies and their promises in terms of cost savings, revenue generation, and profits. Thus, seemingly brilliant, functional, and innovative devices have little chance of succeeding if the same effects can be obtained at lower cost or if the cost is higher than the payback. This effect is further reinforced by the fact that the costs typically accrue immediately whereas the benefits are postponed into an uncertain future. This constraint partly explains the difficulties met by technologies such as ESLs. Other changing pieces of the puzzle are legal rules. What technology can or cannot do is heavily framed by externally imposed rules such as the item-pricing regulation in the United States. When goods have to be price-marked individually, the need for dynamic price displays at the shelf decreases dramatically. Last but not least, evolving social configurations also take part in the overall agencement: the digitalization of the grocery retail sector gives rise to a modified market infrastructure that affords new forms of marketing and consumer practices, which change the division of labor between the involved actors.

All in all, the history of ESLs provides important insight into the technological dimension of prices. The dynamics of prices is not just a matter of hydraulic-like adjustments between supply and demand, as economic models suggest; it is not just a matter of managerial decisions, as management theories propose; it is not just the expression of cultural, structural, and relational frameworks, as sociological theories posit; and it has not become just a matter of digital speed, as contemporary engineers dream. The history of ESLs shows that digital price displays depend on past and present systems and infrastructures, cost constraints and payback schemes, legal frameworks, and human behavior. It also shows that equipment providers play a hidden yet decisive role in this process and that their contribution to the definition of what a price is (or is not) deserves to be made public beyond the well-known but somewhat secondary contributions of socio-economic forces, legal and political schemes, and managerial decisions.

8. Conclusions

We have come to the end of this journey of exploring a century of price fixing in US grocery retailing. In this book we have inquired into the production and dissemination of prices in mundane markets. We have done so by addressing the question: *how are prices fixed?* We have shown that *fixing* prices has a triple meaning. First, fixing prices is about price *setting* in the classic sense of how they are decided upon and imbued with economic values. It involves the various techniques, approaches and strategies in which a monetary value is attributed to the goods and on the different basis which such attribution occurs: for example, on the basis of costs, other goods, competitors' offerings or governmental policies. Second, as we have emphasized throughout this book, fixing prices is about price *posting* in the sense of how they become attached to goods and materialized in retail settings. This includes the shift from oral and negotiated prices to posted prices in various forms – handwritten, printed, coded and digitally displayed – as well as whether prices are attached to the individual products or to adjacent surfaces such as shelves. Third, and finally, fixing prices is about *adjusting* prices, that is, how prices are modified and changed in relation to material and economic conditions. This highlights that prices are not just set and posted once and for all but are subject to adjustments and repairs, for example linked to sales campaigns or changes in the general price level. Our account suggests that fixing prices rests on the interplay of these three dimensions.

During our century-long chronicle, US grocery price display has undergone significant, and at times dramatic, development. It has shifted from oral communication and negotiation over prices to various forms of price display relying on a plethora of price display technologies. These have in different ways contributed to the setting, posting, and adjusting of prices. While some of the forms of price display we have accounted for have been partially replaced over time, many of them are still coexisting with other previous and later forms of price display; images of contemporary grocery stores include a mixture of price display technologies including handwritten prices, printed price tags, and Electronic Shelf Labels (ESLs). Thus, our account has not only been one of newer forms of price display replacing older ones, but also one of proliferation and multiplication of forms of price display.

When we compare the present with the situation a century ago, we find that some issues that were once considered to belong to the past are now reentering the scene. For example, while oral communication and price dynamism were gradually replaced by various forms of price display in the early years of our account, dynamic pricing and voice communication are again hot topics in contemporary retailing. Indeed, voice communication such as Alexa and Google Voice are estimated to become big business (2018, 02, 84–5; 2019, 06, 142) with implications for how price is communicated. Similarly, as discussed in the previous chapter, for the (now not so) recent technology of ESLs (2016, 09, 150–51; 2017, 01, 97–102), we find similar issues as in the early development of the paper label. For example, the initially impoverished (price only) information displayed by ESLs is increasingly enriched with more qualitative dimensions, a development resembling that of paper labels. Despite a tremendous evolution and development over the past century, price technologies remain an area of continuous development and investment among grocery retailers. For example, in a study of 2019 grocery tech trends in the *Progressive Grocer*, Price Management technologies was on the top of the list of prioritized investments (2019, 11, 36). Thus, after a century we may conclude that we will probably never reach a final solution of the issue of price fixing. A look towards the future reveals that we will be likely to see continuous development over the years to come.

Throughout our account the development of price fixing has been tightly linked to three aspects, those of price fixing practices, price fixing materialities, and price fixing digitalization, which have implied various affordances and mitigations for the trajectory of price fixing. In this concluding chapter, we summarize and discuss the overall findings on price fixing in relation to these three main analytical themes in separate sections. First, we discuss the relationships between the various practices of pricing and the mundane governance of price display to wider market changes and power relationships. Second, we discuss the materiality of prices and its importance for understanding prices and the transformation of price fixing in practice. Third, we discuss the gradual and ongoing digitalization of price fixing and how it contributes to our understanding of the digitalization of markets more generally. Finally, we discuss the implications of these developments and their consequences for markets.

PRICE FIXING PRACTICES

Our account has shown how the practices of price display have developed and how they have engaged a multitude of actors with changing identities and relations over time. It has also highlighted the relationship between such practices and wider market changes. First, price display practice relies on various ideas, strategies and devices. Depending on how prices are conceived and enacted, exchange is shaped differently and with different outcomes for individual market relationships and the wider economy. The early history of price display involved a shift from oral prices, via handwritten prices, to printed price tags and every instance of this transition depended on changing practices. In Chapter 1 we showed how the transition to writing prices required a combination of skills, material objects and the body. In Chapter 2, we particularly inquired into the practices of adjusting prices and the interplay of price technologies that favored price fixity or price flexibility. Moving from verbal and individual price negotiations into public price display transformed grocery retail by replacing close ties and slow encounters with more impersonal and faster transactions. The evolution of price display included a wide range of variants including increasingly offensive ones, such as batch sales and loss leaders. In Chapter 3, we showed how such price cutting practices at the individual level proved highly problematic in the aggregate by both triggering and being triggered by economic deflation, which in turn called for governmental intervention and the introduction of resale price maintenance (RPM) policies. These policies in turn called for new forms of price display but also contributed to shift identities and power relationships between different actors, notably suppliers, grocers, consumers and regulators. Chapters 3 and 4 focused on the practices of price display in relation to wider economic changes through the examples of price cutting strategies and price ceiling policies that among other things resulted in making price display mandatory and introducing multiple referents in price displays (comparing your own prices, competitors' prices, and the government's prices).

Second, while our inquiry into price display practices has been situated at the level of US grocery stores, it becomes clear that such practices are not restricted to the grocery managers and staff. On the contrary, our account shows that the evolution of price display practices includes a number of different actors, including retailers, consumers, manufacturers, equipment suppliers, and regulators. For example, throughout our account, equipment suppliers offered various types of equipment on the basis of promises about how the retailers could in turn attract their consumers. Indeed, this is a key characteristic of the "B2B2C" kind of market we find in grocery retailing, where market devices are sold to retailers (B2B) on the basis of promises to improve the retailer–consumer relationship (B2C) (see above, Chapter 2). The evolution of price display involves retailers and consumers, as well as various suppliers of price devices supporting different forms of retail operations. Thus, in addition to retailers and consumers, it is important to take into account other actors in this B2B2C market that influence retailing in different ways. This is important, not least from a societal perspective, since the devices provided by these actors cannot be seen as neutral technical contrivances obediently serving the retailers and their customers. Rather, as our study shows, they have agency to shape markets with a distinctly formative role on the retail sector, its practices, regulations and performance.

Our account also highlights how various forms of price display technologies have been accompanied by changing roles and power relationships in the setting, posting, and adjusting of prices. For example, we saw in Chapter 3 how price display altered the identities of market actors and the power relationships between them. In Chapter 5, we observed the shifting of labeling power between retailers and manufacturers. In Chapter 6, we saw how different or new price display techniques could redistribute power between these actors: for instance how the possibility to include alphanumerical information on price tickets challenged the manufacturers' monopoly on the "literary" description of goods and widened the retailers' ability to engage in product qualification. In the case of the UPC code, such power struggles also played out between retailers and marketing research firms and consumerist organizations. Subsequently, it also provided the means for reversing power relationships by enabling a "wikization" of product codes. In particular, the emerging market infrastructure around barcodes analyzed in Chapter 6 demonstrates the interdependence of multiple practices and actors. In this case, no single actor was in charge of the development, although the UPC committee tried to exert some control over the process. Rather, it emerged from different projects undertaken by manufacturers, retailers and suppliers of retail equipment and the subsequent collaboration within the UPC committee was later accompanied by further developments and additions, such as ESLs and open product databases.

Third, we have explored the mundane governance of price display and the interlinkages between price display practices and wider market changes. In Chapters 3 and 4, we showed how market actors (public and private) specifically combined efforts at the store level to enact price mechanisms that can control global price movements. These accounts speak directly to the issue of how the economy is governed by showing the merits of combining insights from governance and market studies on how market and public actors concretely combine (or not) their efforts, at the store level, to enact price mechanisms that can control global price movements. According to the traditional paternalistic view on policy formation as well as more recent work in behavioral economics (Stiglitz, 2010), the State works like an engineer who preventively and remotely sets the stage on which market actors then act more or less obediently. Our approach to price regulation instead characterizes the process as one in which the government and the market actors not only co-construct the stage, but in which the specific stage props also take on a life of their own as they are appropriated by market actors. The price ceiling experiments we documented thus suggest that State regulation can be flexible like market competition (via continuous adjustments, amendments, exemptions, suspensions, etc.; Letzler, 1954; Nelson, 1954) and that market competition can be rigid like State regulation (through the introduction of technologies that durably shape price display and price competition).

Our analysis of the interlinkages between price display practices and wider market changes contributes to the recent program aimed at studying patterns of "mundane governance" (Woolgar and Neyland, 2013). By mundane governance, Woolgar and Neyland (2013) mean the innumerable socio-technical arrangements that enact and frame larger political stakes like waste management in cities, security checks in airports, or speed controls on roads. Our account follows a similar pattern. On the one hand, it refuses to view governmentality as the implementation of remote, abstract and large-scale political frames. On the other hand, it also refuses to reduce mundane matters to local contexts and indexical situations. Rather, it shows how public policies and mundane practices combine to reshape both social rules and ordinary practices. There is no better word to describe this approach than the adjective "mundane", since it refers both to the ordinary, local and intimate and to the world at large (from the Latin, *mundo*). Therefore, global issues can be addressed at the local level, and, conversely, the local level shapes the global picture. Price display appears as an excellent illustration of this process, given the dual character of prices, which always come in situated material forms with a general and universal meaning. Showing how these opposites interact and shape each other is a fruitful way to describe how the economy is working, locally and globally.

PRICE FIXING MATERIALITIES

Throughout the book we have shown how changes in the materiality of price display allow for changing pricing practices and vice versa. From the early history of price display where printed price tags replaced handwritten prices (Chapter 1), via swing tags and moldings (Chapter 2), batch price holders (Chapter 3), ceiling price tags (Chapter 4), price stamps and price guns (Chapter 5), UPC codes (Chapter 6) and ESLs (Chapter 7), our account reveals the changing materiality of price display and the associated changes in pricing over the past century. We also see the increasing multiplicity of available forms of price display, particularly visible in Chapter 5, and the gradual move from individual devices towards an emerging infrastructure in which numerous devices are interlinked. This is particularly evident in the emergence of the barcode-based market infrastructure described in Chapter 6. However, this increasing interconnectedness was also accompanied by efforts to disconnect some forms of price display, such as individual item pricing.

While some of the more recent technologies have added to the existing pricing infrastructure, others have challenged elements of that infrastructure. For example, Amazon Go (2020, 08, 76–9) use other technologies such as computer vision, sensor fusion, and RFID, which reduce the significance of barcodes for some of its applications. However, paradoxically and despite these technologies, many of the developments still rest on the existence of paper shelf labels for price display (see Buoentempo, 2019), which in turn has seen both development and resistance throughout the studied time period. Moreover, the convenience, smoothness and seeming invisibility of "touchless retail" is not a move away from materiality but rather the opposite, resting on an increased presence of technologies, which may eventually turn into (silent) infrastructure.

Thus, prices are not just abstract aggregate effects, mathematical figures, cultural values, or economic valuations. While prices are "abstracted" through a variety of devices such as pricing techniques, accounting methods, monitoring instruments, trading protocols, and benchmarking procedures (Callon and Muniesa, 2005), they are also material inscriptions (Beunza et al., 2006; Çalışkan, 2007; Muniesa, 2007) whose characteristics and meaning are highly dependent on the underlying writing surfaces, writing tools, and writing techniques. Price is a prominent theme in economic sociology and a large number of studies have highlighted the cultural, relational and institutional factors involved in price formation (for an overview, see Beckert, 2011). Work on the "anthropology of calculation" has moved beyond the classic psychological, social and cultural dimensions of price by exploring its technological dimension drawing on Callon's (1998) performativity program and actor-network theory. In particular, this line of research has emphasized the importance of material devices in formatting the way markets work and prices are formed (Callon et al., 2007). In a similar fashion, recent work in political sociology has highlighted the role of policy instruments, tools and devices in mediating between policy intentions and outcomes (e.g., Lascoumes and Le Galès, 2007; Meyer and Kearnes, 2013; Woolgar and Neyland, 2013; Dix, 2014). Our study of price fixing in the US grocery sector adds to these efforts of unpacking the role of materiality in the economy.

As shown in Chapter 4, the display of prices was a combined effect of the efforts of the Federal Government and the expertise of retail professionals at the shelf level. As such, price display policies and practices move beyond the classic opposition between micro and macro perspectives, or between the abstract "free market" price mechanism and government intervention. Thus, price setting cannot be restricted to abstract processes of competitive or regulative valuation; it also rests on a concrete dynamic of technological and material configuration. This relates both to policy studies addressing the multiple socio-technical arrangements that contribute to enact public policy (Lascoumes and Le Galès, 2007; Woolgar and Neyland, 2013) and market studies attending to the socio-technical infrastructures and "agencements" (Çalışkan and Callon, 2010) at work behind seemingly spontaneous economic transactions. Whereas the first approach sensitizes us to underlying assumptions about the relation between the governing and the governed (Lascoumes and Le Galès, 2007) and to the local and mundane aspects of governance (Woolgar and Neyland, 2013), the second highlights the "mechanisms by which either values and methods of valuations or institutional arrangements can contribute to processes of 'economization'" (Çalışkan and Callon, 2009, 378). The efforts to govern prices both at the retail and government levels show that the pricing of grocery products is reducible neither to social forces nor to economic rationality, but largely performed through the material display of prices as values, understood in the dual sense of numerical signs and ideological worldviews.

Specifically, our account highlights the role of the material in terms of agential bifurcation. Drawing on actor-network theory, recent policy and market studies alike have stressed the contribution of technical objects as specific yet unfaithful (e.g., Callon et al., 2007; Lascoumes and Le Galès, 2007). Objects rarely do only or exactly what we expect them to; they do it differently and often do more than what was intended. As far as acting differently is concerned, consider Latour's classic example of the heavy weights sometimes attached to hotel keys. This device supports the appeal delegated to it – "please leave the key in the hotel reception" – through an egoistic translation: "I will not distort my pockets" (Latour, 1988). But objects also do more. In most cases, what happens is less univocal and somewhat different from what the key example indicates. The delegated message becomes duplicitous; in Latour's terms, objects act both as intermediaries (i.e., faithful messengers) and as mediators (i.e., autonomous adapters). So, technical objects do what we expect them to; price ceiling tags did indeed display the ceiling price. But while performing the expected, technical objects often do something more or else. They obey the script inscribed in them and overflow it at the same time. Ceiling price tags were put to use to display ceiling prices as part of temporary regulations to combat exceptional inflationary pressures (Letzler, 1954) but this contributed to the generalization of price display and to the use of price tag moldings. The price ceiling policy thus propagated the idea that reference prices should be available not only for regulated goods, but for all goods, thus paving the way for the practice of displaying unit prices, like price per weight, that spread in the following decades (overflow). In other words, it is because the action of price ceilings is duplicitous that it is effective: it is because objects faithfully perform what we ask them to do – for instance, displaying ceiling prices – that we take them as passive and under control, and thus often overlook their additional contributions – for instance, generalizing price display. Thanks in part to the price ceiling rules, retailers and consumers came to regard price display as the new normal. It was still possible for retailers not to display all prices, but from this period onward, this practice was marginalized and US grocery retailers embraced open prices and the various forms of price competition that these afforded.

All in all, early price writing practices shed new light on the tension between the materiality of local price matters and the abstract universality of price values. As such, this complements the two opposing dimensions of price fluctuation and price formulation (Callon, 2013, see above) by suggesting a third dimension of price "digitalization", in the double sense that we have highlighted: from handwritten prices to electronic prices, and more generally to "manipulated" prices, both physically and strategically. Our account shows that we should not restrict our attention to either local or global prices, but pay attention to their co-production and mutual adjustment. The lesson is clear: price cognition and price management are dependent on price writing and price "*main*tenance" ("*main*" means "hand", in French). Hence, we need to account for the materiality of prices, for their *hand*ling, be it through manual operations or through electronic procedures and devices as in contemporary retail settings. Indeed, in the light of the evocative results of our study, we suggest that the latter setting presents itself as an interesting site for future research into contemporary versions of the mode of economic organizing we know as markets.

PRICE FIXING DIGITALIZATION

Today, one of the most significant developments related to prices is their digitalization. However, as our account shows, despite several more recent developments in this area, the digitalization of prices has been a long process including a range of changes from manually written prices to contemporary ESLs. This process of indexing, numberizing and computerizing started with the coding of prices explored in Chapter 1 and continued throughout the period up to the encrypted barcodes and ESLs explored in Chapters 6 and 7. Thus, the evolution of price display is a core aspect of the digitalization of retailing and reveals its long trajectory.

Drawing on the etymology of the term "digital" (from *digitus*, finger or toe), it is clear that the display of prices in retail settings rests on a *digitalization* process right from the beginning, even if this process exhibits fascinating social and technical variations over time. In Chapter 1, we focused on one crucial and transitional period: the move from coded to open prices. This period entailed a double development of price "indexing" in the sense of both using the fingers to write the prices and getting rid of handwriting thanks to novel price tag and printing devices. Approaching these mundane developments illuminated the role of the fingers of the invisible hand that animates the market, so to speak. It showed how mundane fingers contribute to the more abstract economic and social mechanisms that most "price studies" tend to favor. In particular, we showed how the technical framing of price writing reversed the meaning of "indexicality". The chapter describes in detail how grocers should use their fingers to write prices in indexical settings not to illustrate the irreducible idiosyncrasy of particular practices, but to make sure that all practitioners, whatever their local situation, perform the same actions and produce the same effects, every time and everywhere, across the US market.

More generally, price tags are and will always be a matter of dexterity. Fingers have not disappeared in the process of price "digitalization", but have been mobilized differently: handwritten precision has been replaced by handy manipulations. Prices must be both flexible and "fixed", but their manipulation should be reserved to professional hands. This process of price "indexing" never stopped. Today, we talk about digital price tags, and the fingers are still there, both in the word "digital" and in the use of digital devices. "Digital" now means precise, fast and clear price display. But the same devices also save the energy of the grocers' fingers. For instance, with ESLs, retailers just have to click on a mouse with their index to change all the prices at once in a store. Digital prices do not replace fingers but reorient them: the time saved with ESLs can be used to rearrange the store and manually display … paper tags and signs, whose less adjustable character contradicts the promises of flexible digital prices (Soutjis et al., 2017). Prices are a matter of "indexical" fingers: mundane hands working hard behind the invisible hand. But our account of the process of price digitalization also shows that the specific techniques, tools, and circumstances under which these hands are working are consequential for the economy.

Throughout the course of this book, which goes from the digital as "what involves fingers" to the digital as "what rests on electronic information", we did not get fewer and fewer fingers, but paradoxically more and more. Over the years, prices have been written, managed and manipulated by the government (see price ceiling), by the law (see item pricing), by the market (see price competition), by economics and management (see price strategies), by databases, algorithms, loyalty programs, and of course, by the retailers who serve as the working hands for all the others, but also add their own creativity to the overall process of price digitalization.

It would be wrong to assume that the shift was from paper to digital, or that the digital necessarily removed paper solutions. It is rather the contrary. We have shown elsewhere why paper labeling, for matters of cost, size, color, attractiveness (etc.) is far from being outmoded by electronic substitutes (Soutjis et al., 2017). Along these lines one of the most successful solutions, especially in the United States where electronic labels have been rather unsuccessful so far, is the proliferation of temporary paper stickers stuck on existing molded ones to stress a particular dimension praised by retailers. In the 2000s and 2010s, these stickers paperized US grocery stores at a level never seen before.

The introduction of ESLs analyzed in Chapter 7 provided features that help grocers speed price change operations, by simply sending computerized orders to the labels. However, ESLs, far from revolutionizing paper labels, rather reproduced their logic by sharing one of their main limitations: that of a one-sided communication scheme, going from grocer to consumer only. During these past 20 years or so, new interactive devices such as self-scanners, barcode and QR-code reading apps challenged this limitation. These innovations participate to furthering the qualitative dimension of product labels, by offering the possibility to extend and enrich the information offered by the labels present on the goods and in the store, but they also introduce the new promises of interactive communication. They do so by adjusting offers to the consumers' profile (when for instance consumers use loyalty cards and agree to share their sales record and personal information), or by helping consumers to select the information they need (in displaying information organized along treelike menus, rather than all at once). Last but not least, digital interactive labeling devices renew the competition for consumer attention between manufacturers and retailers. In particular, the UPC works as a single key that may be used to offer multiple qualifications, depending on the reading apps and the underlying databases, be they connected to the manufacturer or the retailers who compete through them.

Indeed, the two main breakthroughs of the new portable UPC or QR-code readers are their interactive character and their capacity to connect a given code to distinct databases. This feature allows the database owners to hide, select or disclose information according to their interests: for instance, a manufacturer can insist on his brand, while a retailer may prefer to stress nutrition facts (or any kind of information that he sees as a way to increase his goodwill … or profits). In this respect, the UPC raises again the issue of information transparency in marketing channels, by replacing the old-fashioned coding of prices with a similar game now focused on quality. In this respect, electronic interactive labels may appear as deceptive rather than informative, since the competing presentations of the same products reveal the arbitrariness of those who pretend to inform their customers about what these products are. But the UPC also gives the means to reverse this power and arbitrariness. Recently, consumer activists engaged what could be called a "wikization" of product codes. They developed smartphone apps that use the UPC to connect any given product to an alternative database. This database is organized along an open data, wiki-like logic allowing consumers to perform instant comparisons, but also add or access information that is missing on the product package, like for instance, consumer reviews or ratings, or the traffic light grading of foods based on nutritional facts that French manufacturers fought so hard at the political level (Soutjis, 2020). Of course, these systems are for the moment weak and fragile, almost powerless in comparison with those championed by the grocery industry, hampered as they are by the initiative required to use one's smartphone to access the information. However, they point towards a possible extension to the voice of the consumers themselves and thus towards a further re-agencing of the pricing game.

We are often fascinated by the latest technologies, considering them in isolation as if they work fine and have the ability to completely replace existing solutions. But history shows that most new technologies are complementary, limited and temporary adaptations of preceding devices, rather than radically new. Take the case of ESLs: at first sight, they have the power to outmode and replace existing paper labels by lowering the cost of shelf labeling and by allowing instant price adjustments at the shelf level. But replacing paper labels in the ecology of existing store arrangements, as our account suggests, shows that ESLs have to compromise with remote catalogues on the one side and neighboring paper signs on the other, thus severely reducing their prospects (Soutjis et al., 2017).

The more recent digitalization of price display in some regards takes us back to where we started. Among the promises of ESLs is the transformation to fully flexible, individualized, temporary, and responsive prices. Store automation and digital voice technologies promise to remove tedious activities associated with pricing as well as simplifying the adjustment of prices. However, now like a century ago, practices, materiality and digitalization are intimately intertwined. The changing practices of price fixing a century ago were closely linked to changing materialities as well as constituting the first steps in a long-term development of the digitalization of prices from indexing and towards numberizing and subsequently computerizing of prices.

IMPLICATIONS FOR VALUATION STUDIES AND ECONOMIC SOCIOLOGY

We hope to have shown how the introduction, articulation and transformation of price display changed the (US grocery) economy. On the one hand, the move from individual bargaining practices to price setting and price display practices led to the partial replacement of market-based price fluctuations with managerially/manually controlled prices. This control produced relatively stable economic valuations at the store level. On the other hand, the same price display movement created a greater price visibility, transparency, and publicity that led to fiercer price competition in the market at large. This tension created a need for continuous maintenance efforts aimed at combining the contradictory needs of price fixing as price setting, price posting and price adjusting. Managing this tension required so much effort that handwritten prices quickly proved impractical and a wide range of handy devices were introduced with features that would reduce the tension. Since then and as we have shown, these features have been ceaselessly modified and improved, resulting in further changes to the (US grocery) economy.

Our research complements the few extant studies that go beyond the abstract mathematical dimension of prices to emphasize their conventional and material qualities (Grandclément, 2004; Beunza et al., 2006; Muniesa, 2007; Aspers and Beckert, 2011). Specifically, we have shown how the material dimension of prices contributes to the construction of different price mechanisms (Aspers and Beckert, 2011) and to the proliferation of various price-based valuation strategies (Stark, 2009). We did so by historicizing price formulation, illustrating how the continuous introduction and spread of seemingly mundane technical devices for price display contributed to enact quite specific but different pricing regimes in the grocery retail market. Moreover, we show how the retailers and their advisors, as well as the competing manufacturers of retail equipment, reflexively assessed the consequences of these regimes to highlight the merits or shortcomings of specific solutions. We have argued that well-working markets critically hinge on the reflexive efforts of market actors at large to continually test the consequences of and revise the particular price mechanisms that are being enacted. As such, we offer a more specific formulation of Callon's (2009) general contention that well-working markets are those capable of handling their own overflows.

We have moved beyond previous studies of market devices that mostly locate technology before, around, or behind prices, as in the Black and Scholes formula equipping derivative markets (MacKenzie and Millo, 2003), the "credit score card" instrumenting the calculation of interest rates (Poon, 2007), or the pricing algorithms that animate stock prices (Muniesa, 2007). We have shown how policy devices can take on a life of their own as a result of being appropriated, refined and transformed by specific market actors – in our case suppliers of "retail market equipment" – whose expertise lies in supporting the ongoing organizing of the area subject to policy intervention.

In this book, we have moved beyond the price/quality dichotomy that is often implicit within valuation studies, by paying distinct attention to the qualities of prices themselves in the sense of how they are represented and displayed. Thus, we complement previous studies that focus on the multiplicity (Çalışkan, 2009) and materiality (Beunza et al., 2006; Grandclément, 2004; Muniesa, 2007) of prices. Our contribution to the literature on prices builds on Çalışkan's (2007; 2009) notion of "prosthetic prices" – prices that serve as referents for other prices. Like Çalışkan, we show that "global" price movements rest on local actors, practices and devices. However, we complement his work by stressing the material display of prices rather than how their formation reflects economic values (Knorr Cetina, 2006; Grandclément, 2004; Preda, 2006). While Çalışkan's use of prosthesis is not precisely focused on the materiality of prices (see Çalışkan, 2009, 246), our study links the concept of prosthesis squarely to the material qualities of prices. More specifically, we demonstrate that price display techniques play a decisive role in the definition of price levels and also contribute to enact specific versions of the market economy.

Our book thus contributes not only to the anthropology of calculation, but also to the broader anthropology of markets: the socio-material processes of pricing/valuation – with a focus on price fixing – and the associated mundane governance of prices illustrate moments of dispute and contention over valuation in the marketization of grocery products. Here, the history of price display meets Dewey-inspired valuation studies; values are not absolute, intrinsic qualities but emerge from situated valuation practices (Dewey, 1934, 309–25). Specifically, we show how the setting and display of prices transformed both the character of market competition and the identities of the involved actors (see Antal et al., 2015, 2–3). Hence, our account of how price tag technologies and the contested practices linked to them performed or co-configured the US grocery market assemblage goes beyond Granovetter's (1985) notion of the social embeddedness of economic action; it illustrates how markets and their price setting technologies indeed contribute to transform society, notably by promoting a transaction-oriented, rather than relation-based economy.

For instance, our "archaeology" of price display techniques reveals the polyscopic character of prices in retail settings. Contrary to the common wisdom that a given good in a given market has a single price, as in the famous "law of one price" (Isard, 1977; Baffes, 1991), our study supports and complements Çalışkan's insistence on the multiplicity of prices (Çalışkan, 2007; 2009). Throughout this book, we have seen that price display often combines two prices, like the unit price and the package price for a given bundle, the special price and the regular price for a given promotion, or the ceiling price and the actual price during the postwar inflation period. In each of these pairs of prices one works as a prosthetic price – a reference price that allows the customer to appreciate what is on offer. However, the fact that both prices are presented simultaneously using the same material device contributes both to spread the logic of the prosthesis and the acceptability of the offered price: the logic of price display overshadows that of price setting. Price display is thus stereoscopic at the shelf level – the price offered + a reference price to which the former can be compared – and polyscopic at the global level, given the multiplicity of references that can be selected to stage such price "duos". At first sight, this observation just accounts for the mundane details of price display. But on second thought, it has tremendous implications, by unveiling that prices are not one-dimensional. Until recently, the multidimensional nature of the economy was associated with the multiplicity of different "orders of worth" along which goods can be "valued", suggesting that the market and its price dimension was just one possible such order (Boltanski and Thévenot, 2006; Stark, 2009). Our study supports Çalışkan's intuition that the price itself is multidimensional. This means that different types of price competition and, indeed, different economies are enacted depending on which reference prices market actors use and implement at the shelf level.

At the most general level, our account serves to underscore that the relationship between economy and society at a given point is not only sociopolitical but also technological in character. By combining Callon-inspired market studies, Çalışkan's ethnography of price setting, and Woolgar and Neyland's mundane governance, we show that price regulation cannot be restricted to the control of abstract one-dimensional prices or the imposition of external rules on more or less reluctant economic actors, as proposed by economic theory. Instead, the efforts of authorities and market actors in the US grocery sector demonstrate that price regulation depends on the development of technologies capable of reinventing price competition as part of mundane market practices. In Chapters 3 and 4, we saw how they did so by replacing business-to-business price comparisons with comparisons of business to government-controlled price cutting strategies or "ceiling prices", by contributing to the generalization of price display, and by introducing qualitative elements into price labeling. Such efforts to control price fluctuations involve the articulation of business and government expertise, and more importantly, the decisive contribution of price tag manufacturers who devise the technical infrastructures that bridge, animate and transform the two sides.

Moreover, our study contributes to the field of valuation studies by showing that valuation is the outcome of combining specific practices, ad hoc market devices and (now) digitalized solutions, rather than of the somewhat abstract cultural or qualitative processes outlined in the literature. In other words, our findings show price formation as a historically situated socio-technical phenomenon rather than as the product of immaterial and historically constant market forces. Against this backdrop, the use of an idealized framework to first establish and then correct market failures in order to get The Market to work properly appears an unlikely panacea for generating well-working markets. Thus, while recent writings on market design have embraced the idea that the functioning of markets depends on detailed and specific rules (Roth, 2007), they are still handicapped by their reluctance to let go of the ideal, perfectly competitive market as the historically constant gold standard. Here, the observed efforts over time of a variety of market actors to promote, adopt, question, oppose and modify specific pricing technologies hint at an alternative approach. Drawing on Latour's (1996) concept of contextualization, we suggest that the long-term functioning of any market (among other things) hinges on successfully encouraging market actors to continually test the contextualizations of particular price mechanisms, recontextualize them to highlight their shortcomings, and develop alternative solutions. While the long-term effect of this process is likely to be reminiscent of employing a Foucauldian "eventalization" strategy to show the irreducible complexity and idiosyncrasy of price formulation (Foucault, 1991), our account adds a critical reflexive component by suggesting that such efforts should be integrated into the market itself, rather than externally imposed by the researcher.

In conclusion, studies of the economy need to historicize market practices; researchers need to avoid myopic views influenced by the sweeping formulations of economic theory. It is easy to overlook historical detail and simply assume things have always been one way or the other. We have shown that even the formation of prices, which is at the heart of the theoretical edifice in economics, is historically situated. We have also demonstrated that it rests on local practices and mundane technologies that until now have been curiously overlooked and that certainly warrant further scrutiny.

References

Adler, M.H. (1973). *The Writing Machine: A History of the Typewriter*. London: George Allen & Unwin.

Akerlof, G.A. (1970). The market for "lemons": Quality uncertainty and the market mechanism. *Quarterly Journal of Economics*, 84(3), 488–500.

Anderson, O.E. (1953). *Refrigeration in America*. Princeton, NJ: Princeton University Press.

Ansoff, H.I. (1957). Strategies for diversification. *Harvard Business Review*, 35(5), 113–24.

Antal, A., Hutter, M. and Stark, D. (eds) (2015). *Moments of Valuation: Exploring Sites of Dissonance*. Oxford: Oxford University Press.

Araujo, L. (2007). Markets, market-making and marketing. *Marketing Theory*, 7(3), 211–26.

Araujo, L. and Kjellberg, H. (2015). Forming cognitions by investing in a form: Frequent Flyer Programs in US air travel post-deregulation (1981–1991). *Industrial Marketing Management*, 48, 68–78.

Araujo, L. and Kjellberg, H. (2016). Enacting novel agencements: The case of Frequent Flyer schemes in the US airline industry (1981–1991). *Consumption Markets & Culture*, 19(1), 92–110.

Aspers, P. and Beckert, J. (2011). Value in markets. In J. Beckert and P. Aspers (eds), *The Worth of Goods: Valuation and Pricing in the Economy* (pp. 3–40). Oxford: Oxford University Press.

Austin, J.L. (1962). *How to Do Things with Words*. London: Oxford University Press.

Baffes, J. (1991). Some further evidence on the law of one price: The law of one price still holds. *American Journal of Agricultural Economics*, 73(4), 1264–73.

Baker, W. (1984). The social structure of a national securities market. *American Journal of Sociology*, 89(4), 775–811.

Barberis, N.C. (2013). Thirty years of prospect theory in economics: A review and assessment. *Journal of Economic Perspectives*, 27(1), 173–96.

Barrey, S. (2006). Formation et calcul des prix: Le travail de tarification dans la grande distribution. *Sociologie du Travail*, 48(2), 142–58.

Barrey, S., Cochoy, F. and Dubuisson-Quellier, S. (2000). Designer, packager et merchandiser: Trois professionnels pour une même scène marchande. *Sociologie du Travail*, 42(3), 457–82.

Basu, A. and Vitharana, P. (2009). Research note: Impact of customer knowledge heterogeneity on bundling strategy. *Marketing Science*, 28(4), 792–801.

Becker, H.S. (1963). *Outsiders: Studies in the Sociology of Deviance*. New York: The Free Press of Glencoe.

Beckert, J. (2011). Where do prices come from? Sociological approaches to price formation. *Socio-Economic Review*, 9(4), 757–86.

Beckert, J. (2016). *Imagined Futures. Fictional Expectations and Capitalist Dynamics*. Cambridge, MA: Harvard University Press.

Beckert, J. and Aspers, P. (eds) (2011). *The Worth of Goods: Valuation and Pricing in the Economy*. Oxford: Oxford University Press.

Beeching, W.A. (1974). *Century of the Typewriter*. New York: Heinemann.

Bergen, M., Levy, D., Ray, S., Rubin, P.H. and Zeliger, B. (2008). When little things mean a lot: On the inefficiency of item-pricing laws. *Journal of Law and Economics*, 51(2), 209–50.

Bernanke, B.S. and Mishkin, F.S. (1997). Inflation targeting: A new framework for monetary policy? National Bureau of Economic Research, Working Paper 5893, Cambridge, MA.

Beunza, D., Hardie, I. and MacKenzie, D. (2006). A price is a social thing: Towards a material sociology of arbitrage. *Organization Studies*, 27(5), 721–45.

Biswas, A., Dutta, S. and Pullig, C. (2006). Low price guarantees as signals of lowest price: The moderating role of perceived price dispersion. *Journal of Retailing*, 82(3), 245–57.

Boltanski, L. and Thévenot, L. (2006). *On Justification*. Princeton, NJ: Princeton University Press.

Bowker, G.C. and Star, S.L. (1999). *Sorting Things Out: Classification and its Consequences*. Cambridge, MA: MIT Press.

Bowker, G.C., Baker, K., Millerand, F. and Ribes, D. (2010). Toward information infrastructure studies: Ways of knowing in a networked environment. In J. Hunsinger, L. Klastrup and M. Allen (eds), *International Handbook of Internet Research* (pp. 97–117). New York: Springer.

Bowlby, R. (2000). *Carried Away: The Invention of Modern Shopping*. London: Faber & Faber.

Buontempo, F. (2019). Each Amazon Go store I visited in NYC offered something unique, and it made me realize that various retailers should be worried. *Business Insider*, December 19. Available at: https://www.businessinsider.com/we-compared -nyc-amazon-go-stores-each-offered-something-unique-2019-12 (accessed 21 June 2022).

Burr, T.C. (2014). Market-widening: Shaping total market demand for French and American bicycles circa 1890. *Marketing Theory*, 14(1), 19–34.

Butler, J. (2010). Performative agency. *Journal of Cultural Economy*, 3(2), 147–61.

Çalışkan, K. (2007). Price as a market device: Cotton trading in Izmir Mercantile Exchange. In M. Callon, Y. Millo and F. Muniesa (eds), *Market Devices* (pp. 241–60). Oxford: Blackwell.

Çalışkan, K. (2009). The meaning of price in world markets. *Journal of Cultural Economy*, 2(3), 239–68.

Çalışkan, K. and Callon, M. (2009). Economization, Part 1: Shifting attention from the economy towards processes of economization. *Economy and Society*, 38(3), 369–98.

Çalışkan, K. and Callon, M. (2010). Economization, Part 2: A research programme for the study of markets. *Economy and Society*, 39(1), 1–32.

Callon, M. (1986). Some elements for a sociology of translation: Domestication of the scallops and the fishermen of St Brieuc Bay. In J. Law (ed.), *Power, Action and Belief: A New Sociology of Knowledge?* (pp. 196–223). London: Routledge & Kegan Paul.

Callon, M. (ed.) (1998). *The Laws of the Markets*. Oxford: Blackwell.

Callon, M. (2009). Civilizing markets: Carbon trading between in vitro and in vivo experiments. *Accounting, Organizations and Society*, 34(3–4), 535–48.

Callon, M. (2010). Performativity, misfires and politics. *Journal of Cultural Economy*, 3(2), 163–9.

Callon, M. (2013). Qu'est-ce qu'un agencement marchand? In M. Callon, M. Akrich, S. Dubuisson-Quellier, C. Grandclément, A. Hennion, B. Latour, A. Mallard et al. (eds), *Sociologie des Agencements Marchands* (pp. 325–440). Paris: Presses des Mines.

Callon, M. (2016). Revisiting marketization: From interface-markets to market-agencements. *Consumption Markets & Culture*, 19(1), 17–37.

Callon, M. and Law, J. (2005). On qualculation, agency, and otherness. *Environment and Planning D: Society and Space*, 23(5), 717–33.

Callon, M. and Muniesa, F. (2005). Economic markets as calculative collective devices. *Organization Studies*, 26(8), 1229–50.

Callon, M., Méadel, C. and Rabeharisoa, V. (2002). The economy of qualities. *Economy and Society*, 31(2), 194–217.

Callon, M., Millo, Y. and Muniesa, F. (eds) (2007). *Market Devices*. Oxford: Blackwell.

Camerer, C.F. and Thaler, R.H. (1995). Anomalies: Ultimatums, dictators and manners. *Journal of Economic Perspectives*, 9(2), 209–19.

Camerer, C.F., Loewenstein, G. and Rabin, M. (eds) (2004). *Advances in Behavioral Economics*. Princeton, NJ: Princeton University Press.

Carlisle, R. (2004). *Scientific American Inventions and Discoveries*. Hoboken, NJ: John Wiley & Sons.

Chakrabarti, R., Finch, J., Kjellberg, H., Lernborg, C.M. and Pollock, N. (2016). From market devices to market infrastructures. Paper presented at the 4th Interdisciplinary Market Studies Workshop, St Andrews.

Chamberlain, E. (1933). *The Theory of Monopolistic Competition*. Cambridge, MA: Harvard University Press.

Chandler, A.D., Jr (1977). *The Visible Hand: The Managerial Revolution in American Business*. Cambridge, MA: The Belknap Press of Harvard University Press.

Chandler, A.D., Jr (1990). *Scale and Scope. The Dynamics of Industrial Capitalism*. Cambridge, MA: The Belknap Press of Harvard University Press.

Chen, S.-F.S., Monroe, K.B. and Lou, Y.-C. (1998). The effects of framing price promotion messages on consumers' perceptions and purchase intentions. *Journal of Retailing*, 74(3), 353–72.

Chimenti, G. (2020). Conceptual controversies at the boundaries between markets: The case of ridesharing. *Consumption Markets & Culture*, 23(2), 130–53.

Cialdini, R. (1984). *Influence. The Psychology of Persuasion*. New York: William Morrow & Company.

Cochoy, F. (2002). *Une Sociologie du Packaging ou l'Ane de Buridan Face au Marché* [*A Sociology of Packaging, or Buridan's Ass Facing the Market*]. Paris: Presses Universitaires de France.

Cochoy, F. (2004). Is the modern consumer a Buridan's donkey? Product packaging and consumer choice. In K. Ekström and H. Brembeck (eds), *Elusive Consumption* (pp. 205–27). Oxford: Berg.

Cochoy, F. (2008a). Calculation, qualculation, calqulation: Shopping cart arithmetic, equipped cognition and the clustered consumer. *Marketing Theory*, 8(1), 15–44.

Cochoy, F. (2008b). Hansel and Gretel at the grocery store: *Progressive Grocer* and the little American consumers (1929–1959). *Journal of Cultural Economy*, 1(2), 45–163.

Cochoy, F. (2009). Driving a shopping cart from STS to business, and the other way around. On the introduction of shopping carts in American grocery stores (1936–1959). *Organization*, 16(1), 31–55.

Cochoy, F. (2015a). *On the Origins of Self-Service*. Abingdon: Routledge.

Cochoy, F. (2015b). *Une Histoire du Ski. Aluminium, Gens de Glisse et "Coopétition"*. Mirabeau: Editions RF2C.

Cochoy, F. (2020). Open-display and the "re-agencing" of the American economy: Lessons from a "pico-geography" of grocery stores (United States, 1922–1932). *Environment and Planning A: Economy and Space*, 52(1), 48–172.

Cochoy, F. and Dubuisson-Quellier, S. (2013). The sociology of market work. *Economic Sociology, the European Electronic Newsletter*, 15(1), 4–11.

Cochoy, F. and Soutjis, B. (2020). Back to the future of digital price display: Analyzing patents and other archives to understand contemporary market innovations. *Social Studies of Science*, 50(1), 3–29.

Cochoy, F., Hagberg, J. and Kjellberg, H. (2018). The technologies of price display: Mundane retail price governance in the early 20th century. *Economy and Society*, 47(4), 572–606.

Cochoy, F., Hagberg, J. and Kjellberg, H. (2019). The ethno-graphy of prices: On the fingers of the invisible hand (1922–1947). *Organization*, 26(4), 492–516.

Cochoy, F., Hagberg, J. and Kjellberg, H. (2020). The tower of labels: Labelling goods in the US grocery store (1922–2018). In B. Laurent and A. Mallard (eds), *Labelling the Economy* (pp. 233–70). Singapore: Palgrave Macmillan.

Cochoy, F., Hagberg, J. and Kjellberg, H. (2021). Price display technologies and price ceiling policies: Governing prices in the WWII and postwar US economy (1940–1953). *Socio-Economic Review*, 19(1), 133–56.

Cochoy, F., Hagberg, J. and Kjellberg, H. (2022). Reputation, trust and credit: Cultivating shopping practices in early twentieth-century US grocery stores. In V. Howard (ed.), *A Cultural History of Shopping, Volume 6: A Cultural History of Shopping in the Modern Age* (Chapter 7). London: Bloomsbury Academic.

Cochoy, F., Hagberg, J., Petersson-McIntyre, M. and Sörum, N. (eds) (2017). *Digitalizing Consumption: How Devices Shape Consumer Culture*. London: Routledge.

Cochoy, F., Smolinski, J. and Vayre, J.-S. (2016). From marketing to "market-things" and "market-ITing": Accounting for technicized and digitalized consumption. In B. Czarniawska (ed.), *A Research Agenda for Management and Organization Studies* (pp. 26–37). Cheltenham, UK and Northampton, MA, USA: Edward Elgar Publishing.

Cochran, T.C. (1972). *Business in American Life: A History*. New York: McGraw-Hill Education.

Commons, J.R. (1934). *Institutional Economics: Its Place in Political Economy*. New York: Routledge.

Cooper, R. and Kaplan, R.S. (1988). Measure costs right: Make the right decisions. *Harvard Business Review*, 66(5), 96–103.

Cova, B. and Cova, V. (2012). On the road to prosumption: Marketing discourse and the development of consumer competencies. *Consumption Markets & Culture*, 15(2), 149–68.

David, P.A. (1985). Clio and the Economics of QWERTY. *American Economic Review*, 75(2), 332–7.

Démurger, S. (2001). Infrastructure development and economic growth: An explanation for regional disparities in China? *Journal of Comparative Economics*, 29(1), 95–117.

Denis, J. and Pontille, D. (2019). Why do maintenance and repair matter? In A. Blok, I. Farías and C. Roberts (eds), *The Routledge Companion to Actor-Network Theory* (pp. 283–93). Abingdon: Routledge.

Deutsch, T.A. (2001). Making change at the grocery store: Government, grocers, and the problem of women's autonomy in the creation of Chicago's supermarkets, 1920–1950. PhD dissertation, University of Wisconsin-Madison.

Deutsch, T.A. (2004). Making change at the grocery store: Government, grocers, and the problem of women's autonomy in the creation of Chicago's supermarkets, 1920–1950. *Enterprise & Society*, 5(4), 607–16.

Deutsch, T.A. (2010). Exploring new insights into retail history. *Journal of Historical Research in Marketing*, 2(1), 130–38.

Dewey, J. (1934). *Art as Experience*. New York: Minton, Balch & Co.

Dix, G. (2014). Expressing concerns over the incentive as a public policy device. In S. Geiger, D. Harrison, H. Kjellberg and A. Mallard (eds), *Concerned Markets: Economic Ordering for Multiple Values* (pp. 19–45). Cheltenham, UK and Northampton, MA, USA: Edward Elgar Publishing.

Dourish, P. (1922). *The Stuff of Bits. An Essay on the Materialities of Information*. Cambridge, MA: MIT Press.

Dubuisson-Quellier, S. (2013). *Ethical Consumption*. Halifax: Fernwood Publishing.

Duffy, K., Reid, E. and Finch, J. (2020). Sold out? Reconfiguring consumer demand through the secondary digital ticket market. *Consumption Markets & Culture*, 23(2), 174–94.

Du Gay, P. (2004). Self-service: Retail, shopping and personhood. *Consumption Markets & Culture*, 7(2), 149–63.

Dujarier, M.A. (2016). The three sociological types of consumer work. *Journal of Consumer Culture*, 16(2), 1–17.

Durkheim, E. (1950). *The Rules of Sociological Method*. New York: The Free Press.

Edwards, P., Jackson, S., Chalmers, M., Bowker, G.C., Borgman, C., Ribes, D., Burton, M. et al. (2013). *Knowledge Infrastructures: Intellectual Frameworks and Research Challenges*. Ann Arbor, MI: Deep Blue.

Eichengreen, B. and Garber, P.M. (1991). Before the accord: U.S. monetary-financial policy, 1945–51. In G. Hubbard (ed.), *Financial Markets and Financial Crisis* (pp. 175–206). National Bureau of Economic Research, Chicago, IL: University of Chicago Press.

Eisenstein, E. (2005). *The Printing Revolution in Early Modern Europe*, 2nd edn. Cambridge: Cambridge University Press.

Fellman, S. and Propp, A. (2013). Lost in the archive: The business historian in distress. In B. Czarniawska and O. Löfgren (eds), *Coping with Excess: How Organizations, Communities and Individuals Manage Overflows* (pp. 216–43). Cheltenham, UK and Northampton, MA, USA: Edward Elgar Publishing.

Fligstein, N. (1990). *The Transformation of Corporate Control*. Cambridge, MA: Harvard University Press.

Fligstein, N. (1996). Markets as politics: A political-cultural approach to market institutions. *American Sociological Review*, 61(4), 656–73.

Foucault, M. (1991). Questions of method: An interview with Michel Foucault. In G. Burchell, C. Gordon and P. Miller (eds), *The Foucault Effect: Studies in Governmentality* (pp. 73–86). London: Harvester Wheatsheaf.

Friedman, M. (1960). *A Program for Monetary Stability*. New York: Fordham University Press.

Frohlich, X. (2017). The informational turn in food politics: The US FDA's nutrition label as information infrastructure. *Social Studies of Science*, 47(2), 145–71.

Fuentes, C., Bäckström, K. and Svingstedt, A. (2017). Smartphones and the reconfiguration of retailscapes: Stores, shopping and digitalization. *Journal of Retailing and Consumer Services*, 39(C), 270–78.

Garfinkel, H. (1967). *Studies in Ethnomethodology*. Englewood Cliffs, NJ: Prentice Hall.

Giddens, A. (1993). *New Rules of Sociological Method*. Cambridge: Polity Press.

Gijsbrechts, E. (1993). Prices and pricing research in consumer marketing: Some recent developments. *International Journal of Research in Marketing*, 10(2), 115–51.

Goldberg, P. and Knetter, M. (1997). Goods prices and exchange rates: What have we learned? *Journal of Economic Literature*, 35(1997), 1243–72.

Gordon, R.J. (1977). Recent developments in the theory of inflation and unemployment. In E. Lundberg (ed.), *Inflation Theory and Anti-Inflation Policy* (pp. 42–71). London: Palgrave Macmillan.

Grandclément, C. (2004). Bundles of prices: Marketing and pricing in French supermarkets. Paper presented at the 4S-EASST Conference, Paris.

Grandclément, C. (2006). Wheeling food products around the store … and away: The invention of the shopping cart, 1936–1953. Paper presented at the Food Chains Conference: *Provisioning, Technology, and Science*, Hagley Museum and Library, Wilmington, Delaware, 2–4 November. Available at: http://www.csi.ensmp.fr/Items/WorkingPapers/Download/DLWP.php?wp=WP_CSI_006.pdf.

Grandclément, C. (2008). Vendre sans vendeurs: Sociologie des dispositifs d'achalandage en supermarché. Thèse pour le doctorat en socio-économie de l'innovation. Paris: École Nationale Supérieure des Mines de Paris.

Granovetter, M. (1985). Economic action and social structure: The problem of embeddedness. *American Journal of Sociology*, 91(3), 481–510.

Grewal, D., Marmorstein, H. and Sharma, A. (1996). Communicating price information through semantic cues: The moderating effects of situation and discount size. *Journal of Consumer Research*, 23(2), 148–55.

Grewal, D., Monroe, K.B. and Krishnan, R. (1998). The effects of price-comparison advertising on buyers' perceptions of acquisition value, transaction value, and behavioral intentions. *Journal of Marketing*, 62(2), 46–59.

Grossman, S.J. and Stiglitz, J.E. (1976). Information and competitive price systems. *American Economic Review*, 66(2), 246–53.

Güth, W., Schmittberger, R. and Schwarze, B. (1982). An experimental analysis of ultimatum bargaining. *Journal of Economic Behavior and Organization*, 3(4), 367–88.

Hagberg, J. and Kjellberg, H. (2015). How much is it? Price representation practices in retail markets. *Marketing Theory*, 15(2), 179–99.

Hagberg, J. and Kjellberg, J. (2020). Digitalized markets. *Consumption Markets & Culture*, 23(2), 97–109.

Hagberg, J., Kjellberg, H. and Cochoy, F. (2020). The role of market devices for price and loyalty strategies in 20th century U.S. grocery stores. *Journal of Macromarketing*, 40(2), 201–20.

Hagberg, J., Sundstrom, M. and Egels-Zanden, N. (2016). The digitalization of retailing: An exploratory framework. *International Journal of Retail & Distribution Management*, 44(7), 694–712.

Hanna, R.C., Lemon, K.N. and Smith, G.E. (2019). Is transparency a good thing? How online price transparency and variability can benefit firms and influence consumer decision making. *Business Horizons*, 62(2), 227–36.

Hanson, P. (2016). The man who invented Scotch tape. *Priceonomics*. See https://en.wikipedia.org/wiki/Richard_Gurley_Drew.

Hansson, L. (2017). Promoting ethical consumption: The construction of smartphone apps as "ethical" choice prescribers. In F. Cochoy, J. Hagberg, M. Petersson-McIntyre and N. Sörum (eds), *Digitalizing Consumption: How Devices Shape Consumer Culture* (pp. 103–21). London: Routledge.

Harper, R.H.R. (1998). *Inside the IMF: An Ethnography of Documents, Technology and Organisational Action*. San Diego, CA: Academic Press.

Hawkins, G. (2010). Plastic materialities. In B. Braun and S.J. Whatmore (eds), *Technoscience, Democracy and Public Life* (pp. 119–38). Minneapolis, MN, USA and London, UK: University of Minnesota Press.

Hawkins, G. (2018). The skin of commerce: Governing through plastic food packaging. *Journal of Cultural Economy*, 11(5), 386–403.

Hayek, F.A. (1945). The use of knowledge in society. *American Economic Review*, 35(4), 519–30.

Hirschman, A.O. (2002). *Passions and Interests: Political Party Concepts of American Democracy*. Princeton, NJ: Princeton University Press.

Hollander, S.C. (1965). Entrepreneurs test the environment: A long run view of grocery pricing. In P.D. Bennet (ed.), *Marketing and Economic Development: Proceedings* (pp. 516–27). 1–3 September, Chicago: American Marketing Association.

Howard, V. (2015). *From Main Street to Mall: The Rise and Fall of the American Department Store*. Philadelphia, PA: University of Pennsylvania Press.

Hughes, P.T. (1983). *Networks of Power: Electrification in Western Society, 1880–1930*. Baltimore, MD: Johns Hopkins University Press.

Ingold, T. (2008). Anthropology is *not* ethnography. *Proceedings of the British Academy*, 154, 69–92.

Isard, P. (1977). How far can we push the "law of one price"? *American Economic Review*, 67(5), 942–8.

Jacoby, J.R.W. and Olson, J.C. (1977). Consumer response to price: An attitudinal, information processing perspective. In Y. Wind and P. Greenberg (eds), *Moving Ahead with Attitude Research* (pp. 73–86). Chicago, IL: American Marketing Association.

Jenkins, R.V. (1975). Technology and the market: George Eastman and the origins of mass amateur photography. *Technology and Culture*, 16(1), 1–19.

Johnson, S. (2016). Want to know what virtual reality might become? Look at the past. *The New York Times*, 3 November. Available at: http://www.nytimes.com/2016/11/06/magazine/want-to-knowwhat-virtual-reality-might-become-look-to-the-past.html?r=0.

Kahneman, D. and Tversky, A. (1979). Prospect theory: An analysis of decision under risk. *Econometrica*, 47(2), 263–91.

Kahneman, D., Knetsch, J.L. and Thaler, R.H. (1990). Experimental tests of the endowment effect and the Coase Theorem. *Journal of Political Economy*, 98(6), 1325–48.

Karolefski, J. (2016). Are U.S. grocery stores ready for electronic shelf labels? *Progressive Grocer*, 11 October. Available at: https://progressivegrocer.com/are-us-grocery-stores-ready-electronic-shelf-labels (accessed 2 October 2019).

Karpik, L. (2010). *Valuing the Unique: The Economics of Singularities*. Princeton, NJ: Princeton University Press.

Kato, H., Tan, K.T. and Chai, D. (2010). *Barcodes for Mobile Devices*. Cambridge: Cambridge University Press.

Kienzler, M. and Kowalkowski, C. (2017). Pricing strategy: A review of 22 years of marketing research. *Journal of Business Research*, 78, 101–10.

Kjellberg, H. (2004). Wirsälls Marginalanteckning, Eller: Vem Ska Bestämma Priset på Varan? In C.F. Helgesson, H. Kjellberg and A. Liljenberg (eds), *Den Där Marknaden: Om Utbyten, Normer och Bilder* (pp. 205–33). Lund: Studentlitteratur.

Kjellberg, H., Hagberg, J. and Cochoy, F. (2019). Thinking market infrastructure: Barcode scanning in the US grocery retail sector, 1967–2010. In M. Kornberger, G.C. Bowker, J. Elyachar, A. Mennicken, P. Miller, J.R. Nucho and N. Pollock (eds), *Thinking Infrastructures* (pp. 207–32). Bingley: Emerald Publishing.

Knorr Cetina, K. (2006). The market. *Theory, Culture and Society*, 23(2–3), 551–6.

Lancaster, K.J. (1966). A new approach to consumer theory. *Journal of Political Economy*, 74(2), 132–57.

Larkin, B. (2013). The politics and poetics of infrastructure. *Annual Review of Anthropology*, 42, 327–43.

Lascoumes, P. and Le Galès, P. (2007). Introduction: Understanding public policy through its instruments—from the nature of instruments to the sociology of public policy instrumentation. *Governance*, 20(1), 1–21.

Latour, B. (1987). *Science in Action: How to Follow Scientists and Engineers Through Society*. Cambridge, MA: Harvard University Press.

Latour, B. (1988). Mixing humans and nonhumans together: The sociology of a door-closer. *Social Problems*, 35(3), 298–310.

Latour, B. (1996). *Aramis or the Love of Technology*. Cambridge, MA: Harvard University Press.

Latour, B. (2005). *Reassembling the Social*. Cambridge, MA: Harvard University Press.

Latour, B. and Woolgar, S. (1979). *Laboratory Life, the Construction of Scientific Facts*. London, UK and Beverly Hills, CA, USA: SAGE.

Lave, J., Murtaugh, M. and de la Rocha, O. (1984). The dialectic of arithmetic in grocery shopping. In B. Rogoff and J. Lave (eds), *Everyday Cognition: Its Development in Social Context* (pp. 67–94). Cambridge, MA: Harvard University Press.

Le Roy Ladurie, E. (1975). *Montaillou, Village Occitan de 1294 à 1324*. Paris: Editions Gallimard.

Letzler, A. (1954). The general ceiling price regulation—problems of coverage and exclusion. *Law and Contemporary Problems*, 19(Fall), 486–521.

MacKenzie, D. (2004). The big, bad wolf and the rational market: Portfolio insurance, the 1987 crash and the performativity of economics. *Economy and Society*, 33(3), 303–34.

MacKenzie, D. (2017). A material political economy: Automated trading desk and price prediction in high-frequency trading. *Social Studies of Science*, 47(2), 172–94.

MacKenzie, D. and Millo, Y. (2003). Constructing a market, performing theory: The historical sociology of a financial derivatives exchange. *American Journal of Sociology*, 109(1), 107–45.

Maćkowiak, B. (2007). External shocks, US monetary policy and macroeconomic fluctuations in emerging markets. *Journal of Monetary Economics*, 54(8), 2512–20.

Maxwell, S. and Estelami, H. (2005). Introduction, special issue on behavioral pricing. *Journal of Product & Brand Management*, 14(6), 355–6.

Mead, G.H. (1934). *Mind, Self, and Society*. Chicago, IL: University of Chicago Press.

Mellet, K. and Beauvisage, T. (2020). Cookie monsters. Anatomy of a digital market infrastructure. *Consumption Markets & Culture*, 23(2), 110–29.

Meyer, M. and Kearnes, M. (2013). Introduction to special section: Intermediaries between science, policy and the market. *Science and Public Policy*, 40(4), 423–9.

Monroe, K.B. and Lee, A.Y. (1999). Remembering versus knowing: Issues in buyers' processing of price information. *Journal of the Academy of Marketing Science*, 27(2), 207–25.

Mullainathan, S. and Thaler, R.H. (2000). Behavioral economics. National Bureau of Economic Research, Working Paper 7948.

Muniesa, F. (2007). Market technologies and the pragmatics of prices. *Economy and Society*, 36(3), 377–95.

Nelson, S. (1954). OPS price control standards. *Law and Contemporary Problems*, 19(Fall), 554–80.

North, D.C. (1991). Institutions. *Journal of Economic Perspectives*, 5(1), 97–112.

Ohanian, L.E. (1997). The macroeconomic effects of war finance in the United States: World War II and the Korean War. *American Economic Review*, 37(1), 23–40.

Pflueger, D., Palermo, T. and Martinez, D. (2019). Thinking infrastructure and the organization of markets: The creation of a legal market for cannabis in Colorado. In M. Kornberger, G.C. Bowker, J. Elyachar, A. Mennicken, P. Miller, J.R Nucho and N. Pollock (eds), *Thinking Infrastructures (Research in the Sociology of Organizations Volume 62)* (pp. 233–53). Bingley: Emerald Publishing.

Pink, S. (2007). *Doing Visual Ethnography*. London: SAGE.

Polanyi, K. (1966). *Dahomey and the Slave Trade: An Analysis of an Archaic Economy*. Seattle, WA: University of Washington Press.

Pontille, D. (2003). Authorship practices and institutional contexts in sociology: Elements for a comparison of the United States and France. *Science, Technology, & Human Values*, 28(2), 217–43.

Poon, M. (2007). Scorecards as devices for consumer credit: The case of Fair, Isaac & Company Incorporated. In M. Callon, Y. Millo and F. Muniesa (eds), *Market Devices* (pp. 284–306). Oxford: Blackwell.

Porat, M., Surace, K.J. and Milgrom, P. (2008). Method, system and business model for a buyer's auction with near perfect information using the internet. US Patent number 7330826.

Porter, T. (1995). *Trust in Numbers: The Pursuit of Objectivity in Science and Public Life*. Princeton, NJ: Princeton University Press.

Preda, A. (2006). Socio-technical agency in financial markets: The case of the stock ticker. *Social Studies of Science*, 36(5), 753–82.

Presbrey, F. (1929). *History and Development of Advertising*. Garden City, NY: Doubleday.

Progressive Grocer (2019). Audience profile. Available at: https://progressivegrocer .com/audience-profile (accessed 28 November 2019).

Prown, J.D. (1982). Mind in matter: An introduction to material culture theory and method. *Winterthur Portfolio*, 17(1), 1–19.

Puffert, D.J. (2002). Path dependence in spatial networks: The standardization of railway track gauge .*Explorations in Economic History*, 39(3), 282–314.

Roth, A. (2007). The art of designing markets. *Harvard Business Review*, 85(10), 118–26.

Russo, J.E., Krieser, G. and Miyashita, S. (1975). An effective display of unit price information: Can the posting of unit prices change market shares? *Journal of Marketing*, 39(2), 11–19.

Saxon, W. (1980). Richard Drew, Scotch Tape inventor. *The New York Times*, 17 December, Section A, p. 33.

Schatzberg, E. (1999). *Wings of Wood, Wings of Metal: Culture and Technical Choice in American Airplane Materials, 1914–1945*. Princeton, NJ: Princeton University Press.

Schegloff, E.A. (1998). Body torque. *Social Research*, 65(3), 535–86.

Schlereth, T.J. (ed.) (1982). *Material Culture Studies in America*. Walnut Creek, CA: AltaMira Press.

Schnidman, E. (2013). When will the U.S. hit the 1947 wall? Worldpress.org, 1 February. Available at: http://www.worldpress.org/Americas/3956.cfm.

Schwartz, D. (1989). Visual ethnography: Using photography in qualitative research. *Qualitative Sociology*, 12(2), 119–54.

Seligman, E.R.A. and Love, R.A. (1932). *Price Cutting and Price Maintenance*. New York: Harper and Brothers.

Shove, E., Pantzar, M. and Watson, M. (2012). *Dynamics of Social Practice*. London: SAGE.

Simakova, E. and Neyland, D. (2008). Marketing mobile futures: Assembling constituencies and creating compelling stories for an emerging technology. *Marketing Theory*, 8(1), 91–116.

Simon, H.A. (1955). A behavioral model of rational choice. *Quarterly Journal of Economics*, 69(1), 99–118.

Smith, A. (1759), *The Theory of Moral Sentiments*. London: Printed for A. Millar, and A. Kincaid and J. Bell.

Soutjis, B. (2020). The new digital face of the consumerist mediator: The case of the "Yuka" mobile app. *Journal of Cultural Economy*, 13(1), 114–31.

Soutjis, B., Cochoy, F. and Hagberg, J. (2017). An ethnography of Electronic Shelf Labels: The resisted digitization of prices in contemporary supermarkets. *Journal of Retailing and Consumer Services*, 39(C), 296–304.

Spann, M., Fischer, M. and Tellis, G.J. (2015). Skimming or penetration? Strategic dynamic pricing for new products. *Marketing Science*, 34(2), 235–49.

Spellman, S.V. (2009). Cornering the market: Independent grocers and innovation in American small business, 1860–1940. Unpublished PhD dissertation, Carnegie Mellon University.

Spellman, S.V. (2016). *Cornering the Market*. New York: Oxford University Press.

Srivastava, J. and Lurie, N. (2001). A consumer perspective on price-matching refund policies: Effect on price perceptions and search behavior. *Journal of Consumer Research*, 28(2), 296–307.

Star, S.L. (1999). The ethnography of infrastructure. *American Behavioral Scientist*, 43(3), 377–91.

Star, S.L. and Ruhleder, K. (1996). Steps toward an ecology of infrastructure: Design and access for large information spaces. *Information Systems Research*, 7(1), 111–34.

Stark, D. (2009). *The Sense of Dissonance, Accounts of Worth in Economic Life*. Princeton, NJ, USA and Oxford, UK: Princeton University Press.

Stiglitz, J.E. (2010). Government failure vs. market failure: Principles of regulation. In E.J. Balleisen and D.A. Moss (eds), *Government and Markets: Toward a New Theory of Regulation* (pp. 13–51). Cambridge, MA: Cambridge University Press.

Strasser, S. (1989). *Satisfaction Guaranteed, the Making of the American Mass Market*. New York: Pantheon Books.

Strathern, M. (2004[1991]). *Partial Connections*. Savage, MD: Rowman & Littlefield.

Svenska Hemdatornytt (1993). Ny spelfluga: Barcode Battler. *Svenska Hemdatornytt*, 9.

Taylor, B. and Wills, G. (eds) (1969). *Pricing Strategy: Reconciling Customer Needs and Company Objectives*. London: Staples Press.

Tedlow, R.S. (1990). *New and Improved, the Story of Mass Marketing in America*. New York: Basic Books.

Thaler, R.H. (2016). Behavioral economics: Past, present, and future. *American Economic Review*, 106(7), 1577–600.

Thaler, R.H. and Sunstein, C.R. (2008). *Nudge, Improving Decisions about Health, Wealth and Happiness*. New Haven, CT, USA and London, UK: Yale University Press.

Tosh, J. (1991). *The Pursuit of History: Aims, Methods, and New Directions in the Study of Modern History*, 2nd edn. London: Longman.

Trifts, V. and Häubl, G. (2003). Information availability and consumer preference: Can online retailers benefit from providing access to competitor price information? *Journal of Consumer Psychology*, 13(1–2), 149–59.

Twede, D. (2012). The birth of modern packaging: Cartons, cans and bottles. *Journal of Historical Research in Marketing*, 4(2), 245–72.

Urbany, J.E. and Dickson, P.R. (1990). Prospect theory and pricing decisions. *Journal of Behavioral Economics*, 19(1), 69–80.

Velthuis, O. (2005). *Talking Prices: Symbolic Meanings of Prices on the Market for Contemporary Art*. Princeton, NJ: Princeton University Press.

Weber, M. (1978[1922]). *Economy and Society: An Outline of Interpretive Sociology*. Berkeley, CA: University of California Press.

Williamson, O.E. (1973). Markets and hierarchies: Some elementary considerations. *American Economic Review*, 63(2), 316–25.

Witkowski, T.H. (1990). Marketing thought in American decorative arts. *Journal of the Academy of Marketing Science*, 18(4), 365–8.

Woolgar, S. and Neyland, D. (2013). *Mundane Governance: How Ordinary Objects Come to Matter*. Oxford: Oxford University Press.

Zeithaml, V.A. (1982). Consumer response to in-store price information environments. *Journal of Consumer Research*, 8(4), 357–69.

Zeithaml, V.A. (1988). Consumer perceptions of price, quality, and value: A means-end model and synthesis of evidence. *Journal of Marketing*, 52(3), 2–22.

Zelizer, V.A. (1978). Human values and the market: The case of life insurance and death in 19th-century America. *American Journal of Sociology*, 84(3), 591–610.

Zelizer, V.A. (1985). *Pricing the Priceless Child: The Changing Social Value of Children*. New York: Basic Books.

Zelizer, V.A. (1994). *The Social Meaning of Money*. New York: Basic Books.

Index

Printed and bound by CPI Group (UK) Ltd, Croydon, CR0 4YY

16/04/2025

14658489-0003